MW00626216

The Steppe and the Sea

ENCOUNTERS WITH ASIA

Victor H. Mair, Series Editor

Encounters with Asia is an interdisciplinary series dedicated to the exploration of all the major regions and cultures of this vast continent. Its timeframe extends from the prehistoric to the contemporary; its geographic scope ranges from the Urals and the Caucasus to the Pacific. A particular focus of the series is the Silk Road in all of its ramifications: religion, art, music, medicine, science, trade, and so forth. Among the disciplines represented in this series are history, archeology, anthropology, ethnography, and linguistics. The series aims particularly to clarify the complex interrelationships among various peoples within Asia, and also with societies beyond Asia.

A complete list of books in the series is available from the publisher.

The Steppe and the Sea

Pearls in the Mongol Empire

Thomas T. Allsen

PENN

UNIVERSITY OF PENNSYLVANIA PRESS

PHILADELPHIA

Copyright © 2019 University of Pennsylvania Press

All rights reserved. Except for brief quotations used for purposes of review or scholarly citation, none of this book may be reproduced in any form by any means without written permission from the publisher.

Published by
University of Pennsylvania Press
Philadelphia, Pennsylvania 19104-4112
www.upenn.edu/pennpress

Printed in the United States of America on acid-free paper
10 9 8 7 6 5 4 3 2 1

A catalogue record for this book is available
from the Library of Congress.
ISBN 978-0-8122-5117-3

For Lucille
once again

CONTENTS

Introduction

At its height the Chinggisid imperium, commonly known as the Mongol Empire, was by far the largest contiguous land empire in history.[1] And, as the paramount power of the age, its influence and reputation spread well beyond its frontiers. Mongolian courts were thus able to attract natural products and cultural wares from the subarctic to the subtropics. Even after the empire's division, one of its successors, the Yuan Dynasty, continued to exercise such powers. European accounts of Qubilai and his successors flying gyrfalcons from elephants north of Dadu documented and dramatized the Mongols' ability to obtain prestige goods from the principal ecological zones of Eurasia.[2] None of the empire's predecessors or contemporaries enjoyed a comparable range of choices. Among the most beautiful and precious of these resources was the pearl, which came to play a central role in the political and economic life of the empire, a role noted by Marco Polo among many others.

Part I, "From the Sea to the Steppe," investigates the importance of pearls in Mongolian political culture. Since these treasures of the sea had great market value and at the same time carried extensive ideological baggage, their bestowal provided the Chinggisids with a political currency to attract and reward a large and extremely diverse group of servitors from across Eurasia.

The lavish use of pearls in portraits of emperors and their wives documents their value not only as decorative objects—earrings, necklaces, and designs on clothing—but also as symbols of status and power, a topic explored in chapters focused on the acquisition, display, redistribution, and cultural-political meaning of pearls. In addition, I examine subjects that have received little attention to date: foremost among these is the amounts, management, and movement of prestige goods accumulated at the Mongols' highly mobile royal courts and the emergence of what can fairly be called an unrestrained consumer ethos among their core supporters. The creation of rising expectations and their fulfillment constitute key features of Chinggisid statecraft.

This book encompasses the entire history of the empire. For our purposes this can be divided into two stages. The first, the early empire, extends from the formal elevation of Chinggis Qan (r. 1206–27) to 1260, a period of explosive and unprecedented expansion that saw the Mongols' subjugation of southern Siberia, Manchuria, Korea, North China, Tibet, Turkestan, Iran, Mesopotamia, Transcaucasia, the Rus principalities, and the entire steppe zone. The second stage, a lengthy period of internecine conflict, division, and decline, lasted from 1260 to about 1370. Because of rivalries between the ever-multiplying princely lines and the sheer size of their imperium, four autonomous qanates emerged in the course of a protracted and indecisive civil war between the Yuan Dynasty and its ally, the Il-qan state, and the Chaghadai Qanate and the Golden Horde.

The Yuan Dynasty (1271–1368), founded by Qubilai (r. 1260–94), a grandson of Chinggis Qan, controlled the Mongolian homeland, China, and much of continental East Asia. As possessors of the original seat of empire, the Yuan emperors or qaghans were intermittently recognized by other princely lines as the titular sovereigns of the Yeke Mongghol Ulus, the "Domain [or Empire] of the Great Mongols."

The Il-qan state (1256–1335), which included Iran, Afghanistan, Iraq, and Transcaucasia, was founded by Hülegü (r. 1256–65), a grandson of Chinggis and brother of Qubilai. Throughout their history they remained close allies of the Yuan in their joint struggles with rival lines.

The Chaghadai Qanate (1221–ca. 1370), named after the second son of Chinggis, originally embraced most of western Turkistan and later on parts of eastern Turkistan. In alliance with other dissident princes, especially the descendants of Ögödei (r. 1229–41), the successor of the founding father, they were often in conflict with the Yuan.

The Golden Horde (1237–ca. 1500), properly the Domain (*Ulus*) of Jochi, Chinggis Qan's eldest son, was centered on the lower Volga and held sway over the western steppe, the Rus principalities, Volga Bulgharia, the Crimea, and Khwārazm. Its largely autonomous eastern wing, the so-called Princes of the Left Hand descendent from Jochi's eldest son, Orda, controlled central Siberia and the present-day Kazakh steppe and shared a common frontier with the Yuan in the vicinity of the Yenisei River.

The differences that separated the two sets of adversaries extended well beyond family and political antagonisms. There were in addition fundamental differences in their social-ecological characteristics, divergences that have a direct bearing on the principal themes and arguments of this book. First, unlike the Golden Horde and the Chaghadai Qanate, whose core territories were located in or immediately adjacent to the steppe zone, the Yuan and Il-qans shared geographical and cultural space with their far more numerous sedentary subjects, a situation that encouraged differing governing strategies and styles.[3] Second, the Mongolian regimes in China and Iran controlled far more diverse and productive economies than their steppe rivals and therefore had greater access to prestige goods of every kind, including vast quantities of pearls from the southern seas.[4] With these resources they were able to build and sustain the much larger political structures needed to govern settled societies with high population densities.

As regards sources, I have made extensive use of the standard narratives and court chronicles prepared in China and Iran but have by no means exhausted the data on pearls in the Mongols' transcontinental empire. Much remains untapped in local histories, administrative handbooks, treatises on medicine and natural history, encyclopedias, and the literary collections (*wenji*) produced by scholar-officials of the Yuan. Still, despite the limitations and lacunae, the assembled documentation is sufficient to construct a meaningful historical narrative of the subject at large and to ensure that the specific questions raised here are addressed in a substantive manner.

Sources available on the constituent parts of the empire vary significantly in number and quality. The Yuan domain is by a wide margin the best documented, followed by that of the Il-qans, a situation that of course accurately reflects the living cultural and bureaucratic traditions the Mongolian conquerors encountered and exploited in China and Iran. In contrast, the information available on the Chaghadai Qanate and Golden Horde is much more limited in scope and derives in large part from fragmentary, external accounts, since the original body of internally generated sources was smaller in number and of these fewer have survived. The result is an obvious but unavoidable imbalance in geographical coverage. What we do know, however, about the use of pearls and other prestige goods in the latter two realms is consistent with the much fuller data from China and Iran.

The concentration on pearls inevitably magnifies their importance and thereby creates another kind of imbalance. For this reason, I wish to state from the outset that I am not advancing a reductionist argument that "pearls made the empire of the Great Mongols great." Pearls are diagnostic, not determinative. My purpose is to use pearls as yet another window on the Mongols' political culture and its profound influence on the circulation of cultural and commercial wares throughout Eurasia.

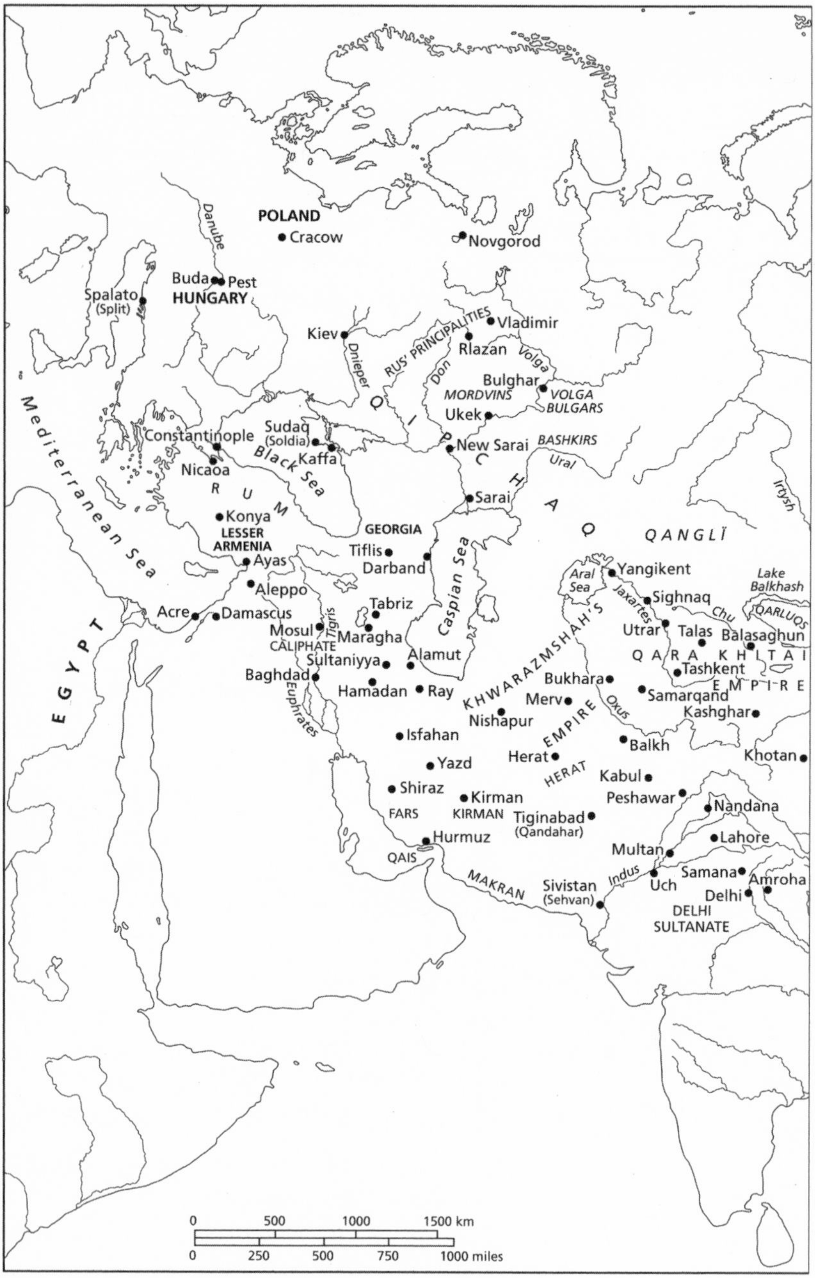

Map 1. Map of Eurasia, ca. 1250. Cambridge University Press.

FOREST PEOPLES
Lake Baikal
Yenisei
Ob
Amur
Onon
Kerulen
Selenga
OIRAT
QÏRGHÏZ
NAIMANS
MERKIT
MONGOLS
TATARS
KEREYIT
Qaraqorum
QONGGIRAT
Liaoyang
Imil
Qayaligh
Almaligh
Beshbaligh
Hami
(Qamul)
UIGHUR
KINGDOM
Shangdu
ÖNGGÜT
KORYO
JAPAN
TANGUT
(XIXIA)
EMPIRE
Yellow River
JIN
EMPIRE
Khotan
Kaifeng
Yangzhou
Hangzhou
Yangzi
TIBET
Fuzhou
Quanzhou
SONG
EMPIRE
DALI
Guangzhou
BENGAL
BURMA
ANNAM
CHAMPA

Part II of this book places the modes of this circulation as well as the nature of the influence exercised by the empire in a much broader chronological and comparative framework in order to identify longer term trends and patterns.

In tracing the movement of pearls into Inner Asia and the steppe over the longue durée, two complementary and compatible perspectives are particularly fruitful. In one, first articulated by Lynda Shaffer, this movement can rightly be viewed as one strand in the larger process of "southernization," the dispersal of cultural traits, including maritime and subtropical products and their associated technologies, from the Indian Ocean littoral northward in the period between the fifth and fifteenth centuries of the Common Era.[5] One might even extend the geographical range and the chronological depth of this movement and argue that southernization was an ancient, permanent, and fundamental feature of Eurasian cultural history.[6] Such an approach offers one further benefit: investigations into the circulation of natural and cultural commodities tend to concentrate on its East-West axis, while the southernization thesis shifts needed attention to the North-South axis.

Addressing the same issue through a different analytical framework, David Christian argues that besides the highly visible and widely acknowledged East-West "civilizational exchanges," equal attention should be paid to the less investigated but no less consequential North-South "trans-ecological exchanges," the movement of goods between zones of the continent with decidedly different natural and cultural histories. And, as he rightly concludes, these two movements readily merge, forming a single interactive, integrated, and continent-wide network of exchange.[7]

By means of these perspectives the movement of pearls can be used to cast additional light on a closely related and equally long-term historical problem, the interconnections between overland and seaborne trade. In the present instance, the Mongolian Empire's active engagement with the southern seas illuminates one example of these interactions, the study of which suggests parallels in the continental circulation of other commodities and precocities both before and after the Chinggisid age.

Other problems can be profitably pursued in the same manner. For one, it will help to establish similarities in the employment of luxury goods in the political cultures of empires through time. As others have observed, under premodern conditions luxuries were necessities in political mobilization, playing an essential role in the creation of ramifying chains of clientage and in the elaboration of court cultures.[8] While the vital importance of luxuries in the political economy of imperial centers is now generally recognized, the consequence of the circulation of such goods for local and regional economies deserves greater attention. In this regard, the history of pearls is again quite suggestive concerning the movement of other kinds of luxury goods and their unintended economic consequences, their secondary effects commonly manifested in the local production of lower-cost substitutes and counterfeits. While a number of studies on specific commodities and regions have appeared in recent decades, a fuller appreciation of the frequency and extended geographical distribution of such production for the economic history of Eurasia calls for a larger, comparative perspective.

Although tracking the circulation of pearls across time offers insights into their long-term price fluctuations and is interesting in itself, these fluctuations have much wider implications, more particularly the relative weight and importance of different modes of exchange—booty taking, tributary arrangements, market mechanisms, and reciprocal gift-giving—in premodern economies. During the Mongolian era all of these modes were in play and all highly interactive, which opens another productive line of comparative research into the circulation of other prestige goods.

Pearls can also tell us much about another little studied but widespread phenomenon, the crafting of cross-cultural marketing strategies under premodern conditions of transportation and communication. In many cases, these strategies drew heavily on a body of myths and tales that were themselves widely diffused across the Old World. In long-distance exchange, as we shall see, all things come with a story, and all such stories have commercial applications.

The story of pearls, of necessity, requires investigation of Mongolian maritime history, and this leads to an important and as yet inadequately addressed question: since the Chinggisids held sway over vast and diverse territories, how did they go about extracting resources from lands with decidedly different environmental and cultural characteristics? To what extent did this entail variations in their policy goals, personnel choices, and techniques of resource mobilization? The answers say much about their adaptability and their success.

Last, in combination these comparisons will help situate the formation of the Mongolian Empire in a proper historical perspective that is sometimes blurred or misconstrued because the Mongols' imperial venture was in some respects groundbreaking and extraordinary. The Mongols, however, did not operate in a vacuum; they had models and made extensive use of them, building upon long-held and widely shared imperial traditions of both nomadic and settled peoples. Once again, pearls help identify and illuminate these connections and continuities, which in turn allow us to answer with greater precision three further and closely related questions, that of Mongolian exceptionalism in steppe history, the Mongols' unprecedented engagement with the sea, and the much discussed "Mongolian impact" on subjects and successors, to whom they left an extremely diversified portfolio of institutions and ideologies for consideration, selection, and assimilation.

PART I

From the Sea to the Steppe

CHAPTER 1

Properties of Pearls

Humans' fascination with pearls is connected with their mysterious origins. The emergence of a beautiful, lustrous object from an unattractive sea creature seems a most unlikely phenomenon. We can begin with a summary of current scientific understanding of the natural properties of pearls and then turn to an examination of the cultural meanings that humans regularly ascribed to them, thereby adding to their value.

In general terms, pearls are calcareous concretions of living mollusks organically produced in response to the invasion of a foreign body, itself usually of organic origin.[1] In reaction to the irritation the mollusk coats the invader, the nucleus, with calcium carbonate in concentric layers over a period of years.

The phylum *Mollusca* consists of more than a hundred thousand living species, many of which produce pearls, commonly from nacre, the aptly named mother-of-pearl. Pearls are first attested in the fossil record about 200 million years BP and become common in the Cretaceous Period, 65–145 million years BP. While many species produce pearls, only a few bivalves produce those of commercial value. For our purposes these can be divided into two categories: saltwater oysters and freshwater mollusks. Of the former, the best known come from the genera *Pinctada* found in tropical seas. Of the latter, pearls are produced by a great number of genera found in the rivers and lakes of Eurasia and the Americas.

As early hominids sought mollusks as a food source, human engagement with pearls goes back several million years. Because pearls deteriorate over time, however, the earliest evidence of human association with them are those excavated from graves located around the head of the Persian Gulf and in Mesopotamia dating to the fourth and third centuries BCE, and the earliest literary references appear later in Near Eastern epics.[2]

The property of pearls most attractive to humans is their luster, reflectivity, and transparency. These special optical properties are connected with their composition, which scatters light within the constituent crystalline structure, and their spherical shape, which makes it appear that reflected light is emanating from the pearl's interior.

As regards their physical properties, pearls are relatively soft compared with gemstones but nonetheless difficult to crush because of their crystalline structure. The color of pearls varies greatly—they may be white, black, red, gold, blue, or green—and generally reflects the color of the interior surface of the shell. Weight and size are equally variable. Their specific gravity is 2.6–2.8, and they are thus light in contrast to gemstones. The largest known pearl measured by its maximum length is 23.3 cm, but natural pearls exceeding 8 cm are extremely rare, and those less than 3 mm have limited commercial value, while those below 2 mm are termed "seed pearls."

The shape of pearls is also endlessly variable: round, teardrop, flattened, elongated, and irregular, called "baroque." A round shape, even in the smaller sizes, is unusual, perhaps only one in a thousand. Since as size increases round varieties become increasingly rare, large spherical pearls have long been the most valuable.

Given the intrinsic attractiveness of pearls, it is not surprising that human communities across the Eurasian landmass responded positively to them or that they readily embellished and magnified their natural attributes, regularly imputed to them extensive spiritual-magical powers, or placed upon them such elevated market values.

The inclination to add value to objects has several important implications that are elaborated in subsequent chapters. First, pearls do not stand alone in this regard; many other commodities have a "prime" or prestige value but no use or utilitarian value. The former, as Colin Renfrew argues, can be attributed to the human proclivity "to give a social and symbolic significance to material goods" that are not adaptive but enhance status and political influence. The possession and ceremonial use of such goods, moreover, is not merely a "reflection" of that status but the means by which it is achieved and broadcast.[3] This perspective is in full accord with political processes frequently observed at Chinggisid courts.

Next, while the purpose of utilitarian objects can often be inferred from their structure and other physical properties, the purpose of purely symbolic goods is more variable, culturally specific, and harder to read.[4] And in selling such goods from distant lands, merchants had to take into account their varied local, regional, and "international" cultural meanings and thereby became deeply involved in the dissemination of these images through space and time.

The images and popular tales surrounding pearls, their high value, strange origin, and unique power are extensively documented. Throughout antiquity and the Middle Ages the wealth of the sea was measured by its yield of pearls; other marine products such as coral and ambergris were valued but were clearly of secondary importance.[5] Their elevated status among the treasures of nature is indicated by the frequent use of pearls in figures of speech to communicate notions of value, beauty, rarity, excellence, and esoteric knowledge in major languages of Eurasia, including those like Turkic that evolved far from the sea, evidence that the pearl culture of the south diffused steadily north.[6] There was in fact a common and coherent set of aesthetic qualities imposed on pearls that crossed innumerable temporal, spatial, and cultural boundaries. While the symbolic and spiritual associations attached to pearls were more variable, the essential point is that everywhere they possessed such properties.

Though pearls as a class of objects were held in the highest esteem, it was also recognized that there was great variation in their individual quality, which ranged from those "fit for a king" to the cheap and unsorted varieties.[7] For the nonprofessional, works on collecting and connoisseurship were composed in Persian, Arabic, Sanskrit, and Chinese.[8] The basic standards were established early and lived long. Already in the first century CE Pliny asserted that the value of pearls is determined by their "brilliance, size, roundness, smoothness and weight," criteria that are found in the ninth-century Arabic commercial handbook attributed to Jāḥiẓ.[9]

Specialists, naturally, developed an elaborate vocabulary to convey information on the qualities of individual pearls to indicate slight variations in shape, size, color, and luster. And, of course, each major trading community had its own, similarly elaborate vocabulary.[10] Consequently, to operate successfully in the international pearl market, a merchant needed to command several hundred technical terms and their equivalents in a number of foreign languages.

In various times and places pearls of different and unusual colors, sometimes used in combination, were in vogue. Sasanian women reportedly dressed their hair with pearls of five distinct colors, and at the court of Maḥmūd of Ghazna (r. 998–1030) pearls of strange hues, some with black dots, were valued and displayed as rarities and anomalies.[11] There is, however, little doubt that white was long the great favorite among elites and connoisseurs for adornment, display, and gift giving.[12]

As for shape, roundness was preferred and tested by rolling a pearl about on a plate.[13] Also much esteemed were any pair of pearls that were identical, especially those extremely rare "twins" found in the same oyster. For the Muslim collector of the Middle Ages, such twins constituted the ultimate matched set.[14]

Size and weight were also critical; they were normally sorted into a dozen grades from small seed pearls to extra-large pearls, the latter known interchangeably in Arabo-Persian as *durr* or *ḥabb*.[15] Those of great size were extolled in poetry and described in prose with a number of stock literary formulas.[16] More concretely and helpfully, pearls are sometimes said to be the "size of sheep dung" in the Mongolian tradition or the size of sparrow eggs or hazelnuts in Islamic literature.[17] It is indicative of the penetration of West Asian standards to the East that Chinese sources also make reference to pearls "as large as hazelnuts."[18]

Since, however, pearls were such a valuable commodity, merchants and jewelers relied on more exact means of determining their weight. In Muslim lands, this was most often expressed in terms of coinage, since official currency had a measure of stability.[19] Pearls were at times weighed by the *mithqāl*, about 4.5 grams, a unit that was also used to establish the mint weight of coins, which for dirhams in the early Muslim era was set at seven-tenths of a *mithqāl*.[20] As a matter of practice, however, the weight of pearls was equated to that of coins in circulation, most commonly the gold dinar.

The final criterion for judging pearls was provenance. This was an important consideration because it was well understood by early specialists on precious gems, such as the famed polymath al-Bīrūnī (973–ca. 1050), that each of the major oyster fishing beds from China to East Africa and the Red Sea produced pearls with distinctive and desirable characteristics.[21] That premodern connoisseurs regularly made clear distinctions among the pearls from across the southern seas that come from only two species, *Pinctada radiate* and *Pinctada maxima,* leads to the conclusion that the slight variations in their development had much more to do with local environmental conditions and harvesting methods than with the kind of oyster producing them.[22]

There were, then, many options available to premodern consumers in Afro-Eurasia. Starting in Northeast Asia, the source closest to the Mongolian homeland, were the "northern pearls (*beizhu*)" taken from mussels in the Sungari and other rivers of Manchuria. Their harvest was a component of the mixed economy of the Jürchens during the pre-imperial and Jin eras (1115–1234), and their extraction, though greatly diminished, continued to the end of the Qing.[23] Japan, as noted by Marco Polo, produced saltwater pearls in white and red that

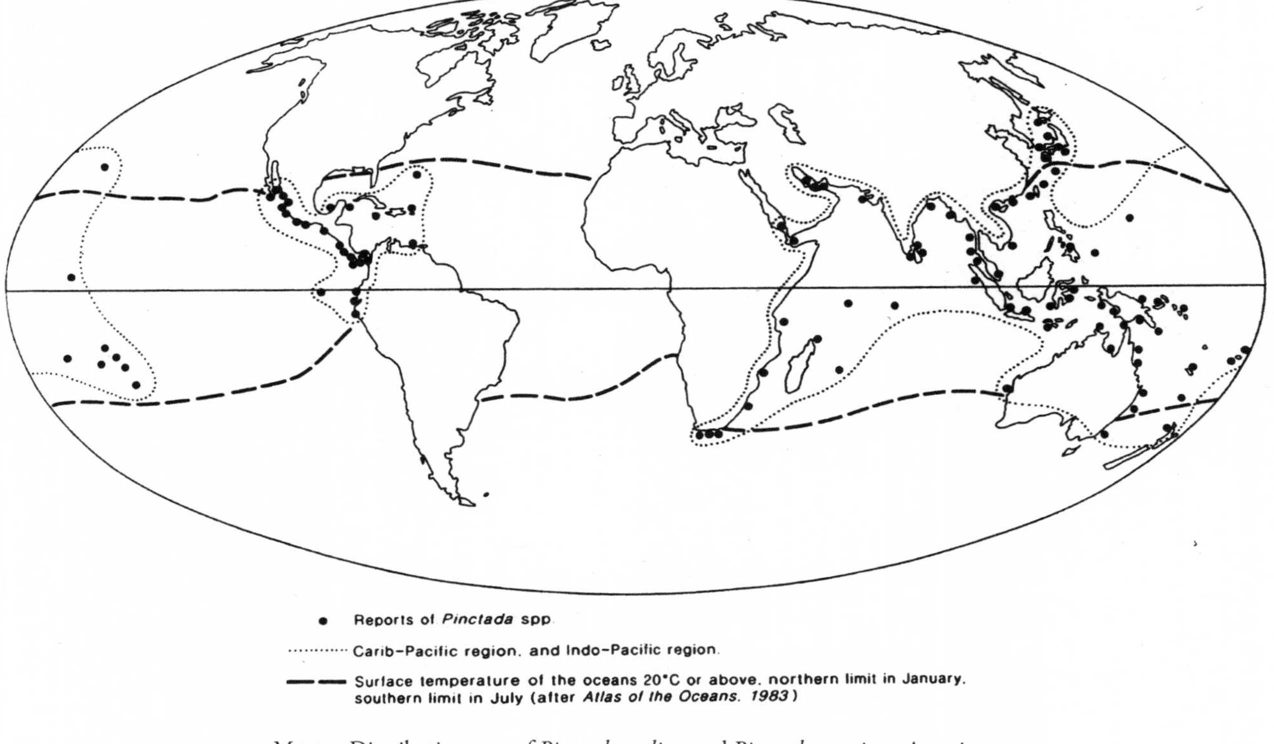

MAP 2. Distribution map of *Pinctada radiate* and *Pinctada maxima*. American Philosophical Society.

were imported to the mainland.[24] China, too, had pearl fisheries along its lengthy shoreline; the most famous were off the Hepu, west of the Leizhou Peninsula, and at Yaizhou, on the northeastern corner of Hainan Island. Both had been worked by indigenous non-Chinese people since the early Han and very likely long before.[25] And in the myriad rivers and lakes found throughout southern and southwestern China there were also abundant supplies of freshwater pearls; these are first attested in Guilin during the Former Han (202 BCE–9 CE) and were still harvested in the early twentieth century.[26]

The fisheries of mainland Southeast Asia and those of the Philippines, Java, and Sumatra were known to the Chinese and Muslims through commercial contacts.[27] Marco Polo's claim that in the "Sea of Chin" there are seven thousand islands around which pearls are fished is an exaggeration but one that speaks to the productivity of maritime Southeast Asia.[28]

India's fisheries were concentrated along the Gulf of Mannar separating the subcontinent from Ceylon. Archaeological evidence indicates that they were first exploited at the beginning of the first millennium BCE, and their trade is mentioned in early Indic literature.[29] From the first century CE onward, a variety of foreign sources single out Ceylon as the principal source of pearls in South Asia.[30] While the island remained productive, Maʿbar (the Cormandel Coast) and Malabar emerged as strong competitors by the late Middle Ages.[31]

The Persian Gulf was also rich in pearls, a reputation that began in antiquity and lasted well into the period of European maritime expansion.[32] There were a number of locales noted for their pearl beds (*maʿdan-i marvārīd*): Ganāfah on the coast of Fārs, Kharak, an island near Basra and, Kishm, another island near Hormuz.[33] Better known were the beds along the coast of Oman and those around the small island of Kīsh/Qays off Fārs.[34] Of all the places in the Gulf "where pearls are born," the beds of Bahrain drew the greatest praise for their quantity and quality, a reputation that lasted into the twentieth century.[35] The fisheries of Aden and the Red Sea, while mentioned, were held to be of secondary importance.[36] To the Muslims and the Chinese, who always took a great interest in the subject, these were the westernmost source of pearls, just as the Philippines were the easternmost.

As to which of these fisheries produced the finest pearls, there were always varying and fluctuating views. These valuations are interesting in that judgments are sometimes based on local pride and economic interest and sometimes on the powerful attraction for goods from distant and mysterious climes. In many instances, of course, such valuations were situational, reflecting changing productivity and market conditions.

Though almost every region had its advocates, there are two that stand out. The primacy of Indian pearls is asserted by the anonymous author of the *Periplus Maris Erythiae* (ca. 50 CE), a view later upheld by others, Chinese and Europeans.[37] The attraction to these pearls may have been conditioned by the belief that Ceylon was the original paradise from which Adam's progeny spread to the rest of the inhabited world.[38] The preponderant opinion, however, held by a host of classical, Muslim, and European authors, favored those of the Persian Gulf.[39] By the Mongolian era this was also the case in China, a view reflected in the listing of the dependencies of the il-qan Abū Saʿīd (r. 1316–35) contained in the *Yuanshi,* in which the first two mentioned are Bahrain (Ba-la-ha-yin) and Kīsh (Qie-shi), the principal centers of pearl production.[40]

On one issue there was general agreement: from antiquity onward, saltwater pearls were deemed superior to, and carefully distinguished from, freshwater varieties, the "bastard pearls" of later English parlance.[41] Their perceived superiority is further underscored by the term "orient" used in Western languages both for an especially lustrous pearl and for the luster itself, usually to distinguish an oceanic pearl, with its greater brightness and luster, from the duller varieties found in riverine mussels of Europe. While jewelers were at times preoccupied with the orient as a measure of the brilliance or "proper" color of other kinds of gemstones, the term is most often applied to saltwater pearls.[42]

A somewhat similar expression of this preference is found in Chinese sources that speak of "brilliant oceanic (*haishang*) pearls."[43] Nonetheless, despite their acceptance of this standard, there was a brief period during the early twelfth century when the upper classes of the Song Dynasty (960–1279) developed an insatiable, almost obsessive desire for *beizhu*, "northern pearls," which they used to decorate their homes and clothing.[44]

In addition, there was a separate class of pearls with an extraordinary property, that of self-illumination. Such claims were made for many gems throughout Eurasia: diamonds that pick up and reflect light, artificial stones made of minerals that phosphoresce when warmed or rubbed, and most notably the "moonlight" and "luminous pearls" frequently encountered in Buddhist, Turkic, and Chinese lore.[45] These moonlight and luminous pearls were counted among the wondrous products of the Hellenistic East, the Daqin of the Chinese sources.[46] While learned skeptics occasionally denied the existence of self-illuminating pearls, belief in them was widespread and enduring, which only served to affirm the mystery and aura surrounding genuine pearls.[47]

Debates over the qualities of individual pearls were ongoing, but, as noted, there were generally accepted standards over much of Eurasia, those of size, roundness, whiteness, and luster.[48] Fabulous prices were paid for those that met or exceeded the established standards; these were styled "royal pearls," a term that goes back at least to the Middle Persian *morwārīd-i shahwār*, literally, "pearl fit for a king."[49] The "great pearl" the Hephthalites seized from the Sasanians in the fifth century that was much coveted by the Byzantine court and in the end sold back to the Persian Great King certainly met this set of criteria.[50]

While by some, the indigenous peoples of South China, pearls were valued above all other objects, they were more commonly measured against other precious products of nature.[51] In the valuation of gems in Islamic lands, only the ruby and the emerald ranked near the pearl.[52] In China, given the reverence for jade, the formula was variable, and on occasion the triad of "yellow gold, white jade, and lustrous pearls" is invoked as the ultimate measure of material and worldly wealth.[53] In ancient India gold held first place and pearls second in the *Veda*'s hierarchy of values.[54]

Gold and pearls were widely viewed as a complementary pair; Shakespeare's "intertissued robe of gold and pearl" describes the dominant standard in rich attire accepted across the Continent.[55] In western Eurasia this pairing was even reflected in commercial practice. In Pegolotti's commercial manual of the 1330s gold and pearls are sold at Tana on the lower Don by the same measure of weight, the *saggio*, about a sixteenth of an ounce.[56] The two not only represented the wealth of the land and the sea but together were associated with the majesty, riches, and reach of great princes. In a few cases, princely possession of pearls in great quantities even served as a stand-in for the actual exercise of maritime power.[57]

The Mongols fully subscribed to these standards. Indeed, in the *Secret History*, besides silver (*mönggü*), gold and pearls are the only natural treasures mentioned, and in the Mongolian version of the Alexander Romance they are presented as the exclusive measures of wealth.[58] And in judging pearls, their criteria were in full accord with pan-Eurasian standards accurately reflected in "The Knight's Tale" where Chaucer depicts Emetrius the king of India swathed in cloth of gold "couched with perles, whyte and rounde and grete," qualities that replicate exactly the Mongols' idea of the perfect pearl and the Persians' notion of "a pearl fit for a king."[59]

CHAPTER 2

Fishing and Processing

Before their sale or distribution, pearls had to be harvested and prepared for market. Preparation involved many stages, including extraction, sorting, valuation, drilling, and stringing. An overview of these processes provides essential background for a number of issues addressed later in the book.[1] Most important, these techniques conditioned in obvious and subtle ways the varied efforts of states to acquire pearls in substantial numbers.

Much lore, of course, is attached to pearl diving, particularly concerning the depths reached and time spent under water.[2] From observations of fisheries in the Persian Gulf over the past two hundred years, it is evident that the pearl beds were three to twenty fathoms deep, with those between five and ten the most regularly exploited. The season was typically late spring and summer when the seas warm up. During this time fleets of dhows with five to twenty on board went to the beds with an "admiral" in overall charge of the operations. Divers, with the aid of an assistant, descended on ropes weighted with stones and a basket attached to another rope to carry oysters back to the surface. The divers, their only "equipment" a nose clip and a knife, stayed under for several minutes, though some observers say five or even ten. The danger from sea creatures was much emphasized in the lore, but in fact the chief threats to the divers' well-being were more prosaic—the bends, cuts from coral, respiratory problems, eye infections, and the like.[3] As the work was arduous, unhealthy, and poorly rewarded, the divers tended to be drawn from local minorities or from imported foreign specialists. In the Persian Gulf, at least in later centuries, the divers were all males, while in East Asia some were females.[4]

Somewhat surprisingly, the data presented by a number of premodern works are in close harmony with recent observations and also provide more detail on the question of fleet size, which they report ranged from twenty to two hundred ships, an indication that the scale of operations was higher in the Middle Ages than in recent centuries. Since this information comes from a wide array of Muslim, Chinese, and European authors, all outsiders to the pearling industry, we have a fairly accurate picture of fishing methods in the Persian Gulf and South India during premodern times.[5]

Off the Chinese coast divers also descended on weighted ropes but had more equipment, leather masks, and even breathing tubes. The major innovation, however, is that by Song times the Chinese began to employ weighted dragnets pulled by junks to dredge and collect oysters in large numbers.[6] The method required closed seasons lasting decades to allow the oyster beds to recover.[7] But even in the absence of such industrial methods, traditional fisheries were regularly depleted, a subject treated more fully in Chapter 9.

Following the harvest, the pearls were prepared for market, a lengthy process consisting of several distinct stages. The first was extraction. In the Gulf and India, oysters were placed on the ship's deck or on shore for several days, since shells were more easily opened and pearls more readily detected and removed from decomposing flesh. The yield of commercially valuable pearls was generally limited, though that of seed pearls, used in medicine and in certain decorative applications, was much higher.

Next came sorting and valuation. The following methods, though only fully described in the nineteenth century by British officials in Ceylon, are in close accord with the more fragmentary information provided by travel accounts from the late thirteenth century.[8] The process involved four basic steps: (1) pearls were grouped by size into ten grades by passing them through a sieve with apertures of different sizes; (2) within each grade, they were then evaluated for shape and orient (luster), at which point expert human judgment comes into play; (3) the pearls are next weighed on scales, higher weights greatly adding to their value, which was established by complicated calculations usually set down in tables; and (4) final prices were now assigned to individual pearls. In the Islamic lands there were very similar instruments and criteria of valuation used by jewelers, lapidaries, and merchants who were regularly attached to imperial and regional courts as resident advisers and treasury officials.[9] As we shall see, this practice was also adopted by the Chinggisids, whose personnel were drawn mainly from the same pool of recruits.

Following valuation, it was common practice to make repairs to improve imperfect pearls. Because of their growth patterns and basic structure, minor blemishes and surface damage could be eliminated by carefully peeling off the outer layer. Color, too, could be manipulated; more particularly, the whiteness

FIGURE 1. Traditional measuring instruments for pearls in the Persian Gulf. Mikimoto Pearl Museum.

of dull pearls could be "restored" or at least enhanced by various chemical and mechanical means.[10]

The following (and very delicate) step was that of drilling, a common practice for the obvious reason that pearls were mainly used as adornment and therefore strung as necklaces or basted on clothing.[11] Since the procedure was so closely tied to a pearl's intended use, a clear distinction was always made between the pierced and unpierced varieties.[12] Drilling, first attested around 300 BCE in Achaemenid territory, is a most challenging task, since a slight misstep can result in ruining a valuable pearl. The essential tool was the bow drill found throughout Eurasia. The usual technique, at least in South India, was to drill one side and then the other so that the two holes met precisely in the middle to prevent "break-out" damage commonly produced by an exiting drill. This, obviously, is a difficult task, one that is further complicated by the crystalline structure of pearls.[13]

The drill itself was usually diamond tipped. Until the discovery of more sophisticated techniques of diamond cutting in the Renaissance, the diamond was mainly appreciated as an industrial tool used in working metal and other precious gems. By the early Middle Ages this appears to be the normal instrument for boring pearls everywhere in Eurasia, since the Chinese of the Tang period obtained their diamonds from India by sea and many of their drills by land from the Persians, which reached them through the Uighurs of Turfan.[14]

The final step, stringing, entailed selecting, matching, and sequencing pearls, sometimes using other materials as spacers.[15] Besides a way of preparing pearls for use as adornments, stringing was a standard method of storing quantities of pearls in royal treasuries, where they were divided into classes, each with a seal indicating its grade and value.[16] Stringed pearls were also used extensively in shipping by sea and land. This preference, especially convenient when handling large numbers of quality pearls, is well attested. A Chinese source reports that in the late ninth century foreign ships arrived daily at Guangzhou (Canton) carrying "strings (*pei*) of 500 pearls," and a century or so later a letter in Old Uighur informs the addressee that a gift of "117 strings of pearls (*salqïm yinchu*)" was in transit.[17]

Both boring and stringing were highly regarded, well-paid crafts celebrated in popular stories and poetry in the Islamic lands, India, and Sogdian Central Asia.[18] In the latter case we have a clear indication of the diffusion of these skills to centers of high demand for pearls, even those distant from the southern seas. In the Mongolian era these operations were conducted in entrepôts on the coast such as Hormuz and in centers inland—Baghdad, Mosul, Tabriz, and Ṣulṭānīyyah. In the latter some were set in jewelry and others sold in bulk to foreign merchants, a pattern that persisted into the early modern age.[19]

CHAPTER 3

Accumulation of Pearls

Like other polities of Inner Asian origin, the Mongols initially obtained luxury items from beyond the steppe by means of plunder. In the Mongolian case the collection of booty was centralized and systematic. Everything seized was enumerated and then redistributed by leaders to followers according to prescribed formulas based on status, rank, and performance.

The first great haul came in 1215 when the Mongols occupied Zhongdu and "seized the Jin palace treasury's pearls, gems and elegant silk textiles." Immediately thereafter, Chinggis Qan sent his chief civil official, Shigi Qutuqtu, "to inventory the Zhongdu treasury."[1] New and equally gratifying returns came during the campaign in Turkestan, where in 1218 the Mongols took from Badakhshan a huge amount of ready cash (*naqūd*) as well as precious gems and pearls (*javāhir*).[2]

One particularly grim episode that says much about the intensity of the Mongols' pursuit of pearls occurred in 1221 at Tirmidh on the upper Amu Darya. When a female captive acknowledged that she had swallowed her pearls she was immediately cut down and eviscerated. On finding several pearls, Chinggis Qan "ordered that they open the bellies of the slain."[3] No wonder a hundred years later the inhabitants of Turkistan still remembered the ruthlessness and thoroughness with which the Mongols conducted searches for hidden treasure.[4]

The quantity of pearls the Mongols took from Baghdad in 1259 was immense and likely unprecedented. Hülegü, the first il-qan (r. 1256–65), secured the treasury of the ʿAbbāsid Caliphate, which was so vast that "precious stones and pearls were like the sand of the sea before him."[5] Among the most prized finds, according to a contemporary Chinese account, were extra-large pearls (*da zhu*) locally called "Jupiters (*taisui*)."[6] But this was not all; during the sack of the city ordered by Hülegü, the victorious troops carried away more gems and pearls from the general population. Since Baghdad was a major pearl-boring center for the Gulf and the Indies, their numbers were great.[7]

The Mongols' method of sacking urban centers is readily apparent. First and foremost, there was a clear-cut division of labor between the common soldiers who pillaged the general citizenry and the Chinggisid rulers and commanders who targeted their counterparts. This was achieved by seizing all treasuries, palaces, forts, arsenals, government offices, and homes of notables, whose contents were inventoried.[8]

Besides government treasuries, ecclesiastical institutions, particularly Eastern Orthodox ones, were also targeted, and for good reason: their churches and monasteries, generously patronized by royal courts, had well-founded reputations for the abundance of pearls adorning icons, crosses, bibles, reliquaries, vessels, miters, and vestments.[9] Many of these were pillaged in the initial Mongolian campaigns against the Rus principalities in the late 1230s and in the sporadic raids and punitive campaigns that followed.[10] It is, then, entirely possible that Hülegü's presentation of a gold cross embellished with pearls to the Georgian Catholicos, as well as other Chinggisid bestowals of church paraphernalia on Eastern Christian ecclesiastical authorities, were recycled booty taken from other Orthodox institutions.[11]

The second major source was the tribute levied on states and territories under Mongolian military pressure as a condition of their submission. This began early; already in 1210 Chinggis Qan demanded from the ruler of the Uighurs "small and large pearls," which were dutifully delivered the following year.[12] In the early 1230s similar demands were placed upon the Korean court and the Baghdad Caliphate.[13] Not surprisingly, by the time of their capitulation in 1243, the Seljuqs of Rūm, fully aware of the protocols of submission, immediately offered their new overlords gems and pearls.[14]

Following the division of the empire in the 1260s, the quest for pearls continued unabated. As the Mongols pushed into southwest China in the 1260s, they began to pressure Annam (North Vietnam) for such tributes, and following their expedition of 1292–93 Qubilai imposed a tribute (*kharāj*) of gold and pearls on Java.[15] During the same decades the Yuan court extended its horizons westward, eliciting high-quality tribute pearls from Maʿbar.[16] Since, however, the latter was an independent polity beyond the Mongols' military reach, such "tributes" tended to merge with princely presentations and diplomatic gifts. This, in fact, had been a normal part of interstate relations in Eurasia for centuries, a practice used not only as a diplomatic courtesy or overture of friendship but also as a means of publicizing a state's natural resources and commercial wares to foreign counterparts. In these exchanges, pearls regularly assumed a prominent role.[17]

Mongolian princes willingly played by these rules, exchanging "gifts" of pearls with foreign courts in great numbers.[18] After 1260 the same practices obtained in the relations between Chinggisid courts, in which tributes, princely gift exchanges, and diplomatic initiatives often are indistinguishable. Certainly, Qubilai in 1288 granted pearls to Qonichi and Udur, princes of the eastern wing of the Golden Horde, because he was seeking allies in the struggle with the hostile Chinggisid lines in Inner Asia. Similarly, the Chaghadai qan Esen Buqa (r. 1310–18) used pearls to improve relations with the Yuan and Il-qans, and in 1326 and 1327 the il-qan Abū Saʿīd sent pearls to the Yuan court to reaffirm their long-standing alliance.[19] Presentations of this kind, often reported as "tributes," commonly signaled new departures and turning points in the complex interrelationships among the four qanates.

The reciprocal nature of these presentations is well illustrated by the exchange between the il-qan Ghazan (r. 1295–1304) and envoys of the Golden Horde during a grand reception held in 1303. Here the representatives of Toqta (r. 1291–1312) handed over twenty-one gyrfalcons to Ghazan, who responded with a pearl worth a thousand gold dinars for each bird.[20] The presentation of local rarities, raptors from the subarctic and pearls from the southern seas, was typical of princely gift exchange throughout Eurasia.

The third means of Mongol acquisition, long-distance trade, which chronologically overlapped the other two, becomes dominant in the latter decades of the thirteenth century as the Mongols' productive "booty frontiers" are largely depleted. And it is at least arguable that commercial channels in combination with government monopolies and tariffs, discussed below, proved their most prolific source in the long term.

The trade in pearls was ancient, extensive, and well integrated, conducted between a series of interlocking networks on sea and land. Evidence of its range and volume is the widespread knowledge of, and intense interest in, the pearls of distant lands. In the early Middle Ages the Chinese and Indians knew much about the sources and uses of pearls in foreign parts, a body of commercial intelligence later acquired by Muslim and European merchants.[21] Because their appeal was aesthetic, economic, religious, and political, pearls crossed markets and were generally in heavy demand. As a result, regions like southern India were able for centuries to obtain foreign goods in exchange for their gems and pearls.[22]

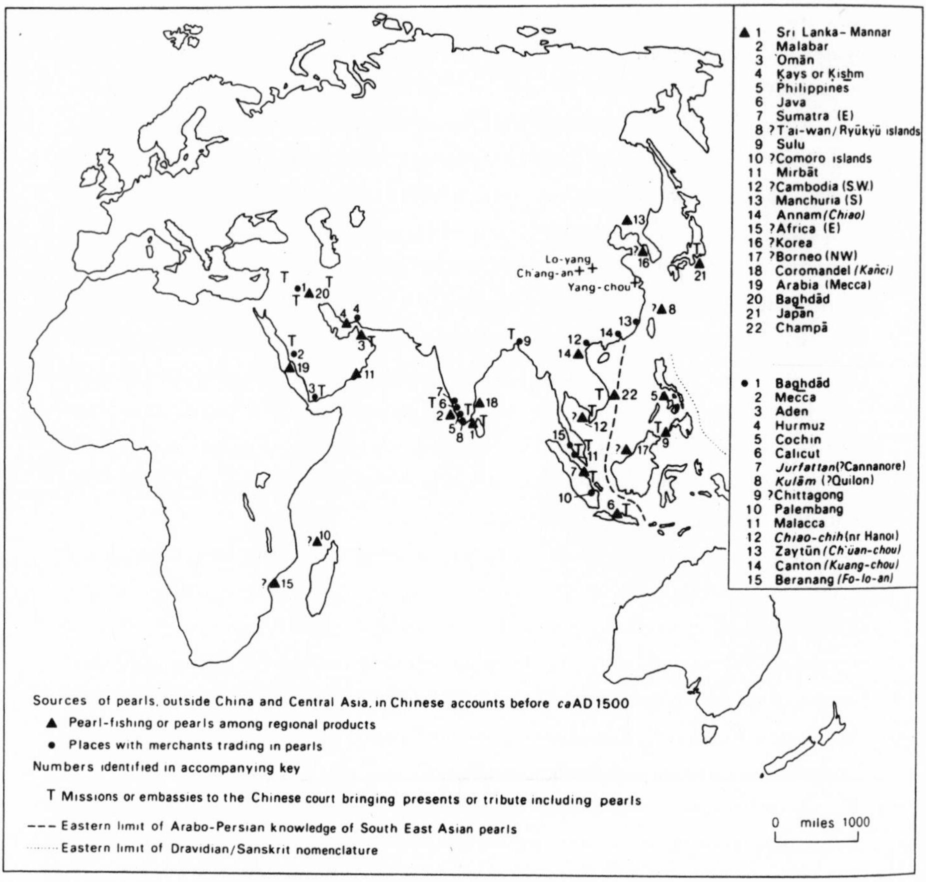

MAP 3. Map of Chinese knowledge of foreign pearl sources. American Philosophical Society.

Another characteristic of the traffic is that merchant companies dealing in pearls were usually composed of individuals with the same ethnic or communal affiliation. Their supplies typically came to them through rulers who tried to maintain a monopoly on local production or through brokers (*banyan, chetty*, and the like) who acted as intermediaries between primary producers, local authorities, and the marketplace. And whenever the opportunity presented itself, the brokers endeavored to buy up the output of a particular source to dominate regional markets.[23] In this they were often successful, for early Portuguese observers identified those dealing in precious stones, coral, and pearls with the richest and most influential among the *chetty* class.[24]

Many different people had a role in this trade—Muslims, Indians, Southeast Asians, and Chinese. Even the Italians, particularly the Genoese, found a niche buying pearls in India and Iran and selling them in Europe and the Golden Horde.[25] Still, there is no doubt that in the Mongolian era the bulk of the traffic was in the hands of Muslim merchants. Their growing dominance in non-Muslim lands was succinctly expressed by the ruler of Maʿbar in 1281 to visiting Yuan envoys: "All Muslim states make full use of their countries' natural products—gold, pearls and precious objects [and with] all their surpluses the Muslims come [here] to trade."[26] The passage provides a snapshot of Muslim merchants' progressive takeover of Indian maritime trade, many of whom Hindu rulers appointed to administer major entrepôts, a process that began in the tenth century and continued into the early modern era.[27] As we shall see, the Mongols did much to encourage their dominance of these networks.

It is hardly surprising, therefore, that Muslim traders were strongly attracted to Chinggisid courts. This is fully borne out by the available information on the amounts Mongolian rulers were willing to invest in pearls. Chinggis Qan's son and successor, Ögödei (r. 1229–41), reputedly purchased twelve trays for the very princely sum of eighty thousand gold dinars.[28] And in 1253 Batu (r. 1237–56), founder of the Golden Horde, requested from the qaghan Möngke (r. 1251–59), ten thousand ingots of silver to buy pearls. The qaghan, however, gave him "only" one thousand and a lecture on the need for restraint.[29]

The major source of these treasures, the Indian Ocean, had by this time developed into an interactive exchange network, what Philippe Beaujard calls "a unified space" in consequence of a series of cycles or pulsations, each characterized by "incrementally increasing expansion."[30] The most complete picture we possess of this integrated market in the Mongolian era comes from Rashīd al-Dīn; as chief adviser and architect of Ghazan's economic reforms, he was vitally interested in the commercial wealth of the southern seas. His knowledge of the subject is indeed impressive. Among other things, he is familiar with the Chinese technical terms such as *matou,* "quay" or "river port," which is accurately transliterated into Persian as *mātū.*[31] More important, he also offers an unsurpassed account of this commerce in his *History of India.* Here he describes an extremely lucrative trade centered on Kīsh and Hormuz, whose networks encompassed Bahrain, Oman, Aden, the Red Sea, and Moqadishu on the African coast. Eastward, the market extended to Gujarat, Malabar,

Ceylon, Maʿbar, Java, Sumatra, Champa (South Vietnam), and the ports of Chīn (South China).[32]

Although not mentioned in Rashīd al-Dīn's account, the Mediterranean world was also connected to these networks through the famous Karīmī merchants of Egypt, whose direct contacts extended to South India, where they had access to goods coming from China. Their fruitful connections throughout the Indian Ocean are confirmed by an anonymous Italian commercial manual of about 1315, which states that in Alexandria and Cairo there were "Oriental pearls of every region in great quantities."[33]

The position of pearls in the larger circulation of oriental commodities is best understood in relation to the Italian commercial term *spezierie*, derived from the Latin *specie*, "kind," which also gave rise to "specie" (coined money) and "spice." For Europeans of the Middle Ages pearls were regularly subsumed under a broad category of goods that included precious metals, coins, aromatics, perfumes, medicines, sugar, spices, dyes, pigments, textiles, ivory, jewelry, and gemstones. Since all had a high value-to-weight ratio, the categorization made perfect economic sense. And, as Peter Martinez stressed on several occasions, collectively these were the prime luxury goods of the age, the backbone of the long-distance trade that connected, stimulated, and sometimes changed regional economies.[34] In the view of some scholars, the maritime trade in these commodities reached its apex under the Yuan and the early Ming.[35] Their arguments are fully compatible with my findings, presented in later chapters, on the volume of pearls acquired and dispensed by Chinggisid courts.

In looking at commerce in natural treasures, it is apparent that states always tried to get their cut. In Iran and China there was a long-held conviction that great sovereigns had to rely on the products of nature, especially gold and pearls.[36] In short, a measure of control over, or a substantial share in, natural resources was assumed to be an inherent right of kings in these two primary seats of empire in the Old World.

This leads to a consideration of the final method of acquisition, different kinds of government monopolies, tariffs, and tax-farming strategies. In the latter case, as Zhao Rugua noted in the early thirteenth century, rulers typically entrusted the operation of fisheries to foreign overseers who recorded the harvest and then apportioned predetermined shares to the local court, the pearl fleets, and themselves.[37] On al-Qatif, an island near Bahrain, an Arabic-speaking Muslim area, fisheries were placed under Jewish officials, and in Maʿbar predominantly Hindu fisheries were in the hands of Muslim merchants.[38] Indeed, this was common practice throughout the western half of the Indian Ocean

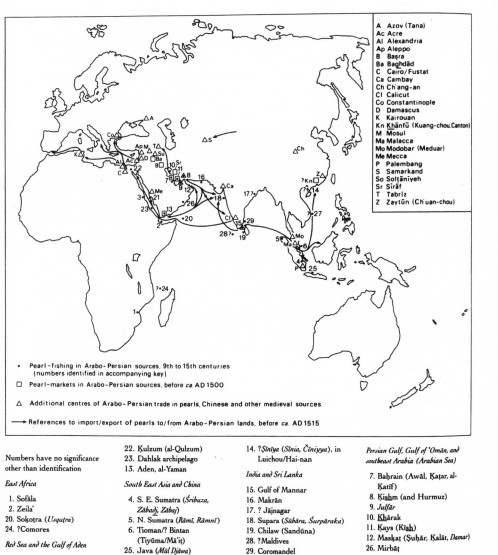

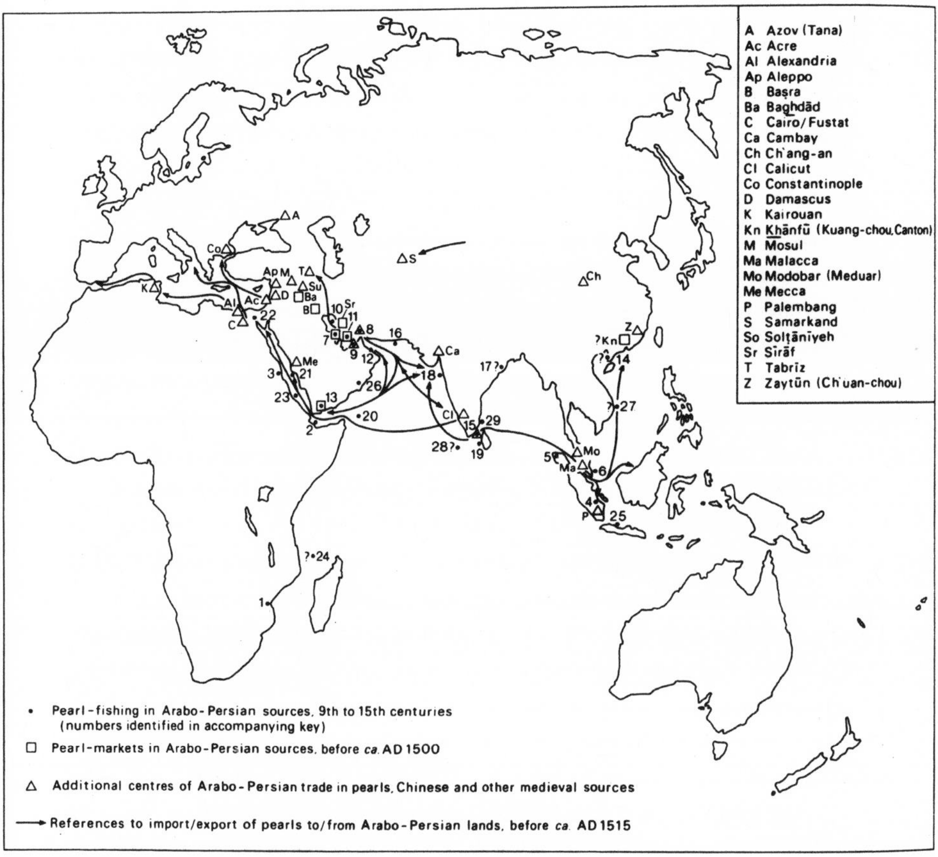

Numbers have no significance other than identification

East Africa

1. Sofāla
2. Zeila'
20. Soḳoṭra (*Usquṭra*)
24. ?Comores

Red Sea and the Gulf of Aden

3. *'Aidāb* (? Adulab)
21. Al-Sirrayn
22. Ḳulzum (al-Qulzum)
23. Dahlak archipelago
13. Aden, al-Yaman

South East Asia and China

4. S. E. Sumatra (*Śribuza, Zābadj, Zābaj*)
5. N. Sumatra (*Rāmī, Rāmnī*)
6. Tioman/? Bintan (Tiyūma/Mā'iṭ)
25. Java (*Mūl Djāwa*)
27. ?*Ṣīnīya* (*Sīnia, Čīnyya*), in Champā
14. ?*Ṣīnīya* (*Sīnia, Čīniyya*), in Luichou/Hai-nan

India and Sri Lanka

15. Gulf of Mannar
16. Makrān
17. ? Jājnagar
18. Supara (*Sūbāra, Śurpāraka*)
19. Chilaw (Sandūna)
28. ?Maldives
29. Coromandel

Persian Gulf, Gulf of 'Omān, and southeast Arabia (Arabian Sea)

7. Baḥrain (Awāl, Ḳaṭar, al-Ḳatīf)
8. Ḳishm (and Hurmuz)
9. *Julfār*
10. Khārak
11. Ḳays (Kīsh)
12. Masḳaṭ (Ṣuḥār, Ḳalāt, *Damar*)
26. Mirbāṭ

MAP 4. Map of pearl trade in the southern seas, ninth to fifteenth centuries. American Philosophical Society.

down to very recent times. Here, virtually *all* maritime pursuits, fishing, collection of ambergris, pearling, and so on were organized by rich merchants who had at their disposal a pool of qualified laborers bound to them through an intricate web of credit and indebtedness that typically lasted a lifetime and often across several generations.[39]

In practice, of course, systems evolved and changed. The history of the Paravan, a caste of Tamil-speaking pearl fishers on the Indian coast opposite northern Ceylon, affords an illuminating example. For centuries they plied their trade under the Hindu kings of Pândya and then in the course of the thirteenth and fourteenth centuries fell under the control of Muslim merchant corporations who dominated the pearl industry in the region until the Portuguese took over in 1534.[40]

Under such circumstances, it is hardly surprising that systems of control and distribution also changed, often becoming composites. In Hormuz, Ceylon, and Quilon, on the southwestern coast of India, rulers over time imposed taxes on private fishers, farmed out fisheries to foreign merchants, and claimed monopolies.[41] In South India, at least, monopolies were sometimes effective. Courts strictly controlled the harvest of pearls, of which they took up to one-half.[42] One method of achieving this end was practiced in early fifteenth-century Ceylon, where the king constructed a large carefully guarded pond from which pearls were periodically extracted. The technique, as described by Ma Huan, might be an early example of "oyster farming."[43]

In the Persian Gulf there was yet another variant, merchant princes who dominated individual ports or islands and played a pivotal role in the operation of the local pearl fisheries. Here between the eleventh and thirteenth centuries island-based polities on Bahrain, Kīsh, and Hormuz (relocated to the island of Jarūn around 1300) gradually replaced mainland ports as hubs of regional and long-distance trade. This was achieved by a variety of means. The merchant princes built up formidable fleets using their wealth from trade and from the pearling industry, which in the case of Hormuz amounted to 20 percent of the annual harvest.[44] Further, they offered themselves as political neutrals able to provide economic services and commercial contacts to their much larger neighbors on the mainland. And equally important, they were attuned to the latest developments in nautical technology that transformed the islands into effective feeder ports providing in quantity foreign commodities that the hinterlands demanded for internal consumption as well as for the overland caravan trade.[45] With these assets they actively competed for control of the Gulf trade and did so throughout the Mongolian period, a topic treated in detail in Chapter 14.

In China, with its history of government monopolies, attempts were made to impose one on the pearl fisheries at Hepu as soon as the Qin reached the southern coast in 111 BCE. While not very successful, sporadic efforts continued into the Song, which set up a government-run fishery on Hainan.[46] In the north, dynasties of Inner Asian origin, the Qitan/Liao (907–1124) and the Jürchen/Jin (1115–1234), used a combination of methods to obtain freshwater pearls, termed bivalve (*gezhu*) or northern (*beizhu*) pearls. They imposed annual tributes on the riverine population of Manchuria, whereas private fishers were required to bring their pearls to government-monopoly tax markets (*juechang*).[47] The large numbers accumulated were used at court and extensively exported to the Song.[48]

The Yuan did much the same; they continued to require private individuals and communities settled on productive rivers to sell their harvest at the government market. In addition, they established a special agency, "Officials for the Management of Pearl Fisheries (*zhuzi minjiang quan*)," that supervised the collection of bivalve pearls.[49] Positions in this agency were hereditary, since the Mongols well understood that the necessary skills passed down within the family.

In the southwest, Marco Polo reports that in the region of Gaintu (Qiandu) in Sichuan there was a saltwater lake, under the strict control of Qubilai's court, in which "many pearls are found." He describes these as white but irregular in shape, often appearing as several pearls bound together.[50] There is, moreover, another mention of production in the region; the *Yuanshi* notes in passing a source of pearls in the land of the Lolos, a generic (and derogatory) name for the Tibeto-Burman peoples of Sichuan and Yunnan.[51]

On the coast, the major establishment was the Guangdong Pearl Fisheries Superintendency (*caizhu tijusi*), established sometime in Qubilai's reign, that controlled some forty thousand households. Because of unspecified "difficulties" it was abolished in the 1320s, and its duties were turned over to local officials. It was then reestablished in 1337 and finally eliminated in 1340.[52] Given its checkered history it seems likely that the superintendency was not productive and that the Yuan court had a more reliable and abundant source of saltwater pearls.

This was indeed the case. By the late Song foreign pearls flowed into China through its major ports—Hangzhou (Quinsai), Fuzhou (Fuqiu), Quanzhou (Zayton), and Guangzhou (Canton).[53] Many of these were from the Gulf or Ceylon, for in 1292 the Yuan authorities discovered that a lama, Yang Lianzhen-jia, had broken into the Song imperial tombs in the mid-1280s and come away with "fifty ounces of big pearls (*ta zhu*)," a term, discussed further on, that regularly designated those coming from the western part of the Indian Ocean."[54]

The Mongols were quick to take advantage of the Song connections and networks. As soon as they reached the south in 1277--78 they set up Maritime Trade Bureaus (*shibosi*) in Quanzhou and Fuzhou. Further, in 1283 the court formally invited foreign merchants to bring their gold, pearls, and other wares, which the bureaus were authorized to purchase for cash. In the following year the Yuan authorities became even more actively involved in overseas trade, providing ships and capital and selecting merchants to go abroad for a wide variety of goods. From the proceeds of the latter enterprises, the government took seven-tenths of the profits.[55] The dispatch in the early fourteenth century of a prominent government official "to investigate thoroughly a Quan[zhou] junk" and "to inspect the pearls" it was carrying points up the court's continuing interest in this trade.[56]

In their search for revenue the Mongols, of course, actively taxed business transactions. The commercial tax, *tamgha*, initially assessed in cash and kind was soon monetized and became a major source of income, "the most liquid (*naqdtarīn*) of the revenues" in the words of Rashīd al-Dīn.[57] Mongols' approach to maritime trade differed significantly from that imposed on domestic transactions. One reason for this was the acquisition of pearls. Toward this end, the Yuan and Il-qan courts both used preferential tariff rates levied on maritime imports to attract desired goods.

In China, Marco Polo says that at Caitan (Quanzhou), frequently visited by ships of the Indies "with many pearls," the kaan took 10 percent.[58] His information is quite correct; as soon as the Mongols occupied the southern coastline Qubilai imposed a ship tax (*bohuo*) fixed at one-tenth in kind for "fine" merchandise and one-fifteenth for "course." As the *Yuanshi* freely acknowledges, the Mongols adhered exactly to the system inherited from the Song.[59] The decision to follow this precedent is hardly surprising, since the Mongols had little experience with maritime trade and since the 10 percent tariff rate represented the traditional share due the qaghan from the proceeds of booty and tribute collection.[60]

The Il-qan court followed a somewhat different path. At Tabriz, its commercial center and sometime capital, silver and pearls were free of customs duties on entering and leaving.[61] Silver, it has convincingly been demonstrated, was exempt because large amounts were reexported to India as part of a sophisticated program of arbitrage and currency manipulation.[62] Pearls, on the other hand, apparently received free passage in order to attract this all-important positional good.

In part, the divergence in their approaches is explained by the elevated pricing practices of the Yuan and by the huge quantities they purchased. To foreign merchants bringing pearls to Chinese ports the 10 percent tariff in kind was well worth paying to gain admission to an extremely lucrative market. But certainly more decisive in explaining their differences is that while the Yuan had an effective administrative presence in all the major ports of entry along its coastline, the Il-qans did not and thus were compelled to work through several layers of intermediaries over whom they exercised limited authority.

In line with the practices of other Chinggisid courts, the Golden Horde also offered attractive tariff rates to foreign merchants and did so, revealingly, for the very same set of commodities. Because their geopolitical situation and their means of access to maritime products differed markedly from that of the Yuan and Il-qans, the topic is examined in different contexts in Chapters 8 and 14.

Finally, it should be noted that the persistent attempts of states to claim a share of these natural treasures inevitably produced efforts at evasion. The ways were varied and equally persistent. Foreign merchants bringing pearls to sell in China tried to avoid tariffs and taxes by posing as tribute-bearers, a very old gambit in this part of the world.[63] On a somewhat smaller scale, pearls always posed a difficult problem for tax collectors and customs officials; because they were easily transported, they could be concealed in small amounts in clothing or disguised as cheap baubles.[64] Further, and again inevitably, bribery was a perennial problem, and so too were the machinations of port officials, who regularly pressured merchants for "gifts" of pearls, a practice with a long history in China.[65] For our purposes, however, successful evasion and official corruption only provided additional channels through which pearls flowed into Chinggisid domains, and this leads to the thorny issue of the quantities they accumulated and dispensed.

CHAPTER 4

Treasures and Treasuries

By means ranging from forcible seizure to market mechanisms, Mongolian courts amassed huge quantities of pearls. The exact numbers will never be known, but the sources provide helpful and at times quite specific information about its magnitude.

As a starting point, it must be stressed that despite the frequent mention of pearls in the sources of the period, there is every reason to believe they are greatly underreported. There are several reasons for this, one of which is ambiguities in vocabulary. In Persian and Arabic texts there are many references to the Mongols' acquisition and display of *gawhar/jawhar*, plural *javāhir/javāhirāt*.[1] The term, which goes back to the Middle Persian *gōhr/gwhr*, "substance," "essence," and "jewel," passed into Arabic and New Persian with the primary meaning of "jewel" or "gemstone."[2] In most contexts, however, it also denotes pearls. For instance, in the Arabic construction *ʿiqd jawhar*, literally, "string of gems," pearls are certainly intended.[3] And when *gawhar* later passed into Turkic in the form *gühär/gävhär*, it did so with the primary meaning of "pearl."[4] Thus, when it stands alone in medieval texts, *javāhir* denotes "precious stones" generally, that is to say, "gems and pearls."

The same semantic ambiguities are encountered with the Arabo-Persian word *muraṣṣaʿ*, "studded [with gems]," for it too could mean precious stones or pearls but once again denotes a combination of the two. In the Muslim sources from ʿAbbāsid through Temürid times, this term is often applied to belts for ceremonial and court use.[5]

In Chinese texts there are similar ambiguities associated with the term *qibao*, "seven treasures," a translation of the Sanskrit *sapta ratna*.[6] Most certainly, then, the term and the concept accompanied Buddhism into China. For the Mongols, at least in the later years of the empire, its Buddhist associations are also evident. Already in Yuan era *erdene*, derived from *ratna*, is encountered in Mongolian translations of Buddhist works, and following the Mongols' conversion to Lamaism in the sixteenth century, Mongolian texts make reference to the seven treasures, which included red pearls (*ulughan subut*), terminology that reflects much older Indic tradition.[7]

But this was only one meaning of the term current in the Middle Ages. From Tang times onward *qibao* was also used to describe any object decorated with multicolored glass and gems of every kind, real and artificial.[8] In this latter sense, it seems likely that the Mongols first encountered such ornamentation among the booty taken from the Jin, whose ruler sat upon "a seven-jeweled throne."[9] Consequently, when Chinggis Qan bestowed upon a successful commander a saddle adorned with the seven treasures, the act had no Buddhist connotations and meant only "studded with multiple gemstones."[10] While many objects adorned with the seven treasures—badges of authority, horse gear, caps, belts, suits of clothing, and tableware—circulated widely during the Yuan, the question of which particular treasures were included cannot be answered by direct textual evidence.[11] But again, given Mongolian tastes and preferences, documented in succeeding chapters, there is every reason to believe that pearls were regularly part of the package.

There is good evidence, too, that the bestowal of pearls at the Yuan court is regularly and substantially underrepresented by the Chinese sources. Several examples can be cited in support of this assertion. The first concerns ʿIsā the Interpreter, an Eastern Christian from upper Mesopotamia in Mongolian service. While his biography in the *Yuanshi* makes no mention of royal bestowals of any kind, we know from a more detailed account of his life prepared by the Yuan scholar Cheng Jufu that at his death in 1308 the emperor offered as funerary gifts paper money, gold, silver, and an "innumerable quantity of pearled clothing and hats," and later when posthumously invested as Prince of Rum (Fu-lin) he received further pearled clothing.[12] From this, two conclusions can be drawn: the extremely generous funerary gifts strongly imply that ʿIsā received similar bestowals in life and that posthumous presentations, while rarely mentioned in the sources, were nonetheless quite common and extensive.

In the second case, it is evident that the common practice of basting court clothing with pearls is not always noted by Chinese texts discussing this attire. In a bilingual inscription of the fourteenth century prepared in honor of a Mongolian official, the Chinese version mentions only his brocade court robe, while the Mongolian text is careful to add that it was "pearled (*subutu*)."[13] The discrepancy is interesting as an indication of the particular importance the

Mongols attached to pearls, and that the matter was not always thought worthy of mention in Chinese texts because court dress was routinely pearled.

As for actual numbers, the available information, although scattered in time and space, anecdotal in nature and using different measures, nonetheless presents a consistent picture of the huge quantities involved. Perhaps the best way to proceed is to sample and evaluate some of the figures reported concerning the productivity of fisheries and the number of pearls possessed by royal courts in other eras and then compare these with data from the Mongolian Empire.

For more recent times, we have the report of John Chardin, a professional jeweler and merchant with a vested interest in collecting accurate data, that in the year 1670 the beds along the Persian coastline by themselves annually produced more than a million pearls, of which the Ṣafāvid ruler received an unspecified share of the larger ones.[14] Here it is necessary to take into account that these beds, though notable, were held to be of secondary importance in the region, following well behind Bahrain and other sources off the Arabian Peninsula. Consequently, it is reasonable to assume that the production of the Gulf as a whole was many times greater than the figure provided by Chardin.

Famous bestowals among elites constitute another indicator of the quantities in circulation. In a well-known episode reported by Ṭabarī and others it is stated that in 805 ʿAlī ibn ʿIsā, the governor of Khurāsān, gave the caliph Hārūn al-Rashīd "gifts" worth thirty million gold dinars.[15] Bayhaqī (d. 1077), who apparently had access to a now lost unabridged version of Ṭabarī's text, says that this presentation consisted in part of three hundred thousand pearls (*marvārīd*).[16] Although the uncertainties surrounding the transmission of this particular data naturally give rise to suspicion, the number of pearls available and the numbers accumulated at imperial centers, though sometimes inflated, were nonetheless quite elevated.

The most stunning piece of evidence in support of this argument comes from the Northern Song (960–1127) and rests on its tradition of bureaucratic record keeping embodied in the *Song huiyao*, an extensive collection of original documents on government operations and finances.[17] This source reports that at the beginning of the dynasty there was established a Storehouse for the Receipt of Pearls (*Shouna zhenzhu ku*) that held those confiscated from the defeated kingdoms in the south and those received through tribute and foreign trade. In 1040, the storehouse, together with several similar institutions, was combined into the Treasury of the Imperial Apartments (*Fengqun ku*). From this repository the emperor in 1068 authorized the withdrawal of 33,436,569 pearls of differing grades to finance the purchase of vitally needed cavalry remounts for the defense of the threatened northern frontier.[18] An astounding figure to be sure, but one based on a reliable and "unintended" source whose sole purpose was to guide internal administration. No wonder there is mention of the Chinese ruler's "palace of large pearls (*durr*)" in a near-contemporary eleventh-century Arabic text, clear evidence that the treasury's immense holdings enjoyed international renown.[19]

Turning to data from the Mongolian Empire, there are several interesting reports from the Il-qan period.

In 1296 the prince of Kīsh, Jamāl al-Dīn, offered Ghazan (r. 1296–1304) two million gold dinars and fifteen hundred *mann* of pearls, about three thousand pounds, for the right to farm the taxes of southern Iran and Iraq.[20]

Next, the testimony of Qāshānī, an Il-qan court official, relates that in 1314–15 the take from Hūrshīf, a secondary fishery (*ghaws*) in the Gulf, was six thousand *mann* of large and small pearls. Equally helpful, we are given information concerning the purchasing power of this specific harvest when he adds that the ruler of Kīsh used the proceeds to hire two hundred boats and twenty thousand mercenaries in his ongoing military confrontations with Hormuz.[21]

From 1340 there is the report of the fiscal officer Qazvīnī that the revenue collected from Kīsh was 491,300 gold dinars.[22] As the island was both a pearling station and a trade emporium, however, we cannot determine the relative contribution of pearls to the total. Nevertheless, their share in the revenues generated was likely quite substantial, since by this time Kīsh had been displaced by Hormuz as the predominant trade center in the Gulf for several decades.

Data from Chinese sources affirm that the quantities available to and controlled by the Yuan court were equally vast. As one measure of this, the "hundred officials," a collective name for the government bureaucracy, were authorized clothing and jewelry decorated with pearls, some of which were bivalve pearls (*gezhu*) of riverine origin.[23] More specifically, from a regulation issued in 1312 on court attire it is known that of the nine official ranks, one through six were allowed to wear pearls.[24] Since the size of the Yuan bureaucracy was about twenty-six thousand, something in the neighborhood of seventeen thousand officials were so authorized, a figure that speaks to the court's ample supplies.[25] And beyond this, there is statistical data based on contemporary records from the reign of Qubilai that fully sustain the argument of abundance.

Mangghudai, a Mongolian official of the Branch Secretariat of Jiangzhe, a coastal province that included Hangzhou, in 1284 presented to court, apparently as a personal gift, "one hundred Chinese pounds (*jin* or catties) of real pearls (*zhenzhu*)."[26]

Shihāb al-Dīn, head of the Maritime Trade Superintendency, in 1289 offered to provide, again as a gift, four hundred Chinese pounds of pearls to the court. The emperor accepted and ordered these be set aside for poor relief.[27]

The maritime province of Huguang reported in 1291 that "for the two years preceding, the commercial tax (*xuanke*) was 90,515 Chinese ounces (*liang* or tael) of pearls."[28] To point out the obvious, this figure represents only 10 percent of the total imported through a single province for a two-year period.

Zhou Mi, a literatus from the south, provides helpful information on a rich Muslim merchant based in Sichuan, Fu Lian, whose family "regularly sent eighty ships overseas." At his death in 1293 he had no male heir, and so the Yuan government confiscated his possessions and found among them 130 piculs (*shi*) of pearls.[29]

A closer look at the units of weights and measures used in the above reports provides further confirmation of the staggering amounts involved. While premodern measures are notorious for their instability and flexibility, we have for the principal ones used here accurate values for the period in question. We can start with the Chinese *liang*. Assuming an average of thirty pearls per ounce, a very conservative estimate, the court's take from Huguang in 1289 and 1290 amounted to just over 2.7 million, and therefore the total number entering the province amounted to 27 million. Next, the *shi* or picul was a Chinese unit of capacity having a value of 94.88 liters in the north and 66.41 in the Southern Song, a value that was left in place following the Mongolian occupation.[30] Thus, if calculated on the northern standard, the merchant Fu Lian left behind about 12,350 liters of pearls, and if on the southern standard, 8,580 liters. However one might calculate the number of pearls per unit of measure, it is evident that many millions are involved.

Equally informative, the picul was the standard dry measure to quantify grain shipments from the southern provinces to Dadu, in one case reported to be 836,260 *shi*.[31] The same practice is found in the eastern Islamic world, where the *mann* of Tabriz, fixed at 260 dirhams or roughly two pounds during the Il-qan era, was the basic measure for both grain and pearls.[32] And even in regions such as Tibet large quantities of pearls (*mun-tig*) were expressed in the basic dry measure (*bre*) for grain.[33] That bulk pearls were almost always treated like grain serves to confirm that the numbers harvested, sold, taxed, deposited, and bestowed were immense. Marco Polo had every right to be astounded at the amounts accumulated by Chinggisid courts.[34]

Given the volume of precious goods the Mongols collected, storage and security became an important issue. When thinking of treasuries in modern contexts, permanent, heavily built, and guarded facilities containing bullion and ready cash come first to mind. While little data exists on practices followed elsewhere in the empire, security for treasuries in Mongolia and North China was normally provided by members of the royal guard. Möngke's appointment in 1251 of two officers "to garrison and guard the palace gates and treasuries/storehouses (*tangcang*) of Qara Qorum" is one clear expression of this.[35] Indeed, these are among the basic and stated duties of the guard from the beginning of the Chinggisid state.[36]

Security was certainly an issue, but royal treasuries of an earlier age diverge from their modern image in several significant ways. First, treasuries still had "public" functions, serving as an extension of the court into which honored guests were invited to view and possibly receive some of the sovereign's riches, a tradition that goes back at least to the Later Han in East Asia and to the Sasanids in West Asia.[37] These facilities provided an effective and glittering stage for the advertisement of royal wealth because they concentrated in one place an array of exquisite and rare objects, the products of nature and culture acquired on home ground and from distant climes.

Throughout much of Eurasia there was considerable unity in their composition: ready money, precious metals, decorated drinking vessels, ceremonial weapons, textiles, furs, medicines, scents, jewelry, gems, and the ever-present pearls.[38] And despite a measure of surface diversity, their contents shared a number of common attributes. All constituted material wealth as well as political capital, potential gifts, and rewards to servitors and soldiers, and most were liquid, especially gems and pearls, which could be used as currency or readily converted into cash. The sale of crown jewels is of course a literary topos and a historical reality, most famously Byzantium's pawning of the royal regalia in 1343 to Venice for thirty thousand gold ducats, which in default of repayment were never returned.[39]

Of the premodern treasuries, those of the Song were probably the most sophisticated; extensive accounts were kept, regular audits made, and a fairly clear distinction maintained between the fiscal resources of the state and the crown.[40] Still, even in this case their composition corresponds closely to West Asian counterparts and to the European conception of *spezierie,* which underscores again the essential unity of the commodities exchanged and, of course, the uniformity of material culture found at royal courts East and West.

Mongolian treasuries certainly embraced the inherited traditions as regards contents.[41] While the Mongols had permanent storage facilities, discussed below, we know, too, that as Chinggisid courts retained their nomadic lifestyle to the end of the empire, they regularly took a sizable part of their treasures on the road during progresses, hunts, and military campaigns.[42] And these, like the permanent facilities of sedentary powers, also lent themselves to display. Two revealing examples, nearly seven hundred years apart, can be cited. In the first, circa 569, Byzantine envoys report that in front of the Türk qaghan's tent "were drawn up over a wide area wagons containing many silver objects, dishes and bowls, and a large number of statues of animals, also of silver, and in no way inferior to those we make; so wealthy is the ruler of the Türks."[43] In this instance the qaghan's display most certainly elicited the desired effect. In the second, Giovanni Carpini, at the court of Güyük (r. 1246–48), records that at the edge of the emperor's camp "more than fifty wagons were placed beyond a hill . . . and they were all filled with gold and silver and silk clothing which were divided between the emperor and his nobles." Yet again, its purpose, to attract attention, project an image of incomparable wealth, and intensify anticipation of rewards, was fully realized.[44]

As neither the Mongolian rulers nor their nomadic adherents, despite an occasional claim to the contrary, possessed the expert knowledge to value, catalogue, or manage gems, there was a pressing need for specialist personnel.[45] On the narrowly technical level it appears they were well served. Like the precious gems they accumulated, the Chinggisids recruited and impressed skilled artisans and jewelers, from East Asia to Europe.[46] Of the latter, we even know the names of two: Cosmas, a Russian goldsmith who made Güyük's pearled throne, and Guillaume Boucher, a Parisian jeweler who in Möngke's reign finished the great drinking fountain/automaton at Qara Qorum.[47]

For the most part, however, the numerous specialists the Mongols collected remain anonymous. During the initial stages of the Mongols' expansion their armies and agents generally collected jewelers and artisans by direct seizure in the immediate aftermath of battle, like any other form of mobile wealth. In subsequent decades, the Mongols increasingly relied upon systematic census taking to register, tax, and apportion technicians of every kind, a search that extended from major cities to small rural settlements.[48]

Their quest began early; during the reigns of Chinggis Qan and Ögödei goldsmiths (*jingong*) were identified and drafted in North China, initially for service with other artisans in catapult units.[49] Next, following the rapid advance of their armies, the Mongols gained control of Turfan, the Tarim Basin, and the eastern Islamic lands, all of which had rich traditions and advanced technologies in the manufacture of jewelry.[50] The Mongols were quick to capitalize on this opportunity; by the time of Ögödei's enthronement in 1229 some three hundred weavers and goldsmiths from the Western Region (Xiyu), Turkistan, and Iran were transported to Hongzhou, located about 180 km west of Dadu.[51] Not surprisingly, the Mongols in the East were soon well supplied with jewelry artisans, including a large staff of lapidaries (*ḥakkākāt*) attached to the imperial treasuries at Qara Qorum.[52]

The number accumulated was substantial. In 1261, on Qubilai's order, more than three thousand households of goldsmiths, agate artisans, and lapidaries (*yugong*) stationed at Qara Qorum, Bai Baliq (on the Selenga River), and other locales in Mongolia were transferred to Dadu, where there was established a "Goldsmith and Lapidary Office (*jinyuju*)" to oversee their activities. Later this office was upgraded to the "Directorate General (*congguanfu*) for Goldsmiths and Lapidaries in Various Circuits," which managed the preparation of precious material for the court and included a dedicated Pearl Office (*zhuzi ju*). In addition, there were other more specialized agencies, such as the Jewelry Superintendency (*jin yu zhu cui tijusi*) subordinate to the Heir Apparent's Retinue.[53]

The major reservoirs of such talent were, of course, great imperial centers. When Baghdad was occupied in 1258, Hülegü immediately placed a Muslim official in charge of all its artisans. Given its attractive powers as the longtime capital of the ʿAbbāsid Caliphate, the city provided a rich haul of renowned goldsmiths, jewelers, lapidaries, and pearl borers.[54] The same can be said of the Song capital Hangzhou, which fell in 1277. It, too, had great numbers of artisans organized into guilds, through which the Yuan, following Song practice, regulated their production and relations with the court, including the Precious Metals and Jewels Office (*jin yu fu*), established in 1280.[55] So, despite the vast booty that came into their possession at the fall of the two capitals, the Mongols wasted little time expanding their capacity to produce ever more jewelry under court control.

The thoroughness of their quest for personnel is clearly illustrated in the experience of Kievan Rus. From archaeological investigations carried out in recent decades it has become apparent that a jewelry industry began among the Eastern Slavs sometime in the ninth or tenth century. Thereafter, a steady growth in the volume and technical sophistication of its products in larger urban centers is noticeable.[56] While these achievements were not always fully appreciated by contemporaries or by modern scholars, it is all the more striking that the Mongols were quick to recognize and exploit this untapped pool of talent. This is evidenced by the fact that in the mid-1250s when the Tatars began a comprehensive census in the Rus Principalities, artisans tried to escape their "counters" by flight westward; among them, a chronicle informs us, were "masters of silver," Old Russian *serebrianiki*, a term that also served as a generic designation for "jewelers."[57]

In other regions of the Golden Horde, where written documentation is lacking, the archaeological data testifies to the Jochids' level of interest in these crafts. Investigations of the two capitals (Sarai and New Sarai) and other settlements of the Volga basin provide unmistakable evidence in the form of workshops, raw materials, and specialized tools for the presence of numerous jewelers, goldsmiths, and lapidaries working in this region. In several cases, such facilities are associated with large urban "villas." Many artisans, apparently, did custom work for princes and notables, while others operated as independent proprietors of their own shops, paying taxes and selling goods to the general public. In any event, this interpretation accords well with what is known from written records concerning the status and activities of relocated artisans in China.[58]

The acquisition, dispersal, and organization of these specialists call for several general and comparative comments to situate the Mongolian experience in historical perspective.

First, although the ethnic background of transported artisans in the Yuan is not always stipulated, it is evident that many, if not most, came from the eastern Islamic lands. A large pool of gem and pearl experts was found in that region, and starting in the 1220s the Mongols began relocating Muslim artisans of every type to their East Asian holdings. The ethnic origins of the specialists in the Golden Horde are in principle even more problematical, but it is likely, too, that many came from the same pool, a conclusion that rests on two considerations. The towns where their activities are documented in the archaeological record are located in the steppe zone, and all were founded by the Jochids at sites without any trace of previous settlement; consequently there were no local craft traditions upon which to draw or any indigenous specialists to draft. The technical personnel perforce came from outside the region. The question of where can be answered with some assurance; on the grounds of style, decorative motifs, and manufacturing techniques, the products from Golden Horde jewelry workshops show close affinities with those of Iran and Turkistan.

Second, while the majority of the imported artisans were from the eastern Islamic world, this does not preclude the presence of specialists from other backgrounds, especially given the Chinggisids' penchant for transporting skilled people between different cultural zones of the empire. And the ethnically diverse pools of specialist personnel that resulted from this practice quite naturally provided an excellent medium for artistic and technical transfers. To cite one well-established example, the rings, earrings, pendants, plaques, and headdresses, some in filigree, produced at the two Sarais and in other Golden Horde sites show an intermingling of Inner Asian, Islamic, and European styles and techniques.[59]

Third, it should be stressed that these foreign artisans, including the jewelers and lapidaries, were transported as families, which in the Chinese sources are always enumerated by the household (*hu*). This procedure, assuredly, was done by conscious design, for, as already mentioned, the Mongols realized that specialized skills were typically transmitted down family lines.[60] Further, and perhaps most important, this practice was consistent with their desire to prevent the assimilation of relocated communities, since the linchpin of their governing strategy was the extensive use of foreign administrators and garrison troops in newly conquered territory.

Fourth, the Mongols' reliance on and acquisition of foreign jewelers has a long and continuous history in the steppe world. In the fifth century BCE the Scythians were much drawn to ornaments fashioned by Greek artisans who readily adapted their products to the nomads' tastes and cultural expectations.[61] In the sixth century the Avars became notorious, to use Arnold Toynbee's apt phrase, as "herders of human-beings" who at times removed settled populations of whole districts into the steppe. Some of these they ransomed, while others were retained to exploit their talents in jewelry making and other crafts.[62] More selective targeting is also on record. In 629–30 the Khazar qaghan sent his agents to Caucasian Albania (Azerbaijan) to gather artisans "skilled in the use of gold and silver, wrought iron and copper" and seems to have done so with the aid of Sasanian cadastral data.[63] The major difference between these earlier efforts and that of the Chinggisids is the matter of scale. And while there were occasional transfers between major cultural zones of Eurasia in earlier times—the Chinese gold- and silversmiths captured at the Battle of Talas in 751 and then sent to the ʿAbbāsid capital to ply their trade—these were exceptional, unplanned events, not the end result of a conscious policy of systematic search, impressment, and relocation such as that carried out by the Mongols in the thirteenth century.[64]

In addition to technicians, there was a need for permanent facilities and administrative personnel. A brief discussion of this subject is necessary to address the crucial question of how well the Mongols managed their newly acquired wealth.

As is usually the case, we are best informed on the situation in the eastern zone of the empire. At Qara Qorum, Ögödei had built a number of wooden storehouses termed *khizānah*, "treasuries," in the Persian texts.[65] And according to the Chinese sources, Qubilai in the course of his reign authorized the founding of a series of treasuries (*tangcang*) located in the new capital, Dadu; while some of these had very specialized holdings, collectively they housed the standard package of ready cash and prestige goods.[66]

In considering this institution in the context of steppe history, it is evident that nomads did not have need for treasuries until they acquired sufficient resources to support permanent political structures. It is hardly surprising, then, that they regularly borrowed both the institution and its nomenclature from sedentary states. In Uighur, for instance, the term for "treasurer," *tsangchi*, combines the Chinese *cang*, "treasury," with the Turkic nomen actoris, *-chi*.[67] The Mongols did much the same; Rashīd al-Dīn uses a comparable hybrid composed of the Arabo-Persian *khazīnah* and the Turkic and Mongolian suffix *-chi*. The resulting form of this title, **khazinechi* or **qazinechi* has an exact parallel in the Old Russian *kaznachei* or *kaznachii*, itself a borrowing from the Turkic chancellery language of the Golden Horde.[68] Here, of course, the direction of transmission is reversed, as in this case a sedentary state received its nomenclature for the office and the institution through the mediation of nomads.

As to those who held this office under the Mongols, we have only the names of three individuals, Tekechüg, Kököchü, and Qundaqai. But even from this meager data it is at least certain that all were of Inner Asian origin.[69] It also seems a reasonable surmise, given the Mongols' patrimonial notions of government, that those appointed were chosen because of their close personal ties to the ruler and not because of their mastery of technical skills relevant to the position, in this case bookkeeping. Further, the rather harsh conclusion that as a class these officials were ineffective and often corrupt finds clear support in the extensively documented fact that while the Mongols were ruthlessly efficient at collecting booty and tributes, the control they exercised over these riches once in their hands was fraught with difficulties, the sources of which, although having quite different origins, soon became entwined and mutually reinforcing.

The first problem, and one that proved insuperable, is linked to nomadic ideas concerning royal possessions. The relationship between the il-qan Abaqa (r. 1265–81) and his senior wife, Bulughan, nicely illustrates the Mongols' attitude. In the course of her lifetime she amassed a trove of fine garments, gold and silver objects, gems, and precious pearls (*la'ālī'-i thamīn*), which came about, Rashīd al-Dīn explains, because every time her adoring husband entered the treasury he "brought out exquisite gems and precious things which he secretly gave to her."[70] Obviously, Abaqa treated the assets of the state as his personal property and disposed of them as he wished. In this he was not alone. From the beginning of the empire to its fragmentation, Chinggisid rulers, unlike those of the Song, rarely made any distinction between government funds and family wealth, with the result that state finances were in perpetual crisis.

All this was further exacerbated by lax administration and by the ever-increasing volume of precious objects flooding Mongolian treasuries during the early empire that made accurate accounting much more difficult and official theft far easier. Again, Rashīd al-Dīn offers illuminating examples. In the early days of the empire, he relates, "officials guarded the treasury and they picked it up and put it down and everything was so disordered that they did not even have a tent and placed it [the treasury] on the ground and covered it with felt. From this arrangement," he concludes, "one can judge the rest."[71] And, in accounting for the financial crisis that engulfed the Il-qan state in the late thirteenth century, Rashīd starts, significantly, by relating what befell the great treasures seized by Hülegü in Iran and Mesopotamia. These, he says, were placed in a castle on an island in Lake Urmiya. Soon, however, many of these holdings, gold and gem-studded jewelry, began to disappear, largely sold off by the castle's keepers to merchants. At the same time, these officials, in return for bribes, willingly made payments for assorted military supplies that were never delivered to the government. A later il-qan, Arghun (r. 1284–91), Rashīd reports, was in consequence of these irregularities moved to found a new treasury, but it, too, soon suffered the same fate.[72]

What happened in these instances would now be called a breakdown of inventory control, though it is fairly obvious that little if any control was ever exercised. In discussing the events leading up to Ghazan's extensive program of economic and fiscal reforms, Rashīd al-Dīn has some caustic comments on the subject. "Before now it had not been the custom for anyone to keep accounts of the treasuries of the Mongolian sovereigns or for accurately fixing the receipts and expenditures." The difficulty, he continues, is that there was a lack of personnel with proper training and that those in charge were given to rampant corruption, more particularly their active and profitable collusion with Chinggisid family members, retainers, and government officials of every rank. "In this way," he ends, "every year from the contents of the treasuries eight-tenths were squandered and two[-tenths] were expended as the sovereign ordered."[73]

Even taking into account the interest Rashīd al-Dīn had in magnifying the problems confronting his sovereign and patron, it is apparent that the Mongols basically ignored the normal accounting procedures used in imperial treasuries in China and the Islamic lands, and the inevitable result was systemic corruption and immense waste.[74]

Throughout his extended critique Rashīd al-Dīn speaks of Mongolian sovereigns generally, not just the Il-qans, and it is most striking that his complaints about lax management find close parallels in the Chinese sources. Here, too, the problems are traced back to the early empire. Already in 1230, the second year of Ögödei's reign, Yelu Chucai, a Sinicized Qitan and chief spokesman of the Chinese faction at court, felt the need to press the emperor to punish "those trading or borrowing government goods" and to put to death "government inspectors who personally steal government properties."[75] Even more illuminating is a statement found in the *Yuanshi,* which comments that at the beginning of the empire there were no officials recording and verifying the receipts and disbursements of the royal treasuries, so that in 1290, just a few years before the institution of Ghazan's reforms in Iran, the Yuan treasuries were reorganized, divided into three subsections: one for textiles, another for gold, gems and pearls, and a third for leather and horse trappings, each with its own personnel.[76] This measure, however, did not bring about the desired relief, for the problems went far beyond the absence of effective inventory control.

Many took advantage of this failing, none more aggressively than the merchants the Chinggisids eagerly recruited as personal financial agents and treasury officials. The staffing procedure under Möngke is related by Juvaynī in a somewhat opaque passage: "A contingent of merchants came [to court] who have brought merchandise to transact business with the treasury of the emperor and these too are of several classes; some value jewels, [another] contingent clothing, some animals and so on."[77] Although left unsaid, it is nonetheless evident that of the many merchants who came to court to offer goods, some stayed on as officials of the treasury. The "twelve wise men" who Marco Polo says appraised and valued gems and pearls at Qubilai's court were likely recruited in similar fashion.[78] Most certainly the combination of an inexperienced leadership with a middle management composed largely of merchants responsible for valuations and accounts encouraged or perhaps guaranteed the spread of the malpractices that so afflicted Chinggisid treasuries.

Further and revealing detail on the court's dealings with foreign merchants is available in the *Yuanshi.* On several occasions it records that when Muslims brought large pearls (*da zhu*) to court, Qubilai rejected their offers, saying that the asking prices were outrageously high and that these sums could be better used "to succor the poor."[79] Viewed in isolation, the passage implies that the

Yuan emperor had developed a different set of priorities and an inclination toward Confucian style of government. But matters were far more complex. First of all, Qubilai's response, a desire to help the poor, was one fully compatible with the Mongols' own patrimonial ethos and style of governance. And second, the court's relationship with merchants was rarely based on simple straightforward business transactions between sellers and buyers conducted in an open, unfettered market.

A noted affair during the reign of Temür Qaghan (1294–1307) throws much additional light on the true nature these transactions. According to the biography of Shang Wen, a high-ranking Chinese official, a merchant from the Western Region came to court in 1303 offering big pearls and rubies (*ya-hu* = Arabo-Persian *yāqūt*), the asking price for which was six hundred thousand silver ingots (*ding*) worth of paper money. Shang Wen strongly objected to the transaction, arguing that the sum involved should be used to alleviate hunger and thereby prevent "disorder in All-Under-Heaven."[80] There is, however, another account of this incident from Rashīd al-Dīn, who was well informed on Chinese affairs through Yuan embassies to the Il-qan court. According to his information, when the offer was made Temür's advisers and brokers (*dalālān*) greatly overvalued the pearls and precious stones (*javāhir*) at six hundred thousand ingots (*balīsh*) worth of paper money, in return for which they received huge kickbacks. At this juncture two brokers not party to the original valuation came forward in protest, arguing that the pearls and gems were horribly overpriced, and the court then ordered Shihāb al-Dīn Qunduzī, formerly of the Maritime Trade Superintendency, to review the matter. He came to the conclusion that the selling price was double their actual market value. Thereupon the merchant and the dishonest brokers were arrested and sentenced to death. In the end, however, judicious bribery allowed them to go free upon return of the overcharges to the treasury, yet further evidence of the high standing and connections of merchant advisers at court.[81]

The apparent differences between these two versions of the affair are readily explained. All large outlays of this type set off debates, some participants arguing about market value and others about fiscal restraint and good government.[82] In his biography it is not surprising that Shang Wen is presented, no doubt quite accurately, as opposing the sale on Confucian principles, while Shihāb al-Dīn opposes it on purely commercial grounds. For our purposes, the major lesson is that merchant advisers' deep involvement in the court's commercial dealings was a certain recipe for corruption and collusion. Nor, it must be added, did this well-publicized international scandal bring a halt to these problems. In a memorial to the throne in 1324, the Chinese military officer and scholar Zhang Gui rails against the merchant middlemen and brokers who "divide pearls into small lots and the selling price [asked] is tens of thousands," an abuse he says first emerged during the reign of Temür.[83] Not unexpectedly, Qubilai, as the formal and honored founder of the dynasty, was exempt from such criticism.

In partial response to these ongoing excesses, members of the Yuan court did make a further effort to restore some order in their wide ranging commercial dealings and arrangements. In 1329 it was decreed that *all* merchants, Buddhists, Daoists, Christians, Jews (Zhu-hu), and Muslims (Da-shi-men = Persian Dānishman) "should again pay taxes according to the old regulations," which obligation, obviously, they had long successfully evaded. The decree itself is of interest on several levels. Most obviously, it categorizes merchants by their communal affiliations, which tells us something about their backgrounds and provides a reminder of the long and intimate connection between long-distance commerce and universalist religions. Next, the decree may suggest that the merchants' ability to escape payment, at least land and head taxes, was in some way associated with the blanket exemptions the Chinggisids regularly offered religious leaders and ritual specialists. Finally, it can be inferred that the larger purpose of the decree was to curtail the Muslims, the most numerous of the foreign merchants operating in China, without singling them out as the principal target. Such an interpretation is borne out by another imperial decree issued two years later that formally exempted the Buddhists from taxation, with the apparent goal of giving them a competitive advantage over the ubiquitous Muslims.[84] But in the face of the court's dependence on the extensive overseas connections the Muslims had and their unparalleled access to desirable positional goods, their influence and their fast practices lasted until the end of the dynasty. The Chinggisids were well aware, as Rashīd al-Dīn presents the matter, that the steady flow of *tamgha*, "commercial taxes," and of *tansuq*, "precious goods," into the imperial coffers was always dependent on their collaboration.[85]

It is most instructive that pearls are continually at the center of the many heated discussions over the purchase of luxury goods and the corruption of brokers and merchants. In the eyes of Chinese officials, pearls came to symbolize, and with good reason, all of the excesses associated with the Yuan court's dealings with foreign, mainly Muslim, merchants.[86] Moreover, it was not only the scholar-officials who harbored strong anti-Muslim attitudes; they were also articulated in biting satirical tales reflecting attitudes among the general populace.[87] Not surprisingly, then, in the opinion of many modern scholars such extravagance undermined state finances and alienated Chinese subjects, major catalysts for the weakening and overthrow of the Mongolian regime.[88]

Yet despite all the price fixing, kickbacks, gross mismanagement, and outright theft, Chinggisid courts still possessed seemingly endless reserves of pearls and other precocities to invest in ostentatious display and conspicuous redistribution.

CHAPTER 5

Display and Redistribution

To determine Mongolian preferences, a brief examination of the Mongols' terms for pearls is needed. In the *Secret History* two words are used, *tanas* (singular *tana*), defined in the Chinese interlineal translation as "big pearls," and *subud*, defined as "small pearls," definitions that are repeated in the *Yuanshi* chapter on court dress.[1]

In the multilingual lexicons produced in the Mongolian era, *subud*, not *tanas*, is always used as the equivalent of the Chinese *zhu*, Persian *marvārīd*, and Arabic *al-lu'lu'*.[2] This strongly suggests that *subud* was the basic native term in the minds of the compilers' Mongolian informants. An alternative view has, however, been advanced. Sir Gerard Clauson argued that *subud* is a metathesized form of the Persian *bussad*, "coral." His explanation is troubling in purely linguistic terms, for it requires both semantic and phonetic shifts, a rather uncommon phenomenon. Further, it rests on the assumption that since pearls are a product of the southern seas and the Mongols are "an inland people," a native term is fundamentally improbable.[3] The latter point, of course, is simply incorrect, because there are riverine pearls in northern Manchuria, the homeland of the Mongols' immediate ancestors. There is, then, no reason the Mongols should not have a native word for pearl, one, presumably, that originally designated the local freshwater variety.

The question of the linguistic relationships of *tana*, as well as the related issue of the geographical distribution of the pearls so designated, also requires consideration, since the term is used ambiguously in the sources. The chief difficulty, of course, is that such a term can be used in a purely descriptive manner to designate any kind of pearl of large size. In a Chinese text of the late twelfth century, for instance, the report that the Jürchen land produces big pearls (*da zhu*) clearly refers to the freshwater variety.[4] More commonly, however, the Chinese and Mongolian use of "big pearl" designates pearls from the western Indian Ocean. Various lines of converging evidence lead to this conclusion. From the pre-Tang period onward, Chinese sources record that Persia (Bo-si) is noted for its "many big pearls."[5] This special usage is continued into the Yuan, when big pearls are regularly connected with Muslim (Hui-hui) merchants.[6] To cite but one example, the Chinese version of a decree issued by Qubilai in 1291 warns that "Muslims offer *tana* pearls (*da-na zhu*) under the pretense of gifts and then seek a price."[7]

The etymology of *tana* also points to its western provenance, for there is no doubt the Mongolian and Chinese forms go back to Persian *dānah*, "seed," and by extension "pearl," a usage that further gave rise to *dānat*, a technical term in the colloquial Arabic of the Gulf to designate the largest pearls.[8] Rashīd al-Dīn makes use of this term in its latter meaning when he tells us that a Chaghadaid qan's senior wife wore "two pearls (*dānah*) of great value," that is she was adorned with the kind most appropriate to her rank.[9]

The principal means of displaying pearls, precious and semiprecious stones in most societies is jewelry. Because the head is the normal focal point in human interactions, the upper body typically becomes the prime location for the placement of such ornaments.[10] For the Mongols this certainly holds true; although fragments of a gold and silver filigree bracelet affixed to a thin copper plate with two inlaid pearls was recovered at Qara Qorum, references to bracelets or finger rings are rare in the literary sources, while those to earrings, necklaces and elaborate headdresses are abundant.[11] Juvaynī, who visited the court of Ögödei on several occasions, says the emperor took many pearl necklaces (*ʿuqūd-i laʾālī*) on his progresses, which he bestowed on servitors.[12] And later, the il-qan Tegüder/Aḥmad (r. 1281–84), a convert to Islam, sent to the Mamlūk court a "rosary (*subḥa*) numbering 150 pearls."[13]

But while necklaces had their place, the Mongols' clear preference in jewelry was for earrings, worn by male and female. Indeed, Mongolian ear ornaments are divided into two types on the basis of gender: the *süikü*, the true earring worn by men, and hung in the normal fashion from a pierced lobe, and the far heavier, more elaborate *süike*, worn by married women, which required a different form of attachment—either a fastener supported by the whole ear or ribbons over the head to prevent elongated or torn lobes.[14]

Some sense of the Mongols' strong attraction to this steppe tradition is conveyed by an incident in 1226 during Chinggis Qan's final campaign. This is dramatically related by Rashīd al-Dīn in his "Collected Chronicles," based on now-lost Mongolian records: "When he reached the country of the Jürchen, the emperor of the Jürchen hearing that Chinggis Qan had arrived sent forth an envoy with magnificent gifts including a number of trays of round pearls worthy of a king and said, 'We submit.' Chinggis Qan ordered that everyone who had a pierced ear be given a pearl. Those present who did not, now pierced their ears and to all they gave [a pearl]. As many still remained, [Chinggis Qan] declared: 'Today is [the time for] gift-giving—scatter them all so that the people can gather them up.'"[15]

The passage, as it has come down to us, raises several issues. First, as to the variety of pearls sent by the Jürchen ruler, the Persian terminology "round pearls worthy of a king (*mavārīd-i ghalṭān-i shāhvār*)" implies they were of oceanic, not riverine, origin. Second, and of greater importance, the mad scramble set off by Chinggis Qan's generosity, however embroidered in the retelling, nonetheless accurately conveys the Mongols' passion for earrings and pearls.

The generations that followed evinced similar enthusiasm. In Turkistan and the western steppe, the ruling elite of both sexes continued to pierce their ears and wear ear ornaments with large, valuable pearls and gems.[16] More dramatically, during operations in Damascus some of Ghazan's troops stumbled across a cache of pearl earrings, and such was their excitement that they immediately divided these up among themselves, ignoring normal procedures on booty collection.[17] A quite different but equally instructive event took place in Iran, where a client ruler was graciously permitted to fasten on Hülegü "with his own hands" an earring adorned with "pearls of great price."[18] As we shall see further on, such an unmistakable sign of intimacy with the throne was only one of the many ways in which the transfer of pearls conveyed powerful political messages.

As is often the case, we are best informed on these matters in China; here the Yuan court introduced measures to monitor the design and use of pearl earrings. Regulations of 1312 on court headgear and jewelry stipulated that of the nine grades of officials, only one through six were authorized to wear pearl earrings, and that only jade and turquoise (*bitian*) could be combined with pearls on such ornaments.[19] Obviously, these were not suggestions for current fashion but rather part of a rigid code of official court dress embedded in Yuan law whose purpose, like military uniforms and insignia, was to provide visual means of identifying individual rank.

Evidence of their regular and lavish use is found in the official portraits of Yuan emperors of the fourteenth century, who wear two earrings, each with a single large white pearl. Their *qatuns*, "wives," or "consorts," are pictured in their life portraits wearing earrings of matched tear-shaped pearls, white and

FIGURE 2. Portraits of the consorts of Yuan emperor Qaishan (r. 1307–11). National Palace Museum.

extremely large, the size of hazelnuts in Muslim and Chinese terminology. Other wives, however, have far more elaborate ear ornaments or *süike*, one consisting of sixty-five matched pearls attached to each pendant.[20] Needless to say, finding matched pearls of this quality and in these quantities required a huge supply from which to select.

Headgear and clothing were also excellent vehicles for displaying pearls, since they could be massed together with stunning effect, a practice encountered at courts across Eurasia.[21] The female headdress of the Mongols was particularly eye catching and often noted. While descriptions focus on the centerpiece, the spectacular elongated boot-shaped "hat," the *boghta*, it was only part of a larger ensemble that featured hairstyles, ear ornaments, and neck and forehead pieces. Their careful integration was essential, first of all to stabilize the heavy and unwieldly centerpiece, which was made secure by gathering the hair in a long hollow tube inside the *boghta*, and by a kerchief that served as an elegant and disguised chin strap.[22]

This elaborate package provided even greater scope for decoration and display. To start at the top, there was an array of plumes, usually three to five. In northern Asia and the eastern steppe feathers were associated from ancient times with shamans and their flights to the Upper World, but also with rulers as an insignia of the authority bestowed upon them by Tengri, "Heaven." As purely a style statement, their pervasive use by the Chinggisids left a legacy that is expressed in the postimperial spread of the practice among their former Muslim subjects.[23]

But while plumes held an honored placed in the decoration of *boghtas*, far more striking and ideologically significant is the multitude of pearls basted on and suspended from female headgear. From the inception of the empire all married Mongolian women of the ruling strata, again following established tradition, decorated their *boghta* with gems and pearls; one, its pearls still intact, came into the possession of Marco Polo and is mentioned in his will.[24]

As time passed more and more pearls were added. An eyewitness, Odoric of Pordenone, around 1320, described the headdress of Yuan court ladies in the following terms: "And all who are married wear upon their heads the foot of a man, as it were, a cubit and a half in length, and at the top of that foot there are certain cranes feathers, the whole foot being set with great pearls, so that if there be in the whole world any fine or large pearls they are to be found in the decorations of these ladies."[25] Odoric's description is fully sustained by royal portraits in which all the *qatuns* are depicted with white, usually round, and carefully matched pearls in compact designs on their *boghtas*. One *qatun* has seventy-seven visible pearls on her headdress itself and forty-four more hanging from her left side; since this was most certainly duplicated on the right, the total is at least one hundred and sixty-five. In every case the hats and dresses are bright red, the preferred background color for showing off pearls in the Islamic world and yet another indication that the Mongols were much attracted to the big pearls of the Gulf and to the prevailing fashion in their display.[26]

Crowns of gold are, of course, closely identified with kingship throughout western Eurasia. Those of great emperors, caliphs, and even minor princes were always festooned with gems and pearls designed to produce a halo effect, a light-show that signaled a sovereign's possession of majesty, royal glory, special good fortune, and a divine mandate.[27] While Mongolian rulers dispensed with crowns of precious metal, royal headgear was nonetheless identified with rulership. The *Secret History*, reporting a family discussion on succession around 1218, states that Ögödei was chosen because he was in constant attendance on Chinggis Qan, who could therefore instruct "him on the great array of the teachings of the hat (*maqalai-yin bauliya*)," that is, he could learn the many principles of governance directly from the founding father.[28]

Still, although their items of headgear, following steppe tradition, were made of felt and cloth, these, too, were richly adorned. In his spurious travels of the late fourteenth century Sir John Mandeville says the great kaan's hat was covered with gems and pearls that were "worth a kingdom."[29] And, in fact, the Yuan regulations on court dress state that the qaghan's hat (*guan*), its aperture, and the silken cords front and back were all basted with pearls, and his ceremonial cap (*mian*) had pearls around the top and on its two pendants, providing the desired aura around the ruler's head.[30]

Clothing, the most visible and widely used marker of royal and aristocratic status, offered even greater scope for massing gems and pearls.[31] In the Mongolian case, the first thing to be noted is that officials and retainers wore similar but somewhat scaled down versions of their sovereign's attire when attending court. Starting in the early empire there are general references to garments of fine pearls (*thiyāb-i marvārīd-i rīz*) at the enthronement of Güyük (r. 1246–48), and in the Yuan there are many more allusions to pearled clothing (*zhuyi*) possessed by individual servitors.[32] Most commonly mentioned are the pearled robes (*zhupao*), garments worn by court and government officials at banquets and other ceremonial occasions. Marco Polo writes of the robes at Qubilai's court studded with gems and pearls "worth more than 10,000 *bezants* of gold," and several decades later Odoric of Pordenone says every courtier has "a coat on his back such that the pearls on it alone are worth some 15,000 florins."[33] The same practices are found at the Il-qan court. At one particularly dazzling affair, a great feast mounted by Ghazan in 1303, his guests, a multitude of foreign envoys, client rulers, and his own officials, were all clad in such robes.[34]

In addition, a number of other kinds of pearled garments are recorded, including those in the style of Buddhist cassocks, foot-length gowns adorned with big pearls (*da-na*), strung-pearl robes, swallow-tailed coats, and an elbow-length pearl netting or mesh.[35] The latter, as the Chinese of the Yuan correctly understood, was a specialty product of western peoples (*xifan*).[36]

Clothing, of course, implies more than just coats; and there are references to bestowals of matching sets of hats and robes.[37] Pearled headgear, called *tanatu tomugh* in Mongolian, was worn in China by Chinggisid princes, favored servitors, and, with some restrictions, high-level government officials.[38]

For the nomads, pants and coats of all styles required belts or sashes. Besides their functional value, belts carried great symbolic power relating to valor, bonding, binding, subordination, and loyalty, all of which can be traced back to the ancient Near East.[39] The usage was adopted by the Iranians and inherited by their Muslim successors. Naturally, these were finely wrought objects, typically made of gold and studded (*muraṣṣaʿ*) with gems and pearls.[40] Belts played an analogous role across the entire steppe zone from the Danube to Mongolia. Their extensive use here is well documented by archaeological finds and by their depiction on the stone statuary produced by the early Türks and later nomads.[41] The Chinggisids continued this ancient tradition, making elaborate use of belts in their enthronement ceremonies and bestowing large quantities on subordinates. All these were studded with gems and pearls and made of silk, precious metals, or, in the western steppe, of high-quality Bulghari leather.[42]

The Chinggisid royal families, of course, possessed great stores of pearled clothing. Their headgear, belts, and even shoes and slippers were so adorned, and their ceremonial robes were decorated with "white pearl fringes."[43] But what of the numbers affixed to individual garments? Does the Mongolian *tanatu*, "pearled" or "basted with pearls," imply a solid field? Such display pieces were attempted, most notably a garment covered with thirty thousand pearls made for the Byzantine emperor Romanos IV Diogenes (r. 1068–71), who, not surprisingly, staggered under its weight.[44] It is possible that the elbow-length pearl mesh, a kind of shawl or bib made from small interwoven pearls, was likewise a solid field.[45] But most usually gems and pearls were arranged in compact designs against a fabric field. All the available evidence, literary and pictorial, indicates that this was the case with the court attire of the Chinggisids and their retainers.

Pearls are also found on badges and insignia. The most numerous were those called *paizi* in Chinese and *gerege* in Mongolian, the generic terms for badges of authority, a practice the Chinggisids adopted in modified form from their Jin predecessors.[46] Initially, these were issued to messengers, envoys, and military officers to authorize access to the imperial post or to requisition food, lodging, and transportation from the general public. Soon, however, the court began to bestow badges on a wide circle of servitors as rewards and status symbols unconnected with official duties, a practice that elicited much comment and criticism.[47] Such badges, also called tiger tallies (*hufu*) in Chinese, came in iron, silver, and gold, and were further differentiated by the number of inlaid pearls. The Yuan court regularly bestowed these on foreign rulers and dignitaries, on their personal retainers, military officers, and civil officials, and even on a distinguished Muslim engineer.[48] Gold tallies with three pearls constituted the highest rank, though a unique tally with imperial symbols was made for Bayan the all-powerful minister (1335–40), who received from the Yuan emperor Toghan Temür "three badges of authority (*pai*) with dragons and phoenixes and inlaid big pearls (*da-na*)."[49]

In all ages royal courts across Eurasia adorned their possessions, whether for ceremonial or daily use, with exquisite decoration, including, of course, gems and pearls.[50] Observers, as intended, were much impressed, but few sought to move beyond the dazzling visual effect to explain the universal appeal and effectiveness of this kind of display. In the introduction to his treatise on gemstones al-Bīrūnī argued that the purposes of royal finery are twofold: to focus attention on the splendor of the ruler and, of equal importance, to raise the hope of servitors and subjects that they might someday partake of these riches. Thus, in his view, great wealth was required to secure and hold the reins of power and to govern efficiently.[51] While details varied in time and space, the formula always remained the same: majesty is most readily demonstrated by a combination of the quantity, quality, and diversity of material riches, that is, by commanding the best of everything a given ruler's world had to offer.

That this characterization is valid can be supported by another body of evidence. It is most suggestive that sources of the Middle Ages are so often well informed on the patterns of display at foreign courts distant in space and in time. Repeated rounds of competitive emulation had encouraged the convergence of court cultures across much of Eurasia, making their fashions and symbols increasingly recognizable and readable.

The Mongols enthusiastically embraced these images as well as the techniques used to create them and regularly met and exceeded the high standards set by predecessors in the steppe and the sown. The royal insignia, staffs, and parasols of the qaghans were lavishly decorated with pearls, as were the personal banners (*qi*) occasionally granted honored officials.[52] And the Mongols did the same with thrones, tableware, wall hangings, carriages, elephant litters, and royal tentage.[53] Thus, wherever visitors at a Chinggisid court might turn, there was always the glitter of gold and the luster of white pearls.

In many respects the most spectacular and astonishing display of all was the number of pearls the Chinggisids bestowed on servitors and court guests. The redistribution of cash and luxury goods was at the heart of Mongolian political culture. Rulers and leaders were expected to share out the proceeds of hunts, raids, campaigns, and tributes with followers. This they did with great fanfare in carefully orchestrated events, great feasts, and princely conventions. Servitors on their part were expected to reciprocate. Thus, at New Year's celebrations Qubilai's large retinue brought gifts of gold, silver, gems, and pearls to their lord.[54] But while there was exchange, it was incumbent on the ruler to demonstrate, or appear to do so, a greater measure of generosity. To meet this obligation, Chinggisid princes periodically showered gifts, most often versions of their pearled royal attire, on their many subordinates.

Some presentations, certainly the most glittering, were collective in nature. These were lengthy affairs involving hundreds or thousands of recipients convoked to mark major events. Great victories, naturally, always called for celebration. Accordingly, in 1279 Qubilai mounted "an assembly of imperial princes in Dadu and apportioned among them the precious gems, drinking vessels and currency seized from the defeated Song."[55] Rashīd al-Dīn describes another gathering, celebrating a political transition. On this occasion, the il-qan Abaqa, after his elevation in 1265, "bestowed upon the royal wives, princes and commanders immeasurable [amounts] of ready cash, gems and pearls (*javāhir*) and precious garments so that the benefit of this reached *all* the soldiers."[56] Here we have a classic case of sequential or serial bestowal, true redistribution, the primary mechanism of political mobilization among steppe peoples by which even those at the lower echelons received, however indirectly, something touched by the hand of their fortunate ruler.

Similar methods were used to obtain support from corporate entities in subject territories. Such was the purpose of the pearled garment given to the Tibetan lama 'P'ags-pa when he became Grand Preceptor in 1253. In addition, the document conveying this office was called the "pearled diploma," and in 1264 the lama received another such diploma that conferred upon him nominal control over all Tibetan clergy.[57] This established a precedent, and henceforth all documents sent to Tibetan ecclesiastical authorities from the Yuan court were "overlain with a netting of strung pearls."[58] The regularization of these presentations was in fact a common practice. For its annual religious festivals, the Yuan court supplied the Buddhist Da Ming Temple in Dadu with funds and pearled, bejeweled gild embroideries.[59] They did so for the same reasons other Chinggisid lines patronized other confessional groups in their domains: successful, organized religions always possessed effective communication systems and exercised ideological influence, both of which were extremely useful in enhancing legitimacy and gaining the obedience of subjects.

Presentations could also be individualized, particularly investiture ceremonies in which the ruler bestows, directly from his own hand, sumptuous clothing on clients and servitors. In its varied forms investiture was a common feature of political and religious life across Eurasia and widely understood as an act of incorporation that established hierarchy, obligations of loyalty, chains of clientage, and command.[60]

In the Yuan, the formal investiture of regional princes, who received rights to incomes from designated agricultural lands (Chinese *fendi*, Mongolian *qubi*), regularly included garments adorned with pearls.[61] Other individual bestowals were prompted by specific personal achievements, military success, exemplary government service, and the like.[62] The context in which qaghans dispensed these awards is well exemplified in the career of Li Ting, a Chinese officer in Mongolian service. Following victories over the Song in 1276, Li and several other commanders were honored at a great feast before an assembly of imperial princes and dignitaries at which Qubilai presented each with a hundred gold ingots, a gilded garment, and a pearled garment. Some two decades later when Temür Qaghan (r. 1294–1307) ascended the throne he and his empress made awards to Li and other key supporters at another gala feast attended by the Yuan elite. On this occasion the honorees each received six bars of silver, a pearled hat, and a pearled elbow-length garment.[63]

These solemn affairs served to honor the recipients' achievements, but of equal import they provided clear guidance to the courtiers in attendance on how best to please their sovereign. Conversely, the same end could be achieved by the recall of such bestowals. In 1328 the Yuan emperor transferred the pearled attire of two disgraced officials to two in high favor, another and very arresting way of educating subordinates.[64]

Clothing was certainly the principal means by which Chinggisid princes signaled their approval and dispensed pearls to subordinates; there was, however, another option—presentations of loose pearls. The practice was begun by Chinggis Qan, who awarded, around 1223, his favorite commander, Sübedei, "big pearls (*da zhu*)," or, in another version of the same event, "a silver pitcher of precious pearls."[65] The practice was continued by Ögödei, who gave large numbers of pearls to his female relatives.[66] One of his bestowals is especially enlightening. At a banquet the brother of a client ruler presented the qaghan with two carboys of pearls (*qarabah-i mavārīd*), and in response Ögödei brought forth a long chest (*ṣanduqī darāz*) of royal pearls (*dānah-shāhvār*) and distributed them by the cupful to all present.[67] As described, this act seems impromptu, motivated by a desire to demonstrate his own generosity and to surpass that of others, a *mentalité* that brings to mind potlach ceremonies and competitions.

But however dispensed, whether basted on clothing, set in jewelry, or transferred in bulk, the primary function of pearls was that of a political currency, which Chinggisid rulers used to attract, reward, motivate, and elevate followers. They were, in short, an essential tool in Mongolian methods of statecraft, "the teachings of the hat." In this, however, pearls were by no means alone. To place these transfers in proper perspective it is necessary to bear in mind that on most occasions they were part of a larger package of royal presentations. Typical is the magnificent feast Ghazan mounted in 1293 at which he bestowed upon the merchant prince of Kīsh, Jamāl al-Dīn, a thousand geldings, fine textiles, vases from China and India, precious gems, and brilliant pearls (*marvārīd-i khūshāb*).[68]

As we shall now see, the huge volume of pearls and other precocities dispensed by Mongolian courts did not satisfy their retainers' ever-growing expectations and only served to incite a desire for more.

CHAPTER 6

A Consumer Culture

Traveling through the southern Altai in 1221, Li Zhichang reports that merchants imported flour from the Western Region that sold locally at fifty ounces of silver per eighty pounds![1] Obviously, by this date the Mongols were eager and unrestrained consumers of foreign goods, including nonluxury varieties, which, in defiance of economic laws, were profitably transported by camel caravan some two thousand *li*, or nearly seven hundred miles.

The rapidity with which the Mongols developed a consumer culture appears congruent with the traditional view that unschooled and unsophisticated nomads learned and adopted such self-indulgent behavior under the corrupting influence of their "civilized" subjects. Such behavior becomes progressively visible in the course of several generations, a line of argument that goes back to the Arab historian Ibn Khaldūn (d. 1406).[2] Indeed, a case can be made for the nomads' susceptibility to sedentary influence exercised in this manner. Zhao Hong, the Song envoy who visited Mongolian authorities in North China in 1221, relates that the younger set, the second generation, had already embraced Turkistani (Hu) clothing and hairstyles.[3] While it is tempting to accept the theory as it stands, there is plentiful evidence that their desire for and choice of prestige goods were formed long before any direct, intensive exposure to the riches and tastes of the sedentary world that followed the initial conquests.

The Mongols' shopping list of priority goods, clearly documented throughout the pre-imperial and imperial eras, informs us that the Mongolian hierarchy of values remained stable for several centuries. The most coveted were herd animals, taken mainly from steppe peoples, and luxury goods acquired from the sown. Chief among the latter were fine textiles, precious metals, and gems, especially pearls. In the latter case, as clients of the Qitans who regularly received big pearls from the ʿAbbāsid Caliphate, the Mongols certainly had some familiarity with the saltwater variety by the eleventh century.[4] We can assume that at this point the aura surrounding such commodities was greatly magnified by their rarity and distant origins, and that consequently, several centuries before the advent of their empire, the Mongols were aware of the material value and spiritual properties attributed to pearls from the west.

Later on, in the mid-twelfth century, the Mongols actually came into possession of these treasures from the hands of the Jürchens, whose ruling strata made extensive use of such items in their personal adornment. In pursuit of clients in the steppe, the Jin court bestowed upon Qabul Qan, a third-generation ancestor of Chinggis Qan, the standard package of royal gifts, "gold, gems and pearls (*javāhir*) and garments."[5] And more immediately and concretely, when the Mongols and their allies defeated the Tatars, around 1195, they seized as part of the booty a blanket basted with big pearls (*tanatu könjile*).[6] While this event became famous in its day, indicating that finds of saltwater pearls were rare in the steppe, it should also be stressed that the Mongols knew exactly what they had acquired, for which they already had a special name.

This is not to argue that their preferences were pristine or purely homegrown. Quite obviously, the Mongols' particular tastes in luxury and positional goods (intended to convey status)were influenced by near neighbors, particularly those of Inner Asian origins. To take but one example, the Mongols' preference for the pearls of the Persian Gulf certainly parallels and mirrors Qitan and Uighur views on the superiority of those from the southern seas over local varieties. And in this specific instance, it seems likely that the influence pearls exerted on the Mongols was closely tied to their imperial associations in the steppe zone.

As I document in later chapters, Mongolian priorities in such matters, the properties and powers of gold, for example, had very deep roots in the cultural history of nomadic and post-nomadic peoples. Consequently, on the eve of their expansion the Mongols were a consumer society in the making with fixed notions about prestige goods held to be the natural accompaniments and ornaments of great empires, notions that were preserved in the historical memory of steppe peoples until activated and made accessible by military success.[7] And this the Chinggisids delivered in spectacular fashion, securing in unprecedented abundance the treasures of land and sea.

Once in command of sedentary lands, the Mongols immediately and avidly indulged their preferences for positional goods. Some of these came through official channels, shares of booty, and court bestowals, but the elites on their own initiatives soon sought more through commercial channels. Concern for adequate supplies began soon after the proclamation of the empire. Around 1215 when the first envoys sent by the Khwārazmshāh Muḥammad to the Mongols arrived in North China, Chinggis Qan received them warmly and then instructed them to relay the following message to their sovereign: "I am the emperor of the East and thou the emperor of the West. Between us let there be a firm treaty of friendship, amity and peace, and from both sides let the merchants and the caravans come and go and let the fineries and wares of my lands be brought to thee and let those of thine lands likewise be directed [unto mine]."[8] Although the passage comes from Jūzjānī, who is repeating stories circulating sometime after the event, the general tone and thrust of the message rings true and is completely consistent with the known facts concerning Chinggis Qan's close relationship with long-distance merchants, a relationship that goes back to the pre-imperial period.

It is also fully consistent with a passage found in the "Basic Annals" of Ögödei's reign in the *Yuanshi,* which presents a vivid picture of the buying frenzy that gripped the Mongolian ruling strata of the second generation: "The imperial princes and all the notables also sent agents to Yanjing (Dadu) and down to the southern prefectures [of the former Jin Dynasty] in quest of commercial goods—[ceremonial] bows, arrows, saddles and bridals. Some [sent agents] to the Western Region and to the Uighurs to seek out and acquire pearls (*zhuji*) and some [sent agents] to the Eastern Sea (North Pacific) for gyrfalcons. Mounted couriers [on these quests] were continuous, [traveling] day and night without interruption, exhausting the populace beyond endurance."[9]

This passage is instructive on a number of points. It affirms once again that the pearls of choice were those imported from the Gulf. Next, it provides a striking example of the importance of transecological exchange, which regularly featured natural and animal products. Further, the access the elite enjoyed to the imperial post for purposes of self-aggrandizement, confirmed by other sources, tells us that within a very short period the Mongols had become compulsive long-distance shoppers.[10] Put differently, in their pursuit of prestige goods the Chinggisids and their retainers enjoyed a transcontinental commercial reach. No wonder Carpini in the mid-1240s was struck by the great wealth their ruling class had amassed in "gold, silver, silks, precious stones and gems."[11]

The quest for ever more luxury items continued unabated in later generations. Rashīd al-Dīn relates that under Ghazan moneylending at usurious rates was rampant, and many notables borrowed heavily to purchase "gems-studded belts, pearls and other expensive goods."[12] Instances of individualized indebtedness accumulated in attempts to keep up or to get ahead are of course commonplace among burghers, merchants, and others with social aspirations.[13] But as pictured in our sources, in the Mongolian case, like that of the ancien régime in France, the entire ruling class became hopelessly mired in debt in the mad pursuit of positional goods.

One useful measure of its scale is provided by another passage from Rashīd al-Dīn, in which he reports that in his time the general populace firmly believed that the perceived shortage of gold in the market place was a direct consequence of the immense amounts tied up in brocade robes worn by the elite.[14] And even if not wholly accurate in economic terms, this perception still provides a useful glimpse into public images and attitudes concerning the Mongolian notables' rampant consumerism.

Their seemingly insatiable desire for more also led superiors to pressure subordinates for pearls, and subordinates to accept bribes from superiors in the same coin.[15] By these means influential and well-placed persons, including two of Qubilai's chief ministers of state, Aḥmad Fanākatī and Sangha, accumulated large personal collections of high-quality pearls. And, of equal interest, once they fell from power their ill-gotten gains were seized and deposited in the treasury.[16] The extent of this kind of corruption and resultant confiscation under the Yuan is revealed in a report submitted by officials of the Censorate (*yutaishi chen*) to the throne in 1282: "We observe that there is an estimated 30,000 ingots [worth of] of paper money, gold and silver, pearls and gems and silk [accruing from] fines for bribery." In response to their memorial, Qubilai "ordered that this should be set aside and given to the poor and destitute."[17] Since the Censorate, the traditional surveillance arm of Chinese governments, was only reinstituted in 1268, the amounts reported represent an accumulation of little more than a decade.

The presentation of "gifts" to influence officials, typically in the form of pearls and similar valuables, was a pervasive and commonly accepted feature of political life throughout most of history. In point of fact, many premodern societies expected and tolerated a certain level of governmental corruption, since officials often did not receive sufficient resources or funds to carry out their primary duties. In the Islamic lands these "gifts," called *nisar*, if kept within reasonable bounds were openly recorded and acknowledged.[18] In the Yuan, however, the practice seems to have reached levels that far exceeded accepted thresholds of tolerance and were thus viewed, quite correctly, as barely disguised forms of bribery conducted on a massive scale.

As Rashīd al-Dīn fully understood, for the Mongols "jewelry (*muraṣṣaʿāt*), gems and pearls (*javāhir*) and garments" were essential markers of wealth and status and therefore an essential ingredient in court politics.[19] Together they formed an integrated package, and everyone of standing was eager to display all three. The same opinion was held by the late Yuan author, Yang Yu, who noted that in China gold, pearls, and brocade cloth were the standard markers of elite status and that the lack thereof was deemed a source of great embarrassment.[20] Their lack also prompted competition and intense jealousy. Another Chinese observer of the same period, Quan Heng, recounts a rather remarkable case of this. In 1358, the last Yuan emperor, Toghan Temür, built a sumptuous dwelling for a courtier, which prompted the palace eunuchs to complain that their lodgings were now inferior. The emperor accepted their argument and in response allowed the eunuchs to remove the gold and pearls from the courtier's dwelling for use in their own![21]

In traditional Chinese historiography, such excess was always viewed as a source and symbol of dynastic decline. This was most certainly the position of Taizu (r. 1368–99), founder of the Ming, who felt it necessary to place a ban on all gift giving among his officials, held to be a baleful legacy of the Mongols, because he was firmly convinced that the practice was instrumental in the downfall of the Yuan.[22]

Attempts to attain status through fashionable and expensive positional goods were, of course, a continuous feature of Eurasian history.[23] The basic social dynamics underlying these consumer cultures were clearly identified and understood long before the emergence of social sciences in the modern era. One of the earlier examples is found in the *Discourses on Salt and Iron* of 81 BCE, which records a debate over government economic policies, where it is succinctly stated that when "notables love precious things, extravagant clothing becomes fashionable among the lower orders"; a later passage adds perceptively that "the rich desire to surpass [each another] while the poor desire to catch up to [the rich]."[24]

Official concern about the dangers this entailed was still very much alive some fourteen centuries later; this is embodied in a decree of the Yuan emperor Buyantu introducing new sumptuary laws in 1314 that state in part: "In the course of recent years the upper classes and the common people have vied with one another for the most extravagant [attire] and [so] superiors and inferiors have become confused. The rules of proper etiquette (*li*) have been subverted and wealth squandered."[25] In this case the principal goal of all such laws, the maintenance of social-political hierarchy, is combined with concerns about widespread financial ruin among all strata of society. In the eyes of a sitting emperor, excessive consumerism was now a major problem and threat to the stability of the Yuan regime.

Episodes of runaway consumerism are common; they are found among sedentary and nomadic people, affect all classes of society, and are by no means unique to any particular place, time, or economic system. The selection of specific categories of positional goods for display is a by-product of what anthropologists call "cultural focus," a phenomenon that has served as a major source of change in both traditional and modern societies. The theory states in part that the cultural traits that receive the most attention and discussion are also those subject to the most variation, elaboration, and competitive emulation.[26] And the most intensive and expensive of these competitions occurred among the elites, particularly when dress and personal adornment were involved. Without any doubt, this was true of the Chinggisids and their courtiers, whose social life was focused on opportunities to display their clothing, jewelry, and pearls. There were certainly many occasions to do so, since the ruling house mounted numerous festivals and ceremonies, some lasting days or weeks, during which attire was changed daily so that guests had ample opportunity to show off and compare their accumulated finery.[27] Most certainly, one of the principal functions of Mongolian courts was to provide venues that were tailor-made for such exhibitions of conspicuous consumption.

It is axiomatic that competitive emulation of this kind regularly leads to excess, most notably the "high" and often irrational fashions sanctioned by royal courts, fashions that frequently become dysfunctional because of increased complexity, size, and weight. One graphic example of this is offered by the elaboration of the *boghta*, which reached such proportions that it had to be carefully engineered and tended to keep it securely in place. Its final and extreme form was presumably reached at the Temürid court. Here Ruy Gonzales de Clavijo witnessed a ceremonial entrance of Temür's senior wife, whose "mighty headgear waved backwards and forwards" so much that her many attendants, to prevent it from falling off, "kept their hands up to the headdress," a vital service three of them continued to perform even after the royal lady had taken her seat. And thereafter, he continues, eight more wives came in procession, all identically attired and attended.[28]

For other women at court this carefully stage-managed fashion parade set the standards of the day, standards that surely inspired attempts to embellish further their own *boghtas* even if they could never hope to duplicate or surpass the dazzling creations worn by the royal ladies. But here again it must be remembered that according to protocol Chinggisid courtiers were not only allowed but actually required to wear slightly scaled-down versions of the frequently enriched royal attire on all ceremonial occasions, and consequently there was always room for additions and improvements.

These considerations bring up the question of the varying pace of fashion change across time. In comparison with the annual new lines of clothing in the modern era, changes in style in earlier days took place over much longer time frames, decades and centuries, and came about more often through elaboration and accumulation than through any conscious attempt at introducing innovation, much less radical departures from the inherited tradition. In most instances, therefore, competitions typically focused on having "more." This is clearly reflected in the fact that the stores of wealth possessed by rulers and elites is characterized by the large numbers of duplicates, especially of ceremonial robes, drinking cups, gems, and pearls. And while very large quantities were actually involved, these figures were further magnified by calculated rumor and outright fabrication. But such figures, however inflated, were oftentimes taken at face value by later generations and accepted as norms handed down by model rulers and thus as quantitative standards to be met and surpassed.

The Mongols, as we have seen, engaged in this kind of competitive emulation that was constantly fueled and focused by lavish court redistribution in which pearls were ever present. But for them, matters went much deeper than mere display, for they imputed to pearls and other precious materials a variety of miraculous powers. Indeed, it can be argued that the Mongols themselves measured the success of their imperial venture in terms of their acquisition and accumulation of such wondrous, even portentous goods. A cluster of sources from the thirteenth and fourteenth centuries—Chinese, Armenian, Syriac, and Old French—all accurately express this attitude by reiterating the claim that in pre-imperial times the Mongols were exceedingly poor, with a very limited and homely repertoire of material culture, and then going on to assert with emphasis that they came to enjoy great rewards and wealth in direct consequence of the achievements of Chinggis Qan. Most tellingly, the primary measuring stick used to document the stark differences between the two eras is the replacement of their coarse native attire with the sumptuous wear produced and extracted from settled societies.[29]

The uniform views of these authors, none of whom witnessed the transition, assuredly echo the historical memories of their informants, memories that can be used as a rough guide to the perceptions of the second, third, and fourth generations on the transformative character of the empire's rise and unparalleled expansion. For the servitors of the Chinggisid, this entailed much more than a mere change of clothing styles or increase in material wealth. The true meaning and profound significance of the event was clearly understood and articulated in the mid-1260s by Juvaynī, who asserts categorically that this sudden and miraculous transformation from poverty to plenty was brought about solely by "the banner of Chinggis Qan's good fortune (*dawlat*)."[30] The nature of this very special good fortune and its intimate interconnections with the potent spiritual properties inhering in positional goods is taken up next.

CHAPTER 7

Fecundity and Good Fortune

For the Mongols, pearls had a special potency. It was believed, among other things, that they promoted virility and fertility. This is why Maḥmūd Yalavach, governor of North China, on a visit to the aging Ögödei and his favorite wife "scattered a great amount of royal pearls (*la'ālī'-i shāhvār*) upon their heads."[1] Pearls, "seeds," like rhinoceros horn, served as an aphrodisiac. Consequently, they were an appropriate wedding gift that strengthened the reproductive powers of bride and groom. In Qitan, Uighur, and Mongolian traditions the bride was the primary recipient, while among the Temürids it was the entire wedding party.[2] Found as well among many sedentary peoples, the elite practice of scattering pearls as a symbol of chastity and as a form of sympathetic magic to ensure a fruitful marriage may have given rise to the modern practice of scattering rice, a much less expensive white seed, at weddings.[3]

By itself, however, such an explanation for the Mongols' attraction is incomplete and inadequate. To grasp the full implications of the association of pearls and fertility, it is necessary to examine in detail Rashīd al-Dīn's account of the Mongols' mythical ancestress, Alan Qo'a, in which shells are equated with wombs, and pearls with the seed of life, semen.

Rashīd al-Dīn introduces his extended remarks on this ethno-genetic tradition, which drew on old Mongolian records and native informants, with the following statement:

> The tradition of the masters of story-telling (*ārbāb-i ḥikāyat*) is such that Dobun Bayan, husband of Alan Qo'a, died in his youth. But, since the Divine Decree of the Creator, who is without equal, was thus that there would appear on earth a sovereign, a powerful,

> ever-successful Lord of the Fortunate Conjunction (*sahib qirān*) who would bring under his mandate all kingdoms of the world and enclose all the recalcitrant in the collar of obedience. His spirit would be so powerful that he would be able to rule the world and be the ruler of its peoples. After him, all the sovereigns and emperors on the face of the earth would be from his progeny just like a shell which has within it an incomparable pearl (*durr-i yatīm*) nurtured through the years. . . . The [Creator] perfected the pure womb of Alan Qo'a, brought forth the shell of the pearl of the noble birth of Chinggis Qan and created in it his true essence from pure light.[4]

For Rashīd al-Dīn, his sources, and his informants, this is a vital matter, since in several later passages he returns to this theme, asserting that in consequence of their immaculate conception the lineages descendant from Alan Qo'a were the most esteemed among the Mongols.[5] In detailing their divine descent and attributes he elaborates: "The will of God on High was such that the pearl (*gawhar*) of the being of Chinggis Qan in the course of passing days and lengthening months and years was nurtured in the shells of the loins of his ancestresses. To Qaidu Qan who gave rise to the lineage of Chinggis Qan, He [God on High], gave prosperity and good fortune and bestowed [upon him] help, strength and care so that there came to him wives, dependents, flocks and herds beyond counting as well as three sons born to him favored by good fortune."[6] Finally, Rashīd al-Dīn sums up the properties of the Chinggisids in the following manner: "And like an incomparable pearl (*durr-i yatīm*) among precious gems, he [Chinggis Qan], by his nobility and exquisite qualities stood out from other people. . . . And his great heirs and famed lineage on the six sides of the seven climes [of the world] became possessors of imperial crowns and thrones and princes of fortunate kingdoms (*mamlakat-i bakht-yārī*)."[7]

Even though this history was prepared at the behest of Ghazan, under whom the conversion of the Il-qan elite made rapid progress, such traditions still had meaning and relevance. It is not, then, by chance that Rashīd al-Dīn is careful to associate Ghazan himself with this glorious line of descent as "a great pearl (*durr*) of the sea of the Chinggisid dynasty."[8]

In evaluating this data, the first issue that needs to be addressed is how Rashīd al-Dīn viewed his material. On other occasions he understood and explained fanciful steppe beliefs as metaphors and phraseology. Certainly, he had ample ground for doing the same in this case. For centuries Muslim authors and poets have used pearl and shell metaphors to emphasize the purity and luster of noble lines and persons.[9] And the incomparable or orphan pearl (*durr-i yatīm*), possessing unrivaled properties of size, shape, and brilliance, was regularly invoked for similar ends.[10] Consequently, it is likely that Rashīd al-Dīn and his Muslim readers did not take the account literally and understood the references to shells and pearls as figures of speech used to convey the superlative but wholly *human* qualities of the Chinggisids. The Mongols, on the other hand, surely saw matters in a different light; to understand their perspective we need to look more closely at the variants of this myth through time and then situate the available "options" in the context of their imperial ideology.

As a point of departure, we can compare Rashīd al-Dīn's version of the myth with the presentation in the *Secret History*. Most obviously, there is a common core: in both, the lineage of Chinggis Qan issues from Alan Qo'a in a virgin birth decreed by Heaven, Tengri of the steppe peoples. In the *Secret History*, however, she is repeatedly visited and impregnated by a "resplendent yellow man . . . whose radiance penetrates [her] womb" and who then departs on "a moonbeam or a ray of the sun." But while light and radiance are essential elements in both versions, its source differs. In the *Secret History* the "radiance" comes through the agency of the Golden Man, while in Rashīd al-Dīn the "pure light" comes directly from the Creator. Lastly, and again obviously, there is no reference to pearls in the *Secret History* account.[11]

If we now turn to other, and later, versions, it is the storyline of the *Secret History*, somewhat modified, that prevails. The variants begin early; writing in 1271, the Armenian monk Kirakos says he heard that Chinggis Qan "was not born of human seed" but born of a divine light that penetrated his mother.[12] Since to the best of my knowledge this claim does not appear elsewhere, the transference of the virgin birth from a mythical ancestress to Hö'elün, Chinggis Qan's biological mother, may be a means of Christianizing and thus intensifying Chinggis's miraculous descent. Or, of course, it may only be a simple misunderstanding; religious beliefs and concepts crossing cultural-linguistic barriers are frequently misunderstood and transformed.

More calculating and studied are the variations of the myth invoked in Temür's search for legitimacy, which can be reconstructed from genealogies, narrative histories, and inscriptions produced in Arabic, Persian, and Uighur during and after Temür's reign. These, too, follow the *Secret History* version, claiming descent from the "Radiant Being" and Alan Qo'a, but also introduce many revisions and contradictions in these efforts to connect Temür and his lineage, the Barulas, to the Chinggisids and their divine origins, an enterprise that continued down to the sixteenth century in Mughal India.[13]

The multiplicity of versions and variants clearly increased through time, but there is no reason to assume all go back to a single prototype. In introducing the Mongols' ethno-genetic myth Rashīd al-Dīn states that his information comes from the "masters of story-telling," and his use of the plural indicates there were a variety of oral and written versions from which to choose. Consequently, there is little purpose in trying to reconcile or harmonize the discrepancies, for there was never an "authentic" original story that later versions "corrupted." Rather, as with epics and other productions based on oral transmission and tradition, there was always an evolving repertoire, a menu of versions to draw upon that could be adjusted to meet the moods and needs of new audiences.

Inasmuch as Mongolian religious life in the twelfth and thirteenth centuries was highly syncretic, an admixture of the Tengri cult, Shamanism, veneration of the Sun and Moon, and a multitude of local deities, it should occasion no surprise that their ethno-genetic myths and imperial ideologies bore the same composite character. Moreover, this was long part of the steppe tradition. As Peter Golden argues, among the early Türks the existence of distinctive variants of these creation myths helped facilitate political mobilization by providing flexibility and an "ideological umbrella" when forging disparate ethno-linguistic components into a nomadic tribe, confederation, or state. Since all steppe polities were ethnic conglomerates, variant myths of origin were not only inevitable, they were also a major asset.[14] Equally helpful, individual components of these stories were typically multivalent, allowing recipients to read into them expected and satisfying meanings. After all, politics, including the kind practiced in the present day, is about building coalitions of differing and sometimes antagonistic constituencies; in order to do this successfully, variable, adaptable messages are absolutely essential. And in the specific case of the Mongolian Empire, whose political and military elite was certainly the most diverse in premodern times, pearls possessed the needed range of spiritual and symbolic meanings.

As to why there was a "pearl variant" on the menu and thus available to Rashīd al-Dīn, an examination of the Chinggisids' imperial ideology is in order. Its chief characteristic is its extreme brevity, which in the following Persian-language version is accommodated on the face of a coin issued in Tbilisi in 1252:

By the Might of God on High
By the Good Fortune of the Emperor of the
World, Munkū (Möngke) Qā'ān[15]

All the elements of this formula are articulated in Rashīd al-Dīn's version of the ethno-genetic myth, which says that Chinggis Qan's birth, engendered by the perfect pearl in an immaculate conception, was part of a heavenly design that bestowed upon Chinggis special good fortune and a mandate for dominion on earth.

It is particularly noteworthy that in Rashīd al-Dīn's accounting there is a clear and repeated equation of pearls with good fortune. For the Mongols, this equation is rooted in the basics of their adaptation to the steppe environment and their pastoral mode of subsistence. One key feature of the mode was the heavy reliance on dairy products—butter, curds, yogurt, and koumiss. The great importance of these in their diet is signaled in the Mongols' fivefold color classification of foods, in which the white varieties hold first place. White, "the mother of color," was identified with lactation and herd growth, and herd growth was the major measure of prosperity and good fortune.[16]

The contemporary sources provide several helpful perspectives on the political significance of white during the formative stages of the empire. According to his Chinese biographer, at the birth of Muqali, later Chinggis Qan's viceroy in North China, a white vapor arose from inside the tent, signaling his brilliant future.[17] White, however, was not only a symbol: white objects beckoned, ensured, and indeed created good fortune. Such was its power that white underwrote the success of the empire from its very inception. In 1206 when Chinggis Qan was elevated at a great convocation (*yeke quriltai*), they hoisted his white battle standard (*chaghan tuq*) with the nine tails to open the proceedings that formally proclaimed the new state.[18] And following his death in 1227, his all-powerful spirit, his charisma, or good fortune (*su*) continued to affect the fortunes of the empire and became identified with, and resided in, his white standard, appropriately renamed *sülde*.[19]

The intimate and vital connection between the color white, good fortune, good government, and dynastic legitimacy is most explicitly made in a passage found in the biography of Yelu Chucai in which the minister addresses Ögödei thus: "Your Highness has recently mounted the throne [so] you should vow not to deviate from the White Way (*dao*)." The emperor, the passage continues, "followed this [advice] as it is the [Mongolian] national custom to revere white for white is the *cause* of good fortune."[20]

These beliefs were institutionalized and enshrined in annual festivals accurately described by Marco Polo. One was held in August outside the summer capital of Shangdu, where Qubilai ceremonially tended his large herds of white mares and sprinkled some of their milk in the air and on the land to appease the spirits and to ensure the fecundity and prosperity of all living things. A second, held at Dadu in February, celebrated the coming of spring, the Mongols' New Year, still observed today as Chaghan Sara, the "White Month." On this occasion Marco Polo relates that Qubilai's servitors bring him pearls and other presents "of white things and with white things" and that his servitors exchange "white things" among themselves so "that they may have good luck."[21]

Such annual celebrations are recorded as well in the Il-qan realm. Variously called the "Sabbath of the White" or the "White Festival," these were organized by the early rulers and continued under Ghazan.[22] Vaṣṣāf's contemporary account of the New Year's celebration of 1303 describes, like Marco Polo, a great throng of guests engaged in gift exchange and attired in white, pearled apparel.[23] In a very real sense, the Mongols were actively and systematically engaged in making their own luck.

The association of "white things" with good fortune has another and important implication for Mongolian political culture: every time a Chinggisid prince bestowed pearls they enhanced the recipients' luck on two distinct levels. First, the pearls by themselves had this effect and, second, their provenance transferred some of the royal line's immense fund of good fortune (*su*) to their servitors. Just such a transfer is portrayed in the account of a bestowal at a gala feast held in 1277, at which Mangala, son of Qubilai, presented the Chinese general Wang Piwei with a golden goblet and sable coat, and the prince's consort presented the general's wife with "a hat and dress strung with pearls," after which she declared: "Because of the [royal] make of your lady's dress, your lady is truly a fortunate (*fu*) person."[24] Significantly, the *fu* in this passage is the same character used in Chinese versions of the Mongols' ideological formula to translate *su*.[25]

Good fortune, like the pearls themselves, was consequently a dispensable commodity and had to be dispensed with great liberality. Providing high-ranking recipients with personalized bestowals in grand settings was a standard way of dramatizing these transfers, but it was obviously impossible for the Chinggisid princes to bestow gifts individually on their numerous followers. By means of sequential redistribution, however, they could transfer goods from their own hand down the chain of command to the rank and file. Properly arranged and staged, this, too, effectively dispersed a ruler's charisma and good fortune to underlings, a procedure that provided a powerful bonding agent creating an ever-widening circle of servitors and adherents.

Because of their intense lustrousness pearls were held to be especially potent. The same quality underlies the Mongols' attitude toward porcelain. One of the earliest indications of interest comes in 1263 when Qubilai demanded from the ruler of Annam "white porcelain wine cups" as tribute, the only manufactured goods among a lengthy list of natural products.[26] And later when the Mongols gained unlimited access to China's extensive domestic production, it is telling that although they did not make extensive use of porcelain, the preferred variety was *luanbai*, or "egg white" ware. The same can be said of jade; it, too, had limited appeal for the Mongolian elite, but the jade in their possession was predominantly white in color.[27]

From this it can be concluded that while all "white things" helped to engender good fortune, not all were equal; for the Mongols there were hierarchies, differing levels of potency. Most certainly, Berke Qan's royal pavilion tent covered with bleached felt or the eight white yurts (*chaghan ger*) established by Qubilai for the veneration of Chinggis Qan and his relics delivered far greater benefits than the humble herders' tent coated with chalk, clay, or ground bones "to make it gleam whiter."[28]

The preferences of the Mongols in these matters yield yet another important conclusion concerning their conceptions of the color and potency of pearls: it was not as a class of objects that pearls possessed such power—only the white varieties produced good fortune and fecundity. Proof of this can be found in the portraits of the Yuan *qatuns* whose innumerable pearls are *all* white, never other shades or colors.

While many peoples, Turkic nomads, Iranian oasis dwellers, and others, held the color white and pearls to be auspicious and to attract good fortune, so far as I am aware only the Chinggisids made this belief an integral part of imperial ideology.[29] It therefore seems very likely that foreigners and many of the Mongols' subjects viewed pearls in a somewhat different light, as a royal gem, an expected possession of great princes, but not, at least initially, as a means of engendering imperial good fortune. Under these circumstances the elaborate ceremonial transfers of pearls regularly mounted to achieve this end may have functioned as vehicles to propagate and educate outsiders about a central tenet of their imperial ideology.

Beyond this, the Chinggisids' vast accumulations of high-quality pearls served to advance and document another basic tenet: the dazzling displays of great quantities of the chief treasures of land and sea, gold and pearls, provided eye-catching and unmistakable evidence of the extent and attractive powers of the Mongols' imperium, thus validating the claim of a heavenly mandated dominion on earth. In an age of limited literacy, the visual and ceremonial communication of political propaganda, what Pierre Briant calls *vitrine idéologie*, "showcase ideology," was a vital tool in the search for adherents and legitimacy.[30]

CHAPTER 8

Pearls After the Empire

In the course of the fourteenth century the regional qanates experienced crises and disintegration: Mongolian rule in China, Turkestan, and Iran came to an end, while the Golden Horde, greatly weakened by Temür's assaults, survived into the next century. The Mongolian Empire was no more, but it had made a deep impression on the historical memory of its many subject peoples, producing an afterimage that exerted influence on the policies and political cultures of its successor states, sedentary and nomadic. What, then, of the Mongols' massive accumulation and display of pearls—did this extend the geographical range of the popularity and political uses of pearls? The problem can best be pursued by comparing conditions south of the steppe with those to its north.

Following Yuan precedent, the early Ming pursued an active commercial policy across the southern seas. Their sources of pearls extended from Southeast Asia to the western reaches of the Indian Ocean.[1] From Aden (A-dan) and Hormuz (Hu-lu-mu-si) the Ming acquired various kinds of gemstones and quantities of big pearls (*da zhu*).[2] The Ming court was itself a major consumer.[3] Regulations on court dress in the *Mingshi* detail the quantity and quality of pearls authorized on the hats, belts, and robes of the royal house and its officials.[4] Similar stipulations governed the headgear and pearls of the Ming empresses.[5] But while the Ming court's preferences in, and display of, pearls continues many features of Yuan practice, there is one notable difference: not surprisingly, jade, which receded into the background under the Mongols, comes again to the fore under the Ming as a favored partner of pearls, the normal Chinese formulation regarding the wealth of the land and the sea.

Although the commercial ties the Chinese had with the Persian Gulf declined following the termination of Zheng He's voyages in 1433, their reserves were certainly substantial; in 1449 the Ming court bestowed upon the qan of the Western or Oyirad Mongols fifty-six hundred (or sixty-five hundred) big pearls (*tanas*).[6] Saltwater pearls of some kind continued to circulate into the early Qing. As late as 1659 there is a Russian diplomatic report that Beijing was well supplied with gemstones and pearls, all coming "from the south."[7] But this is also the period when the provenance of pearls becomes increasingly problematical in North Asia in consequence of sweeping changes in their nomenclature: in Chinese "eastern pearl (*dongzhu*)" replaces the earlier "northern pearl (*beizhu*)," while *tana* comes to designate "mother-of-pearl" in Mongolian and "freshwater pearl" in Manchu.[8] Consequently, when the Manchu emperor honored a Mongolian ally with *tanas* in 1620 it is difficult to determine what was intended.[9] These shifts in terminology are apparently tied to the embrace of freshwater pearls by the Manchus as a statement of ethnic identity and a symbol of their homeland.[10]

Overall, the impact in North Asia, while certainly detectable, is muted and did not constitute a dramatic new departure; the patterns of use, featuring the combination of fresh- and saltwater pearls and the interplay of local and international fashions, are consistent with practices found for centuries at the royal courts in the region, whether of Chinese or Inner Asian origin.

Similar continuity can be found under the Temürids, the Mongols' successors in the eastern Islamic lands. As was true of the Ming, they, too, had access to productive pearl fisheries in the Gulf and India. And, of course, the founders' far-ranging campaigns produced more in the form of booty.[11] In combination this allowed the Temürids, like their Chinggisid precursors, to amass and put on display huge numbers of high-quality pearls. With these they adorned their jewelry, headgear, clothing, furniture, wall hangings, tableware, and one-of-kind display pieces.[12] Of the latter, the most spectacular was a large artificial tree with a gilt trunk the size of a man's leg and branches bearing fruit of precious gems and "many great round pearls of wonderful orient and beauty."[13] As the Sasanid and ʿAbbāsid courts famously featured similar artificial trees, this spectacular creation enjoyed an impeccable imperial lineage in West Asia.[14]

The high level of continuity in this instance is only to be expected, for Temür consciously emulated Mongolian traditions, presenting himself as a dutiful imperial son-in-law (*küregen*) trying to restore the broken empire while at the same time drawing upon and assimilating the rich resources of the Perso-Islamic cultural synthesis of the preceding centuries.

In contrast to the continuities south of the steppe, in the north there are signs of significant change, particularly noticeable in Moscovite Russia. This can best be understood by briefly exploring the principality's intimate, centuries-long relationship with the Golden Horde, whose rulers, like Chinggisids everywhere, energetically sought to secure large supplies of pearls from all available sources.

Without direct access to the open seas, the Golden Horde received its pearls through a variety of channels, including long-distance trade. Most of the merchants involved were Muslims with close official connections to the court. But there were Greeks and Italians on the scene as well; operating from centers in the Crimea and at Tana, they, too, trafficked in pearls.[15] From their places of origin in the Indian Ocean pearls made their way to the Golden Horde by a number of different routes. The first ran from India overland through Turkistan to Khwārazm and Sarai. The next came through the Red Sea, across Mamlūk Egypt, longtime ally of the Jochids, and from there to Constantinople and the northern ports of the Black Sea. Lastly, there was a land passage from the head of the Gulf across Iraq to eastern Asia Minor and then by ship to Caffa and Tana.

The latter route, dominated by the Genoese, was particularly active. This was made possible because they constituted the major European presence in the Il-qan domains from the late thirteenth century to the disintegration of the regime. Their sanctioned quarters in Tabriz and in the small independent Greek kingdom of Trebizond enabled them to become intermediaries in this lucrative transit trade. As a result, and despite the intermittent hostilities between the Il-qans and the Golden Horde, pearls and other wares regularly flowed into the western steppe from the southern seas in the hands of European traders.[16]

There were strong incentives to do so, since the Golden Horde offered extremely attractive tariff rates. Like the Il-qans, they collected customs on all goods entering their realm except for gold, silver, and pearls, an exemption that lasted from around 1289 into the 1330s.[17] And a decade later there was still only a nominal 0.5 percent duty placed on the pearls imported by the Genoese.[18] Rates like these say something important about the intensity of a court's desire for gems.[19]

Princely presentations and diplomatic gifts further augmented their supplies. A hoard, dating to about 1350, unearthed near Simferopol in the Crimea, contained more than three hundred items of gold jewelry and female headdresses adorned with pearls and other precious stones may be just such a gift. Since the pieces exhibit clear Mamlūk stylistic affinities, and since they enjoyed good relations with the Golden Horde, the find is reasonably interpreted as a princely presentation lost in route to Sarai.[20]

Another and major source was booty, which in the Golden Horde retained its importance well into the fourteenth century. On the complex and convoluted nature of such sudden transfers of wealth, one transfer is particularly instructive. Following the breakup of the Mongolian regime in Iran in 1335, one of the regional contenders for power was Malik Ashraf, a descendant of Chuban, the powerful minister of the last il-qan, Abū Saʿīd (r. 1316–35). By 1349 the malik, who controlled Azerbaijan, had amassed a huge fortune of precious metals and gems through looting and the confiscation of subjects' property. In 1357, as the invading Jochid forces under the personal command of Jani-Beg Qan (r. 1342–57) crossed the Caucasus, Malik Ashraf, his army rapidly disintegrating, fled with his treasures, which his few remaining retainers soon plundered. When Jani-Beg heard of this, he immediately sent out agents to track down the malik and make a careful search for his riches. Some of it was recovered, more specifically the treasury of gems and pearls, which the qan took back to the Horde.[21]

By these varied means the Jochids managed to accumulate substantial reserves of gems and pearls. There are several lines of evidence sustaining this conclusion. First of all, there are two well-informed and contemporary Italian sources that speak directly to the issue; one, a commercial manual of circa 1315 states plainly that merchants can find in Tana "Oriental pearls of every region," and the other, a business letter from 1343 reports that an Italian merchant purchased "as many pearls as cost 17,000 *bezants*" at Urgench in Khwārazm.[22] Given their wide availability on the open market in major cities, pearls must have been plentiful also among the Jochids and their servitors.

The second line of evidence, from some decades later, fully supports such an interpretation. This is found in a contemporary Russian cycle of tales relating the fall of Mamai, the non-Chinggisid kingmaker in the Golden Horde. In 1380, the Russians defeated Mamai, taking away great loot, jewelry (*uzoroch'ia*), gold, brocades, and damasks, and in the following year the Chinggisid qan, Toqtamish (r. 1376–95), defeated him in the steppe north of the Crimea. On this occasion the victorious qan seized "his riches, gold and silver, pearls and gems, all in great numbers, and divided them among his retainers." Mamai then fled to Caffa "with great riches, gold and silver, gems and pearls" and was killed there by the Genoese, who confiscated his remaining treasure.[23]

The constant recycling of booty is itself of great interest; it is quite conceivable, though not demonstrable, that pearls confiscated by Malik Ashraf subsequently passed through the hands of Jani-Beg and his successors to Mamai, Toqtamish, and finally the Genoese, a case of the sequential expropriation of the expropriators. More certainly, owing to the continuous and ever-intensifying power struggles within the Golden Horde, great treasures like that of Mamai were repeatedly seized, redistributed, and dispersed, with the result that quantities of pearls ended up in regions with limited previous exposure to products of the southern seas. One such was western Siberia, where in the early 1580s Cossacks found in the encampments of the Qanate of Sibir great riches, including precious stones and pearls.[24]

At the time of the breakup of the Horde there were, however, other forest people, the Volga Bulghars and the Eastern Slavs, with a much longer and more intense exposure. This is attested by the Russian *zhemchug*, derived from the Chinese *zhenzhu* as mediated through Bulgharic Turkic *yĕnchĕk*, a linguistic relationship that strongly suggests a shared experience with pearls dating back centuries before the Mongolian conquest.[25]

To judge from the available literary sources, among the Eastern Slavs, following their conversion to Orthodox Christianity in about 990, pearls are more frequently mentioned in connection with religious than with political display.[26] But during and after the period of Mongolian domination, there is evidence of their increasing political use at the Moscovite court. Tatar influence on this shift is detectable, which is hardly surprising, since the principality was a dependency of the Horde. In consequence, Moscovite princes made regular trips to Sarai in the discharge of their obligations to the qan and were thus extensively exposed to the court culture of their overlords, from whom they received formal investiture in office, which in Chinggisid tradition always required bestowals of richly decorated court attire.

While Russian sources provide much general information on the Horde, these reports often lack detail. We know, for example, that starting with the initial conquest in the late 1230s down to the fifteenth century, Russian princes and Golden Horde qans "by custom" continually made presents to one another, but what was exchanged is not specified.[27] There is, however, one likely bestowal to the princes of Moscow still extant, the so-called cap or crown of Monomakh. Made of gold and bedecked with pearls, the cap, according to sixteenth-century Russian sources, is said to be the gift of the Byzantine emperor Constantine IX Monomachus (r. 1042–55) to the Kiev prince Vladimir Monomakh (r. 1113–25), which, obviously, is a chronological impossibility. And further, on stylistic grounds, the cap has close affinities with later Islamic traditions in jewelry making that became prevalent in the Golden Horde. Consequently, there is a growing consensus that the cap was either inspired by this tradition or that it came as a gift from a Tatar qan to a Moscovite prince.[28]

There is, in addition, some literary evidence indicating what Russian princes very likely received from the Horde or, of equal significance, what they choose to emulate. According to his testament, Ivan Kalita of Moscovy (r. 1328–41), the Jochid's first chief fiscal agent in the Russian principalities, bequeathed to his sons and daughters golden goblets, golden plates, a sable pelisse, silk mantles, and a golden Italian belt all decorated with gems and pearls.[29] While we cannot prove their provenance, we can reasonably expect that some of these came as gifts from Özbeg (r. 1312–41), the qan Ivan so loyally served. Even the Italian belt, which likely came through the Crimea or Tana, may well have been a bestowal from the qan. The wills and testaments of his immediate successors point in the same direction. These princes left their heirs bulk pearls as well as pearl-adorned helmets, clothing, belts, tableware and earrings.[30]

Gifts, however, were not their only source of their pearls; booty and tribute are also in evidence. As noted previously, in 1380 after their defeat of Mamai the Russians seized great treasure, and it can fairly be assumed, since the primary meaning of the old Russian *uzoroch'e* is "jewel" or "jewelry," that pearls were involved, particularly in light of what he lost the following year.[31] More certainly, by the sixteenth century the Moscovite princes had obtained quantities of pearls from the Golden Horde's successor states, especially from the Qanate of Kazan, the direct descendants of the Volga Bulghars. In 1508, after a successful Russian attack, its qan sent an envoy to Vasily III (r. 1505–33) with "gifts" that included a pavilion tent covered with pearls and gems, one that originated in Ṣafāvid Iran.[32] The princes' greatest haul came in 1552 when Moscovy defeated and permanently occupied the qanate. And, adhering closely to Mongolian patterns of booty taking, as soon as resistance ended, the Russian sovereign, Ivan IV (r. 1533–84) surveyed the state treasury and had it sealed and sent it to his capital, while the Russian troops "seized also unmeasurable amounts of gold and silver and pearls (*zhemchug*) and precious stones" from the general population. In addition, they were allowed take from the qan's private quarters some of his personal possessions, pearled wall hangings and precious pearls (*bisar*).[33] Not surprisingly, at the victory parade in Moscow, Ivan wore "a gold crown adorned with large pearls (the cap of Monomakh?)" and similarly decorated attire.[34]

Commercial connections provided further supplies. Europeans who were in Moscovy to trade in the mid-sixteenth century noted that its ruler obtained pearls from the Gulf and India, some through English hands, and that the tsar aggressively tried "to engrosse" or corner the market for pearls.[35] So, like earlier Mongolian courts, the court of Moscovy attempted to establish quasi-monopolies on imported pearls to turn a profit and to ensure adequate stores of this important political currency.

What, then, did the Moscovite court do with its growing stock? By the late fifteenth century there is explicit testimony that among other positional goods, pearl-decorated cups and textiles were exchanged between Russian elites and their prince.[36] When West Europeans arrived in Russia in the next century, their observations affirm this picture and add some illuminating detail. They relate that notables at the court of Ivan IV were attired in gold brocade robes that were bedecked with pearls, as were their hats, collars, capes, boots, bracelets, and horse trappings, fashions that survived into the seventeenth century.[37] Naturally, the pearls of the grand prince were of the highest quality, "very large, round and orient" in the words of an English merchant, phrasing that echoes Clavijo's descriptions of those in possession of Temür, another noted successor of the Chinggisids.[38]

Since, however, pearls also had a visible presence at the Byzantine court, we are confronted with the long-debated issue of the relative importance of Byzantium and the Golden Horde in the development of Moscovite political culture.[39] There was, of course, considerable interplay between Byzantium and the Golden Horde, but in attempting to weigh their respective influence we must keep in mind that while Moscovite princes for more than two hundred years repeatedly visited the Horde, *none* set foot in Constantinople.

In the thirteenth century, their audiences in the Horde often concerned renewal of investiture made necessary by the death of a qan, and in the fourteenth the trips mainly concerned the delivery of tributes. In reporting these events, the Russian chronicles routinely and laconically say a certain prince *ide k ordu*, "went to the royal camp (Mongolian *orda*)," which in fact is a very apt characterization, for the Jochids still followed a nomadic lifestyle.[40] This meant, in turn, that the Rus princes and their retinues spent extended periods at Sarai and in the sumptuous encampments in which the court made annual rounds throughout the Volga basin.[41]

Yet another important channel of influence, also documented in the Russian sources, were the envoys (*posoly*) that princes sent as semipermanent representatives to the Horde. By the mid-fourteenth century these officials are increasingly called *kilichei* and are now sent mainly by the Moscovite princes with rich gifts to negotiate assorted matters with the Jochid ruler. As their title goes back to the Mongolian *kelechi*, "speaker" and by extension "interpreter," "spokesman" or perhaps "mouthpiece," they were certainly well named.[42] They, too, spent long periods in the Horde, and given their title and the nature of their duties, were likely chosen in the first place for their knowledge of the languages and customs of their Chinggisid hosts, and therefore constituted excellent mediums for the transmission of Golden Horde political culture to the Moscovite court. In consequence of this extensive and first-hand experience, it is hardly surprising that Russian notions of imperial grandeur, particularly in its visual and material manifestations, so closely parallel that of the Horde, their most immediate model.

In explaining Moscovy's eager embrace of pearls, it should also be remembered that because of their widespread sanctification and long association with imperial rule, here as elsewhere they were multivalent, conveying different but nonetheless authentic and comprehensible messages to a variety of subject peoples. Thus, a pearl-bedecked tsar affirmed his orthodoxy and legitimacy for his Slavic servitors and subjects, and at the same time for his growing number of Tatar retainers and clients it affirmed him as the rightful successor to the qans of the Golden Horde. Their acceptance of this succession is unmistakably expressed in the title the Tatars adopted for the Moscovite ruler, *belyi tsar*, "the White Emperor," which was first bestowed on Ivan IV by the Noghai Tatars in the mid-sixteenth century, a practice later followed by the western Mongols, who styled the early Romanov rulers *yeke chaghan qan*, "the Great White Qan."[43]

Inasmuch as white was the color symbol for the west and the source of good fortune among steppe peoples, the Moscovite tsar had become in their eyes the Fortunate Qan of the West. This, moreover, accords well with the self-image of the Moscovite rulers, who, from the time of Ivan III (r. 1462–1505), claimed for themselves possession of luck (*zdrovie*) and good fortune (*schastie*).[44] And, appropriately enough, as the Russians moved eastward in the seventeenth century their envoys to various Mongolian rulers attributed the success of these missions to their sovereign's special good fortune, a claim that Tsar Alexei in 1659 instructed his envoys to communicate to the Manchu emperor.[45]

From this data, four conclusions are warranted.

The Chinggid era is the first time pearls assumed a massive presence and permanent place in the political life and court culture of states centered in the forest zone north of the western steppe.

Viewed in a somewhat different perspective, this was the first time such states, thanks to Chinggisid precedents, practices, and priorities, had access to large stores of pearls, and their influx into the northern forests under the Golden Horde constitutes yet another stage in the long-term process of southernization.

In contrast to their expansive phase, when the Mongols relied exclusively on external sources of gems and pearls, in their decline phase Chinggisid rivals relied increasingly on internal sources; that is to say, they seized these items from one another. Such abrupt, disruptive transfers of wealth are also diagnostic of the decline phase of many imperial regimes.

Last, the Mongolian Empire's expansion generated massive concentrations of pearls and gems, and the disintegration of the empire generated equally massive dispersals, both of which dramatically affected the distribution, availability, and price of pearls.

PART II

Comparisons and Influence

CHAPTER 9

Prices of Pearls

The history of pearls in the Mongolian Empire provides a useful window on more general and long-term historical phenomena, the innumerable side effects and unanticipated consequences of the circulation of cultural and commercial wares in premodern Eurasia. To achieve productive observations about these phenomena requires broad cross-cultural and historical comparisons. By design, these comparisons concentrate on the interactions between polities, ethnicities, and communities that differ in scale and complexity, since the crucial issue here is the impact of transcontinental commerce and cultural standards on local tastes and local economies.

In Chapters 9, 10, and 11 a number of these effects are identified and briefly examined. These case studies demonstrate that this was a recurrent and widespread phenomenon and that sufficient documentation exists for such investigations, some of the most enlightening of which is found in nontraditional sources.

The first of these comparative studies treats long-term fluctuations in the value of pearls and other gems. Information on the price of pearls in antiquity and the Middle Ages is sporadic and distorted. Characteristic are the figures given in traditional Islamic literature, which, following well-established Indian lapidary traditions, are usually much inflated, designed to underscore the magnificence of a specific gem or to broadcast the great wealth of its owner, typically a famed prince.[1]

These practices begin early and the numbers reported are extraordinary, as the following brief sampling illustrates:

A string of pearls valued at a hundred thousand pieces of gold in ancient India.

A thousand flawless pearls each worth four thousand silver dirhams bestowed by a Sasanid king.
A string of pearls valued at a million gold dinars in early ʿAbbāsid times.
Another string of pearls, valued at eighty thousand [dinars or silver dirhams?], in Fatimid Egypt.
And most astounding, a large pearl that sold for seventy thousand gold dinars under the ʿAbbāsids.[2]

In viewing the list as a whole, several commonalities stand out; all the valuations come from much later sources and typically relate to royal possessions, purchases, and presentations. The literature transmitting this information consists for the most part of works devoted to rarities and wonders written for the entertainment of the upper classes. But such tales are also perpetuated in works of a more popular nature. In the Persian encyclopedia of Dunaysarī, prepared in the Il-qan realm during the latter half of the thirteenth century, there is a short discussion of pearls available in the Persian Gulf, and it, too, pays particular attention to those commanding extremely high prices.[3] Since his work was intended for a general audience, and appropriately written in a simple, direct style, it certainly reflected and sustained popular views of pearls as objects "worthy of a king's ransom."

Clearly, there is a certain synergy at work here: fabulous values enhance the majesty of the prince, and such majesty in turn enhances the fame and worth of the precious gems he possesses and dispenses.

The impulse to inflate was in fact general and even affected specialists like al-Bīrūnī, who on occasion could not resist drawing attention to storied pearls purchased at a great price by a great prince.[4] When speaking of his own time and place, however, his valuations markedly change, for he now provides realistic, market-driven prices for individual pearls as determined by weight, shape, luster, and provenance. And in this context, even those of the highest quality cost only around a thousand dinars.[5] His data, moreover, is compatible with the statement found in an anonymous early thirteenth-century Persian geography that reports the same figure as the usual asking price for the very best Chinese varieties.[6]

For the Mongolian era some realistic pricing data is also available. Tao Zongyi, writing in the late Yuan, says that a certain pair of pearl earrings had recently sold for thirty-odd silver ingots.[7] Francesco Pegolotti, circa 1330, is even more helpful, providing examples of the prices and weights of pearls sold in Persia and the Mediterranean region.[8] But even taking into account this welcome deflation of value to realistic levels, there is no doubt that profit margins remained high and pearls continued to invite major investment. And on the vital matter of merchants' expectations there is some hard data available; according to the sworn statements of the principals in a lawsuit, a company of Italian merchants in 1343 purchased 102,000 *bezants* worth of pearls in Delhi.[9] Merchants might well hope for, but did not require, fabulous or inflated prices for pearls in order to anticipate substantial returns on investments.

While certainly useful, this kind of information is limited and scattered, and consequently it is nearly impossible to reconstruct year-by-year price histories for pearls in any particular region or market in antiquity or the Middle Ages. Nonetheless, something can be said about the varied forces at work, natural and human, that account for the recurrent and often extensive changes in their price across the centuries.

One major source of change was the volatility of supplies, which tended to fluctuate widely and sometimes wildly due to the repeated overexploitation of established beds. As a result, there was considerable comment on, and sensitivity to, this variation. Inquiring about the harvest from a small fishery off the coast of Fārs, the il-qan Ghazan was informed by a court official that in a good year it might return about 750 *mann*, a year later perhaps 450, and in the third year only 250.[10] There was, however, only a limited understanding of what caused the variation. One traditional view is reported by al-Bīrūnī, who says that in his day the pearl beds of Ceylon (Sarandīb) were largely depleted and that local opinion held the oysters had "migrated" to Sufala on the east coast of Africa.[11]

For a modern explanation of why harvests were so irregular, several fundamental features of pearls' natural history must be taken into account.

First, many oysters have to be sacrificed for a small number of pearls. Even assuming the very best ratio, that one oyster in ten contains a commercially viable pearl, this nevertheless means extensive wastage and major reductions in breeding populations. And if, as seems far more likely, the ratio is one in a hundred or a thousand, the devastation is proportionally greater. Its magnitude is well documented in Ceylon, where overfishing was a perennial problem; here in 1905 alone a grand total of 49,250,189 oysters were taken in pursuit of pearls.[12]

Second, while other high-value stones are products of extremely long-term cosmological and geological processes, pearls result from relatively short-term biochemical processes. So, unlike diamonds or rubies, whose supply is finite, pearls constitute a renewable resource. It is, therefore, not by chance that terms like "harvest" and "crop" are regularly used in the pearling industry. And, as is true of other renewable animal products—feathers, fur, and ivory—used for human adornment, there is a pronounced tendency to assume an infinite supply and to engage in overexploitation, an attitude effectively conveyed by the German *Raubwirtschaft* (plunder economy).[13] Not surprisingly, pearls, both fresh- and saltwater, have been subject to ruthless exploitation, and, for the most part, conservation was forced on producers, who only reluctantly and sporadically adopted protective measures in the aftermath of drastic declines in harvests.[14]

Third, while diamonds are forever, pearls are not. They are in fact quite fragile, given to general deterioration and to damage, a vulnerability often remarked upon by early naturalists, poets, historians, and merchants.[15] This in turn meant they were often destroyed in substantial numbers during raids and military operations. Al-Bīrūnī, who accompanied Maḥmūd of Ghazna on his annual forays into northwestern India, notes that when out of religious zeal an "idol temple" was fired, the pearls were destroyed beyond recognition, while the rubies survived.[16] Although of secondary significance, such deterioration and destruction still had an effect on the availability and price of pearls.

Fourth, and to bring the story to its conclusion in the modern age, since it is relatively easy to replicate the natural processes involved in the development of pearls, large-scale human-controlled production, perfected by Mikimoto, became possible.[17] And this development in combination with the overexploitation endemic to traditional fishing practices meant the natural pearl industry finally collapsed in the course of the late nineteenth and early twentieth centuries.[18]

Natural forces in combination with production methods were therefore the fundamental factors responsible for the repeated and sometimes extreme fluctuations in supplies that conditioned the price of pearls in the long term. But once on land, the stock of pearls, whatever its size and composition, was further subject to alternative and ever-changing modes of exchange that frequently and decisively influenced their availability, distribution, and value. The place to begin such an analysis is with the arguments of Philip Grierson and Anthony Cutler that in the medieval West there were three dominant forms of circulation—trade, gift exchange, and booty collection—and as a corollary, the patterns in the distribution and possession of valuables cannot be understood as the simple by-product of a series of commercial transactions.[19] Their formulations, in my view, can be usefully applied throughout Eurasia in premodern times.

Certainly, basic market forces were always part of the mix. Since large, round, white, and lustrous pearls are the rarest produced by nature and the most highly valued by humans, their long-term price structure was continuously shaped by fundamental laws of supply and demand. So, too, was the shorter-term price structure. During the Middle Ages and the early modern period in areas with abundant supplies, such as South India, pearls were bought and sold on the open market, used as a medium of exchange in commercial transactions, and regularly came into the hands of the lower classes.[20] The same was the case in China during the imperial period. One of the earliest expressions of market forces at work is found in the *Discourses on Salt and Iron* of 81 BCE, where it is noted with disapproval that the massive and insatiable tastes for finery lead "artisans to strive for excessive ingenuity," while others "bore into mountains for gold and silver or plunge into the deep for pearls (*zhuji*)."[21] That this quest was not a monopoly of the upper classes is made evident in later Chinese sources that report pearls were available in open markets and hawked on the streets, at times cheap enough to be in the possession of commoners.[22] This was the case even in Turkestan, far from any sea; at the great celebration Temür held in Samarqand in 1404 there were merchants in the bazaar offering gems and "lustrous pearls" to the general public.[23]

Their value-to-weight ratios and their liquidity made pearls an attractive form of currency for travelers. It was, for instance, standard practice for those on pilgrimage to Mecca to carry pearls rather than cash, some of which were provided gratis by royal courts, the Mamlūks, Il-qans, and others.[24] And when at the end of the journey great numbers were sold to brokers to cover expenses, this depressed the market throughout the entire region. We should also bear in mind that the final price of these particular pearls was determined by a countervailing market force that placed limits on the extent of their depreciation—their sanctification by association with the Holy City.[25] As a result, Mecca became a major center of pearl exchange, which led Ma Huan into the mistaken belief that the Heavenly Quarter (Tianfang) was itself a major center of pearl production.[26]

Luxury items of every kind are particularly susceptible to changing fashions. While these shifts in earlier times were less frequent than those of today, they are still noticeable in the historical record. Among the more famous cases is the mania for pearls in Rome during the first century CE, which, as Pliny caustically notes, swiftly and dramatically drove up their prices.[27] And even in Iran, where pearls were plentiful and long mainstays in personal ornamentation, a new fad that incorporated pearls in female hairstyles increased their demand and price in the late sixteenth century.[28] Such changes in fashion, both large and small, were a permanent feature of, and influence in, the marketplace.

Although supply and demand were undoubtedly important, there were other nonmarket modes of exchange that regularly bypassed and/or replaced steps in what we think of as the normal business chain leading from primary producer to broker/wholesaler to retail merchant to customer. Together, these disruptions regularly affected in unintended and unpredictable ways the market value of pearls and gems.

Gift exchange offers one example of this. As already documented, at the courts of the Chinggisids such exchange could assume massive proportions. Here, as at other imperial centers, there were high concentrations of elites constantly vying for the sovereign's favor and exchanging prestige goods with one another. Under such circumstances there are periodic sell-offs of valuables prompted by hard times, political crises, and changes in fashion. Quite naturally, the most liquid of the assets, gems and pearls, predominated, with the result that markets quickly became saturated, and prices declined precipitously.[29]

At times, elite sell-offs became institutionalized. Something like this occurred in Dadu, where by imperial decree a special market for "pearls, gems, and jewelry" was established in 1327.[30] That Tao Zongyi, a contemporary, is able to accurately describe a wide variety of gemstones from the Western Region and provide their Arabo-Persian and Indian names is one indicator of the volume in circulation during the last decades of the Yuan.[31] Mandeville, writing in Europe shortly thereafter, might well have heard a distant echo of these extensive sell-offs, for he notes the cheapness of gems and pearls at the great kaan's court, whose numbers he says "pass man's estimation."[32]

The last mode of exchange, booty collection, is often ignored or held to be marginal or extraneous to formal economic analysis and therefore deserves more extended treatment. When considered at all it is usually associated with the depredations of barbarians and nomads, but sedentary polities also enthusiastically engaged in the pursuit of plunder. In fact, some of the most productive booty frontiers in Eurasian and world history were worked by "civilized" powers whose methods of collection, if not their range of action, were similar to those of the Mongols.

Mesopotamia, over which the Roman and Persian empires in their various guises fought for centuries, was one such frontier from which endless loot was extracted, including large hauls of pearls.[33] While great wealth was extracted from captured cities and their inhabitants, also rewarding in the search for precious stones was the systemic looting of the dead in the immediate aftermath of battle.[34]

Equally famous and quite likely even more productive of gems and pearls was the northwestern frontier of India. Ancient nomads began the seizures in the early centuries CE, and in the Middle Ages Muslim states, most notably the

Ghaznavids (977–1186), took up this profitable enterprise on a regular basis, acquiring much treasure from courts, shrines, and temples. These annual forays were motivated in part by India's reputation for the beauty and magical power of its gems and in part by the belief that the temples, besides their external decorations, contained storage facilities and treasuries, which functioned as proto-banks.[35] Although the figures given in Muslim sources on the amount of booty extracted from India may be exaggerated to glorify Maḥmūd and his successors, there can be no doubt about its magnitude, as is clearly evidenced by the opulence of their court in Afghanistan.[36]

There is, I believe, a discernible dynamic at work here. To a certain extent the looting was stimulated by the many legends and tales concerning the number, value, beauty, and magical properties of the gems in the possession of the temples, monasteries, and shrines of India.[37] Some of these, to be sure, were the by-products of boasts by invaders about the great treasure seized to magnify their success and reputations. But it is also true that the Indian administrators and inmates of these establishments were actively engaged in creating their own legends about their holdings—a huge emerald whose incredible luminosity allowed one to read at night well represents these efforts.[38] They of course made these claims of immense material and spiritual wealth to attract new adherents and donations, but in so doing they unwittingly attracted the attention of local bandits and foreign invaders.

North China was another such frontier, an arena in which Inner Asians were continually active. Its riches, real and imagined, repeatedly attracted steppe and forest peoples southward, where they formed hybrid border regimes and on occasion great empires. And in the course of these rounds of raiding and conquest they regularly pillaged their predecessors' wealth and treasuries. When the Jürchens occupied the Qitan's Upper Capital in 1119 they systematically plundered the burial vaults of the Liao emperors and found much gold, silver, gems, and pearls. About a hundred years later the Mongols seized the Jürchen's accumulated pearls in Zhongdu, and in 1368 when the Mongols fled back into the steppe, they hurriedly carried with them some but not all of the Yuan court's precious gems (*paoyu*) as the victorious Ming forces entered Dadu.[39]

Such recycling of plunder, as already emphasized, was in fact common across Eurasia. Some notion of its frequency, and the concomitant concentration and dispersion of gems and pearls, can be gained by looking at the kingdom of Georgia from the eleventh century through the fourteenth. With the arrival of the Seljuqs in 1065, Georgia's regional courts and ecclesiastical establishments were repeatedly sacked by the invaders, who, like the later Mongols, targeted precious metals and gems. Subsequently, with the restoration of unity and formation of a formidable Transcaucasian empire, the Georgians went on the offensive, reclaiming and accumulating great amounts of gold, gems, and pearls from their Muslim rivals through booty collection, ransom of prisoners, and imposition of tributes. In the Mongolian period they initially lost pearls through the same channels and then a short while later recouped many of these losses at Baghdad and other locales, as clients and military allies of the Il-qans. Finally, when the Il-qans converted to Islam at the end of the thirteenth century, Georgia's accumulated treasures, always including pearls, were looted once again, seizures that continued into the Temürid era and beyond.[40]

To obtain a complete and balanced picture of booty taking in the transference of vast wealth, we must revisit the issue of mobile treasuries. The first thing to be noted is that peripatetic kingship was not a monopoly of the steppe and was common in the sedentary world as well. Al-Bīrūnī, as usual, offers some insightful comments on the subject. The normal preference of kings, he states, is to carry precious gems on progresses and campaigns, since they are lighter and take up less space than precious metals. It is therefore a matter of logistics, which in turn explains for him why "precious stones are the accessories of kings."[41] In this al-Bīrūnī is quite correct. The classical sources frequently mention the practice among the Persians, starting with the Achaemenids, the political model for its many successors in the Near East.[42] As a direct consequence of this practice, whenever sedentary rulers took to the field great treasures were made available for the taking. In 590 when the Byzantine troops overran the Sasanian royal camp they came away with a rich haul of gold and pearls, and in the period 792–813 the Byzantines and Danubian Bulghars seized the others' mobile treasuries on three occasions.[43]

Nomadic rulers, for the same logistical reasons, and because of followers' expectation of regular redistribution, adhered to the same practice. Qubilai, while still a prince, took along a large supply of pearled garments when he campaigned in southwestern China in the early 1250s.[44] Temür also brought huge quantities of clothing, precious gems, and pearls (*gawhar*) into the field for this purpose, and it is hardly surprising that when his troops were defeated in 1400 by Mamlūk forces in Syria, the victors came away with much gold and pearls.[45] In some cases, victorious forces quite literally followed trails of strewn treasure left by defeated rulers in the course of their hurried flights.[46] Most obviously, this was done to reduce weight and increase speed but also in hope of distracting pursuers.

The choice of precocities taken to the field raises another important question. In conformity with al-Bīrūnī's analysis, the logistically friendly precious stones are always included, but why the large amounts of sumptuous clothing, which are cumbersome and make heavy demands on transport animals? The answer is that investiture was continually used to recognize special service and publicize new appointments and promotions, and was therefore integral to command and control of nomadic armies. Without the regular redistribution of this specific combination of rewards, steppe armies soon became disaffected and disintegrated.

Since without doubt the booty frontiers of the Mongols far outstripped those of their predecessors, extending as they did from Korea to Mesopotamia, they obtained incalculable amounts of mobile wealth from the continent's richest courts and economies. Most noted is that accumulated and stored at great capitals, provincial cities, and royal courts, but much was also seized on the move. The reason for this is easily identified: the Mongols' rapid expansion generated massive movements of sedentary, nomadic, and seminomadic populations fleeing the onslaught, most particularly the elites, who took with them their most portable forms of wealth.

The extent of the resulting turnover is well exemplified in the history of the Khwārazmian state, the major objective of the initial phase of the Mongols' westward expansion in the period from 1219 to 1231. These sudden and recurrent shifts are catalogued at length in the biography of Jalāl al-Dīn, the last Khwārazmshāh, written by his retainer Muḥammad Nasawī, an eyewitness and participant in many of these transfers, whose account can be verified and amplified by independent sources.

From these it is clear, first of all, that when members of the ruling house and other elites left their homeland under Mongolian pressure they did so with large amounts of precious metal, coined money, gems, and pearls (*javāhir*). Further, while on the run Jalāl al-Dīn acquired for his mobile treasury additional assets, again in the form of coin and gems through "gifts" from temporary clients, tributes levied on local rulers, and plunder seized throughout Khurāsān and Transcaucasia. At the same time, however, he also suffered major losses. Some occurred because the weight of the treasures was so great that it was necessary to jettison gold and coin at river crossings to escape the Mongols, most famously on the Indus in 1221. Other parts of the mobile treasury were lost in confrontations with the pursuers, who were quick to seize and redistribute these spoils. Finally, when Jalāl al-Dīn died in 1231 with only a few expensive gems and pearls in his possession, those of his adherents who survived fled to the Mamlūk kingdom with the remnants of his treasure or took it to the Mongolian court to obtain forgiveness and favor.[47]

All in all, during the course of the 1220s incalculable and unprecedented amounts of negotiable and transportable wealth were dispersed, transferred, and lost over a huge swath of territory from Turkistan to Transcaucasia. One measure of its immensity is that even the Mongols' careful searches missed sizable quantities. This is indicated by the profitable and regular practice of excavating and washing soil around the larger cities of Turkistan in the sixteenth century to recover precious metals and gems buried in the 1220s.[48]

While this massive dispersal of liquid wealth entailed transfers between a number of different ethnicities, polities, and social classes, the chief beneficiaries, of course, were the Mongols. Although forcible seizure is naturally viewed as the antithesis of the free market, such seizures could have appreciable and dramatic effects upon them. Already in the 1250s Juvaynī, a contemporary observer, noticed that Mongolian notables had amassed so many gems and pearls (*javāhir*) that in the markets around their centers prices fell precipitously.[49] Conquest often has this effect. In the aftermath of Alexander's plundering of the East, there were so many gems in Macedonia that here, too, prices were greatly depressed.[50]

Somewhat unexpectedly, rampant corruption, generated by the sheer volume of these seizures, also produced noticeable price fluctuations. During the reigns of Arghun and Gheikhtu, provincial governors regularly sent to the treasury "gem-studded belts, pearls, and other high-priced wares" in pursuit of favor and personal gain. The couriers to whom they were entrusted, however, sold them in search of quick profits at low prices or pawned them as mere trifles, and consequently the demand for pearls and gems (*javāhir*) collapsed. In this instance, the incessant demand for ever more gems did not raise market prices but rather depressed them. According to Rashīd al-Dīn, these practices were so extensive that the true market value for precious stones only rebounded after the implementation of Ghazan's fiscal reforms in 1298.[51]

A small-scale but nonetheless informative illustration of the interactions between modes of exchange, their velocity, and the volatility they produced, is provided by Nasawī. He relates that at Khabūshān, in western Khurāsān, the Mongols overtook and killed a party of wealthy Khwārazmians in 1222. They did not, however, stop to search for spoils, most likely because they were on a tight military schedule. The common people of the area then collected the gems and pearls (*javāhir*) from the dead and sold them at a small local bazaar at very low prices. Some of these were purchased by a certain Naṣr al-Dīn, the mayor of the nearby town of Nisā. Shortly thereafter, he related directly to Nasawī that among them was a diamond (*ālmās*) he bought for seventy dinars, which he subsequently presented to Jalāl al-Dīn, at which point he discovered that the stone was actually valued at four thousand dinars. Thus, within a year, this gem changed hands and status from private property to spoils of war to a market commodity and finally to a politically motivated gift.[52]

The existence and interaction of these modes of circulation brings up another important question: Are there sequential patterns in their dominance, and do these constitute evolutionary stages? In the effort to understand large-scale political formations and their characteristic systems of exchange, there is often a focus on identifying a dominant mode variously labeled tributary, redistributive, feudal, and so forth. But to me, the evidence points to the prevalence of mixed systems that coexist with, compete with, and complement one another. It could hardly be otherwise, for such admixture was built into the very structure of pan-Eurasian exchange. At the eastern end of the Silk Road, trade goods were acquired largely by means of plunder and tribute, and thus through military investments, while at the western end their final price was determined by market competition. The same thing can be said of the transecological exchanges; when northern products, acquired by means of coerced tributes and the archaic "blind trade," reached the south, they were routinely sold on the open market or presented as princely gifts. Consequently, commodities that traveled over extended distances normally did so through variable combinations of modes. But even those moving over much shorter distances did as well: from the eyewitness testimony of Kirakos we know that in Transcaucasia during the 1240s Mongolian commanders routinely sent a favored merchant prince "gifts from their war booty," that is, they eagerly invested these forcible seizures in commercial enterprises.[53]

These extensive interactions, while difficult to chart and disentangle, are responsible for the cycles of concentration and dispersion of precious stones and pearls that had far-reaching effects on their value. But even this is not the end of the complications; as we shall see next, the demand, distribution, and cost of pearls was also conditioned by widely diffused mythologies concerning their origins, properties, and powers.

CHAPTER 10

Myths and Marketing

Merchants, of course, also influenced prices and manipulated markets, including those for pearls, and had many ways of accomplishing this. On occasion they honored rulers and notables with sumptuous gifts, provided free "samples" of their wares, an equivalent of the modern "loss leader" designed to open doors to new markets.[1] Most often, however, merchants strove to maximize the price and profit on their goods by hard bargaining and artful salesmanship. In the case of pearls and gems, they were greatly aided by the rich lore and myth surrounding precocities.

The belief that precious stones and pearls had esoteric properties and magical powers that exercised beneficial influences on their possessors was universally accepted in traditional societies, including their educated classes—religious leaders, literati, and naturalists.[2] Thus, while much of this lore was popular in origin, over time it became enshrined and authenticated in learned literature. In the classical sources precious stones were widely held to ensure good health, attract good fortune, and ward off a great variety of evils.[3] In later centuries, Muslim works on mineralogy, which drew heavily on Greek, Iranian, and Indian literature, were, most tellingly, admixtures of natural history, commercial advice, and fantastic tales concerning precious gems.[4]

Chinggisid courts took more than a passing interest in this literature, especially the Il-qans, under whom several manuals were produced. The earliest of these, the *Tanksuq-nāmah-i īl-khānī* (The Treasure Book of the Il-qans) by Nāṣir al-Dīn Ṭūsī (1201—74), was compiled in the 1260s for Hülegü. This work, covering metals, minerals, and gems, made extensive use of al-Bīrūnī's *Kitāb al-javāhir* (Book of Precious Stones).[5] In 1301, another servitor, the court historian Qāshānī, issued under his own name what might be termed a "revised edition" of the former. Entitled *'Arā'is al-javāhir va nafā'is al-ṭā'ib* (Treasures of Precious

Gems and Perfumes), it describes the location of fisheries, mainly those within the Persian Gulf, the wind and water conditions prevailing at these sites, the diving techniques, growth of pearls, their placement inside the shell, their nomenclature, size, shape, and color, and other criteria used in their valuation.[6] There is also evidence for a third treatise. According to a bibliography of Rashīd al-Dīn's works, dating to 1310–11, his agricultural manual, *Kitāb-i Āthār va Āḥya'* (The Book of Monuments and Living Things), contained in its original form information on the extraction and benefits of gems and pearls, chapters that have been lost.[7] Obviously, at the Il-qan court, which possessed extensive collections of jewels, works on lapidary subjects enjoyed an ongoing popularity.

The Yuan court also had access to a number of as yet unidentified Islamic manuals on the topic. In 1273 the Northern Observatory (*Bei sitian jian*) attached to the Imperial Library Directorate (*Mishu jian*) reported its holdings of Muslim scientific works as consisting of 290 items (*bu*) classified by subject matter. One of these headings, transliterated *zhe-wa-xi-la*, answers to the Arabo-Persian *javāhir* or *javāhirāt*, plural forms of "gemstones and pearls." The accompanying Chinese annotation states that the holdings contained five such items that treat "the discrimination and recognition of jewels."[8] While there is no way of positively identifying any of the titles, it would be extremely surprising if the collection did not include al-Bīrūnī's *Book of Precious Stones,* as his stature in this field was unchallenged in the Muslim world.[9] It is also possible that Ṭūsī's treatise was among these titles: it was available for transmission sometime before Hülegü's death in 1265, and as Ṭūsī was the preeminent Islamic astronomer of his day, it seems likely that Muslim scientists assigned to the Northern Observatory would take a special interest in all his works.

In any case, since al-Bīrūnī's treatise exerted a pronounced influence on all subsequent Muslim writers on minerals, this means that both the Il-qan and the Yuan court drew upon a common body of learned literature for authoritative information on gems and pearls. This is hardly surprising, for the teams of specialists who evaluated precious stones at the two courts were drawn largely from the same pool of recruits, Muslim merchants and lapidaries.

Both the learned literature and the popular lore devote much attention to the ever-miraculous origins. The mystery of pearls begins with the mysteries of the deep, a realm of wonders populated with strange creatures and powerful nature gods, a place where anything imaginable was possible.[10] Perhaps the most widespread and long-lived theory, first recorded by classical authors, asserts that oysters come to the surface seasonally, open their shells, and absorb rain or dew, which is then transformed into pearls.[11] Climatic conditions therefore determine the quality of pearls; this, of course, was in full accord with much ancient and medieval thought, which held that environmental conditions exercised a fundamental influence on the behavior of all living things.

A variant of this theory, while acknowledging that the best pearls are produced in the rainy season, asserts that they are actually engendered by a small crab-like creature that brings food to the oyster, which then forms within its shell a "root" giving rise to the pearl.[12] The basics of these theories of generation are repeated in medieval Muslim and Jewish sources, and by the sixteenth century they were well known to Europeans.[13]

Although the above theories, ascribed to the Greeks, were widely accepted, there was an alternative explanation advanced by al-Bīrūnī, whose views on the question were the most advanced in premodern times; he argued that pearls developed within the body of the oyster, thereby openly rejecting the prevailing wisdom.[14] It is both notable and revealing that despite al-Bīrūnī's reputation and authority, this particular argument gained few adherents and soon became marginalized. The easy explanation for this rejection is that he was ahead of his time, but it is also true, as I discuss shortly, that merchants and the pearling industry had a vested economic interest in perpetuating and propagating inherited lore, not recent advances in natural history.

In East Asia there was an equally rich lore. In Chinese mythology, the mysterious Kău people lived at the bottom of the sea, and their tears were transformed into pearls.[15] And even when the generation of pearls was brought onto land, the process remained quite wondrous, for the Chinese believed that in the distant and exotic West there were pearl-producing trees and precious-gem trees with pearl-like seeds.[16] But the most widely held and enduring belief is that pearls were "conceived in moonlight," an idea obviously prompted by the moon's shape, color, and brightness. Oysters once again come to the surface, open their shells to follow the course of the moon, and absorb its essential light, which perfects the "soul" of the embryo pearl.[17]

Pearls naturally bore the imprint of their mysterious origins. Their special properties were many. Some were self-illuminating, emitting moonlight, and some, even after removal from the sea, continued to grow, at least in a proper spiritual setting.[18] Notions about their potency and powers are ancient. In early India pearls, produced by clouds, snakes, fish, elephants, and oysters, were thought to bring good fortune, fecundity, and victory, and to counteract poison.[19] They were even prophetic; the possession of special pearls allowed one to tell the future.[20]

Significantly, much of the lore about pearls found in popular and bookish traditions was shared across cultures.[21] One common theme, already touched upon, is the belief that pearls have their origin in globular forms of water—rain, dew, and teardrops. Not surprisingly, in a number of South Asian languages the words for pearl and tear are closely related.[22] The pearls formed from teardrops shed by an icon of the Virgin Mary in fifteenth-century Byzantium speaks to the westward advance and assimilation of this mythology.[23]

Such movement, however, was far older than this. The predominant theories of pearl formation came into contact and began to merge in late antiquity; this is evident from the report of Ammianus in the fourth century CE that the Indians and Persians believed oysters come to the surface and open their shells, their simultaneous exposure to *dew* and *moonlight* producing the pearl.[24]

A somewhat different admixture is reported in the Chinese sources of the same period. In the early dynastic histories and on the famed Eastern Christian stelae of 781 at Xi'an, the Chinese text of the inscription lists among the remarkable products of the West "the pearl of the brilliant moon (*ming yue zhu*) whose halo illumines the night."[25] In this instance, the attributes of the pearl combine Chinese notions of their generation, Iranian concepts of coronas signaling royal good fortune, and Christian haloes identifying sacred personages. As pearls moved across boundaries they often acquired new ideological readings while retaining the older messages of their place of origin.

The Far West was no exception; the long-accumulated and shared lore of pearls in the East had a pronounced effect on European attitudes and perceptions, which were fully crystallized during the voyages of exploration. To be sure, explorers eagerly sought out and exploited New World pearls, but as Donald Lach observed, it was gold that came to symbolize their quest for riches in the Americas, while the Orient became for them a land of gems and pearls much prized for their symbolic, ornamental, magical, and medicinal values, a perception that faithfully reproduces the images and beliefs circulating in the Muslim world and Asia.[26]

Of their various attributes, one of the most esteemed was their curative powers. In West Asian medical traditions the entire oyster, shells, flesh, and pearls, had medicinal applications.[27] In powdered form, pearls had great potency and were used in the treatment of an assortment of ills, most commonly of the eye, an application found as well in Europe and India.[28]

The Chinese also used pearls in treatments of the eye and in the elixirs of life prepared by Daoist alchemists.[29] Their use in healing was common as well in

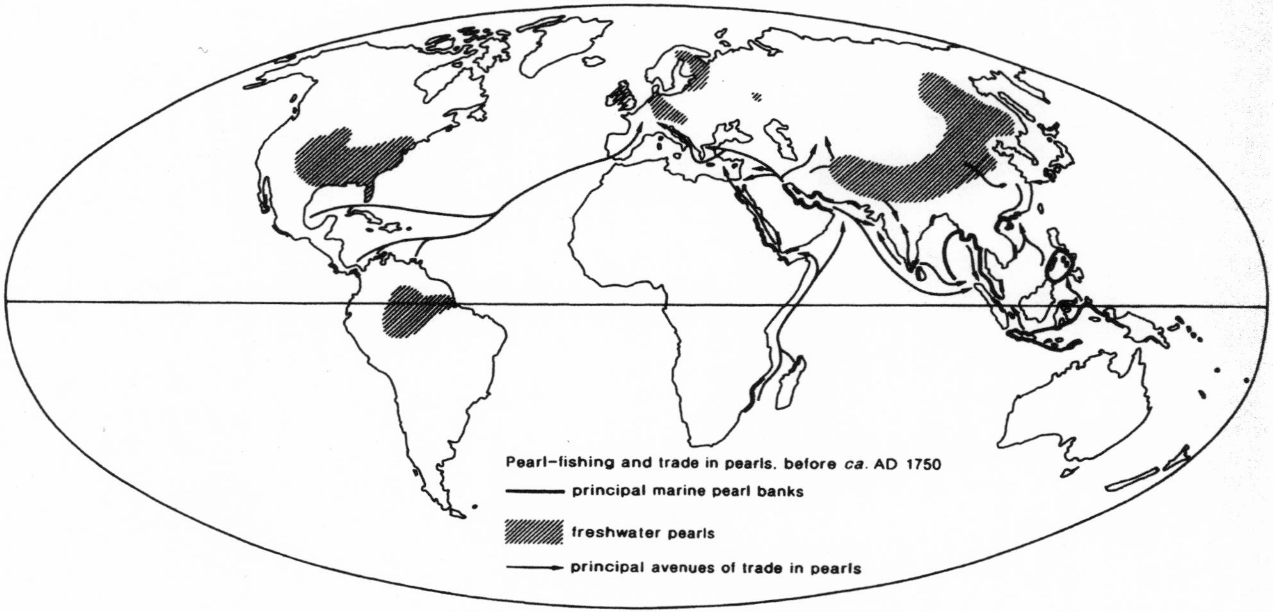

MAP 5. Map of global trade in pearls, ca. 1750. American Philosophical Society.

the subcontinent, and from there it spread into Inner Asia in the pre-Chinggisid period through Indian medical texts translated into Khotanese, Uighur, and Tibetan. In later centuries pearls remained a fixture in Tibeto-Mongolian pharmacology, enjoying popularity into the twentieth century.[30]

By the late Middle Ages a similar pattern of acceptance and use of pearls is found in Europe. In the Western tradition, precious stones, for purposes of medical application, were divided into those originating in the ground—rubies or emeralds—and those of animal origin—pearls or corals. All were employed as amulets to ward off ills and evils and all were taken internally, normally in powdered form, to treat specific ailments. Their popularity in the Far West again reflects the continental dissemination of these beliefs and usages.[31]

One commonality in the pharmacological traditions of Eastern and Western Christians, Muslims, and the Chinese was a decided preference for unpierced pearls.[32] The reason for this is the belief that their healing powers were compromised by perforation, which permitted much of its vital force to escape.[33] The unpierced varieties, handled by specialized dealers in the Islamic lands, were the smaller and cheaper seed pearls that were in any event difficult to bore and consequently the favored source of powdered medicines.[34] European records of the late medieval ages make frequent reference to *perle da pestare,* sold by the pound, which indicates a fairly high level of consumption.[35] Their extensive use for this purpose explains why Western merchants consistently placed pearls and gems together with drugs under the heading *spezierie*.[36]

Possessing such potency, pearls were naturally hard to acquire. Juvaynī cites an Arabic verse, one of many on the theme, which says that the sea drowns pearls, while carrion floats on the surface.[37] The sea in other words hides it treasures and offers them protection. In the classical sources sharks collectively guard oysters because they greatly admire pearls. And when divers manage to obtain one, an admiring shark seeks them out and extracts revenge. This, it is explained, is why pearls are so expensive.[38] The theme of voracious sea monsters devouring divers is encountered elsewhere; even those pearls believed generated on land are guarded by fearsome creatures.[39]

It follows from this that human acquisition of pearls was itself a miraculous feat achieved by special means, of which there are endless variations reflecting local religious and magical practices. In the western portions of the Indian Ocean, land-dwelling animals, foxes, and birds, occasionally deliver pearls into human hands.[40] But more commonly sea creatures are the chosen instruments. In a cycle of Arabic tales popular during the tenth to thirteenth centuries, a Muslim divine, while traveling on ship, is accused of theft and in response invokes God to summon to the surface innumerable pearls in the mouths of fish to prove his innocence.[41] More widely known, however, is a method, reported by Pliny, that turns on the belief that oysters, like bees, live in colonies and if one captures the "king," one controls the entire "swarm."[42] In an obvious adaptation, a thirteenth-century Persian geography repeats this older tradition in its essentials but has a "king of pearls (*shāh-i gawharān*)" lowered into an oyster bed, where it attracts to itself other pearls like a magnet attracts iron filings. Predictably, one of these "kings" was in the possession of another, much storied king, the Sasanid Khusro II Parviz (r. 591–628).[43]

In China, emphasis was sometimes placed on direct human agency, heroic divers who plunged seven hundred feet into the deep to obtain pearls.[44] But more often, and in conformity with tales from the West, animal assistance was involved. Already in Han times there were stories of fishers who ride elephants into the sea, spend the night with the "shark people," and then collect pearls wept by sharks.[45]

The development of the northern pearl craze in Song China sheds further light on the subject of animal assistants. First of all, this fad brought forth or made popular a highly inventive acquisition myth. Contemporary Chinese sources report that it was widely believed that they could be obtained with the help of gyrfalcons trained to capture swans that fed on oysters and thus had pearls in their crops. In consequence, the Qitan court, in pursuit of profit, pressed its Jürchen clients to extract from the Five Nations (Wuguo) inhabiting the lower Ussuri and Amur basins ever more gyrfalcons. What is even more interesting and significant, however, is that these same sources record a direct linkage between mythologies of pearl formation and the actual techniques of acquisition. Because of the belief that moonlight, which reached its peak in the eighth month, was essential in the generation of pearls, the Liao government insisted that the Five Nations dive for pearls in the rivers of northern Manchuria during the tenth month under difficult winter conditions. In combination, these impositions precipitated a general revolt among the subject peoples that gravely weakened the Liao.[46]

From this extensive body of shared and related lore merchants had an abundant supply of material from which to draw in the conduct of cross-cultural commercial ventures. And it can be demonstrated with textual evidence that these similarities were products of conscious dissemination, diffusion with intent, phenomena with important theoretical implications.

The British archaeologist Andrew Sherratt has argued for "a focus on consumption rather than on production" in identifying and analyzing longer-term historical change. Consequently, scholars must give serious attention to trade and exchange that takes into consideration "culturally defined luxuries," not just bulk goods normally categorized as "necessities." New patterns of consumption, it is important to recognize, are transferred and transformed across time and space because, Sherratt concludes, "regimes of value like the goods themselves can be diffused."[47]

This kind of diffusion, its longevity, operational range, and cultural dynamics are nicely illustrated in merchants' reliance on popular mythology in the marketing of pearls and gems. The employment of this lore for commercial ends is particularly well documented in Tang China. In the capital, Chang'an, and other inland and coastal cities there was a large Persian and Sogdian (Hu) presence catering to Tang society's intense fascination with all things foreign and exotic. Chinese popular tales of the era consistently attribute many marvels and magical powers to the pearls the Iranians purveyed: they could find water in deserts, bring good fortune, and allow possessors to walk on water or to change their body size at will. The merchants themselves were seen as dealers in wonders, as alchemists and magicians who found treasures at the bottom of the sea. Tales of their acquisition of pearls from the sea-dwelling Dragon King, also described in Buddhist legends and portrayed in a seventh-century tomb mural at Kucha on the northern rim of the Tarim basin, testify to the extended geographical distribution of such tales and to the mythological integration of the overland and seaborne commercial circuits.[48]

The supernatural powers imputed to these merchants and their pearls were broadcast widely in the popular media and most certainly constituted a major business advantage. The question of whether merchants cynically made up and manipulated such lore to promote sales or whether they shared their customers' beliefs in the special properties of precious stones is both answerable and instructive. Individual attitudes are unknowable, but collectively the Sogdians, the preeminent long-distance merchants of the pre-Islamic period, were much entranced with gems and their varied powers. Al-Bīrūnī cites a work in Sogdian that contains a list of multicolored stones, which when ground into powder serve as potent amulets that ward off trouble, encourage success in business, stimulate sympathy from others, and so forth. The work in question, the *Tūbūsta* in al-Bīrūnī's Arabic text, can be identified with a surviving fragment of a Sogdian lapidary entitled *twbwsth*, or more likely *nwbwsth*, a treatise apparently of indigenous Inner Asian origin.[49] Thus we have good evidence that the sellers were firm believers in the power and efficacy of their product, always an asset in attracting customers and closing sales.

The geographical mobility and commercial utility of this lore is further documented in an early thirteenth-century Persian geography which relates that in the South China Sea there dwell a people who annually come onshore with pearls, trade them to Indian merchants for iron and steel, and then return to the depths.[50] The inspiration for this tale, embroidered and adapted to foreign markets, can be traced back to two Chinese traditions: first, to the Kău people, who, as noted, live under water and weep pearls, and, second, to the pearl fishers of Hepu, whose bronze boats were closely associated with gods and sorcerers, since only they could command the magical power to make metal float.[51]

This intimate and enduring linkage between folklore and precious stones in Eurasia is clearly illustrated in the movement and image of diamonds. Just over a century ago Bertold Laufer convincingly demonstrated that while the product itself came from India, the lore surrounding its acquisition originated in the Hellenistic East. The first mention of the legend, which certainly reproduces a version of far greater antiquity, is encountered in the writing of Epiphanius, bishop of Cyprus (ca. 315–403). Its storyline, yet another acquisition myth featuring animal assistance, consists of five basic components: the source of the diamonds is far-off "Scythia"; they are found in a deep and inaccessible canyon; humans throw into it large amounts of carrion; birds bring up the meat, to which the stones adhere; humans capture the birds and obtain the diamonds. The tale is next encountered in two variants preserved in a work of the Tang scholar-official Zhang Yue (667–730), both of which recount the arrival of diamonds in China during the early sixth century. In the first, which goes back to a learned court official, the source of the diamonds is Fu-lin, the Eastern Roman Empire, and in the second, related by merchants from Funan (modern-day Cambodia) the source is correctly placed in western India. In both versions, however, the method of acquisition faithfully reproduces that found in the account of Epiphanius.

The legend obviously enjoyed considerable appeal and staying power, for in subsequent centuries it appears, with only minor modification, in a variety of Muslim lapidary works and popular poetry.[52] The mythology, moreover, was still very much alive in the Mongolian era when, fittingly, it was recorded by a man of the Far East, Chang De, Möngke's envoy to Hülegü, and by a man of the Far West, Marco Polo, one of Qubilai's envoys to the il-qan Arghun.[53]

For our purposes, this myth of acquisition has a number of telling characteristics, most of all its longevity, geographical and cultural mobility, and dissemination through a variety of media—religious and learned literature and commercial channels. In the latter instance it bears emphasizing that it is conveyed by Southeast Asian–based merchants who bring, as a package, Indian diamonds and Hellenistic folklore to Tang China.

Commercial utilization of myths about precious stones is a very old game. As Quintas Curtius noted in the first century CE, the Indian seas cast up gems and pearls in abundance, and the Indians, to their own profit, successfully spread the desire for such goods to foreign peoples.[54] Evidence of their success can be found in the growing demand for Asian gems in the Mediterranean. This was sufficiently strong that gemstones were prepared in South India specifically for Greek and Roman consumers, a development indicating that intermediaries, brokers and merchants, were imparting accurate marketing information to producers and processors.[55]

Specifics of their marketing strategy in the West is spelled out in detail by Arrian in the first century CE: the Indians, he says, cleverly connected Indian pearls (sea margaritas) with Hercules, who during his travels and quests discovered this "new form of womanly adornment," which he bestowed upon his daughter. The result was the large-scale purchase of this treasure by "rich and prosperous" Greeks and Romans.[56] The Indians, or more accurately their merchant intermediaries, thus successfully exploited the image of a celebrity, a true superstar of the age, to target a specific demographic in a foreign market.

Pliny, for his part, attributes other successful marketing strategies to the Persians. In his view, it is above all the Magi, a class of itinerant ritual and spiritual specialists, who are responsible for perpetrating endless falsehoods about the magical properties of precious and semiprecious stones.[57] Among many others, Pliny cites spurious claims that certain gems make athletes invincible or individuals invisible, while some counteract witchcraft or confer upon the possessor the gift of prophecy. These falsehoods, he says with disdain, many in Rome found convincing and purchased these miraculous gems in quantities.[58] In this criticism he was not alone; merchants' propensity to lie, to create illusions, was frequently noted and condemned. To Eunapius, a fifth-century writer, information from merchants was useless, since they would say "what they wished to profit therefrom."[59]

These critical and sometimes caustic comments bring us back to the matter of merchants' sincerity and honesty. Of course merchants manipulated and deceived, but such behavior is hardly evidence they did not believe in their products. In any case, we should not hold merchants to higher standards than the purveyors of religious beliefs, whose techniques of proselytization regularly combine zealous faith, artful performance, and calculated manipulation of their message, all of which are designed to target yet another kind of demographic—potential pools of converts with differing cultural characteristic and expectations. Furthermore, it should be pointed out that despite all the dire warnings across the centuries, these strategies continued to be used and continue to be successful down to our day.

In viewing the foregoing material from the perspective of advertising history, several points stand out. For those importing and selling gems and pearls there was an array of popular beliefs to be co-opted and culturally adjusted in the pursuit of profit. In presenting their wares to the public, merchants "authenticated" the special properties of gems by appeal to cultural heroes, to specialists in magic, and to learned literature, which allowed them to create new demands and penetrate new markets. All this, of course, anticipates many of the key principles of modern marketing and was available to well-schooled merchants without any investment in what we now think of as advertising.

To complete the picture of gem merchants and their markets, let me address several additional issues concerning the modes of consumption, purchasing power, social aspirations, and market behavior of buyers. Merchants, of course, endeavored to shape markets to their advantage, but markets were sometimes advantageously shaped for them. For the individual seller, certainly, an enormously wealthy prince "mad about precious stones" was the ideal customer.[60] But for the industry at large better still was the sudden emergence of the nouveau riche, of which those engendered by the early successes of the Roman and Mongolian empires stand out as prime examples. In both cases the beneficiaries of this expansion were unsophisticated and gullible, given to competitive emulation and possessed of disposable income that initially seemed inexhaustible. For the Mongols, as the contemporary sources make abundantly clear, the mad scramble for positional goods, most notably pearls, led the Chinggisid elites to actively seek out merchants and pay much-inflated prices for their wares. In the end, however, this resulted in increasing indebtedness, from which the merchants, also operating as moneylenders, obtained further profit.

Of the gems so marketed, pearls stand out for their appeal, which reached across most of Eurasia. The principal reason, perhaps, is their versatility; they could be worn as an ornament simply for their lustrous beauty, as a marker of status, or as a protective talisman and could be ingested in powdered form for better health. Few if any other gems could make the same combination of claims. And, of course, they came from a very mysterious place that, like all other extreme environments, always imbued their natural products with magical powers and spiritual force.

The data further suggests a number of conclusions that have wider application for the study of cultural and commercial history.[61]

First, many other products traveled with tales and mythologies that made them highly desirable and easier to sell. Of these, spices offer a most instructive example. From their arrival in the Mediterranean in Roman times various magical and healing powers were ascribed to them, and a number of the claims made on their behalf can be traced back, like those for gems, to Indian sources.[62] And we should bear in mind that much of this ancient lore was still in play in the early modern age, driving the demand for spices and the European quest for alternative oceanic routes to the East.[63] Even less visible industrial materials like ambergris and asbestos traveled with equivalent lore. In these cases as well, the attached tales are sufficiently complex and specific for independent invention to be precluded and their transcontinental diffusion assured.[64] In light of the frequency and persistency of this phenomenon, it is difficult to escape the conviction that every product crossing a cultural or ecological divide did so accompanied by its own set of fabulous stories and origin myths.

Second, these associations arose very early; by the third millennia BCE, the movement of textile and textile technology between the Iranian plateau and Central Asia was already encoded in mythology.[65] This phenomenon has therefore been with us from the beginnings of the urban revolution, and very likely from the very beginnings of long-distance exchange in exotic goods deep in prehistory.

Third, in many if not most cases, the producers, conveyers, and consumers of these goods and their associated lore are native to different cultural zones of the continent. Consequently, knowledge of this body of lore, like that of foreign tongues, exchange rates, weights, and measures was a normal part of merchants' stock-in-trade, all essential tools in the demanding business of cross-cultural commerce.

Fourth, calculated shifts in the focus of cross-cultural advertising provide good evidence that merchants often possessed a repertoire of potentially useful tales and myths that were called forth situationally. Most illuminating in this regard is the history of northern ivory, walrus tusks and narwhal horn, known as "fish teeth." These two materials, never clearly distinguished from each other by sellers or buyers, first came south in quantity during the Liao Dynasty (907–1125).[66] Harvested by hunting peoples of the arctic and subarctic, the product reached southern markets through intermediaries in the forest zone and then entered east-west commercial channels by land and sea. Initially in demand as sword hafts, fish teeth were soon and effectively recast as a potent medicine in the guise of "snake horn" that unfailingly detects and/or counteracts poisons in all its forms. In this latter application its growing popularity rested on the widely accepted principle that "poison neutralizes poison," a belief jointly held by Chinese and Muslims. The transformation of this commodity from industrial material to antitoxin is clearly a result of a conscious change in marketing strategy initiated by enterprising merchants trying to boost sales, an instance of a very old tale being successfully attached to a very new product.

Fifth, the merchants conveying these commodities had a vested interest in mystifying and exoticizing their wares and therefore the lands in which these originated. They were certainly well positioned to do this; in traditional societies well-traveled individuals were assumed to have special knowledge of distant places and extraordinary objects, and, as an occupational-social category, none were more widely traveled than merchants. As messengers from far places they could plausibly present themselves as "experts," competent judges in all matters concerning intercultural standards of excellence and the authentication of the special properties attributed to foreign products.[67]

Sixth, the recognition that merchants were simultaneously purveyors of foreign wares and foreign lore leads to a final and perhaps most significant conclusion: the creation of images of distant lands and of distant peoples, "the other" in contemporary academic jargon, was very much an interactive and collaborative process involving multiple actors and multiple motives.

CHAPTER 11

Substitutes and Counterfeits

For high-value luxury items like pearls, authenticity looms large in the calculation of their worth. The issue of substitutes and counterfeits also has immediate relevance to the ongoing debate concerning the nature and consequences of long-distance trade in the premodern world. Were the consequences of such exchange, principally conducted in precocities, limited, as many have argued, to small numbers of rulers and urban elites, leaving the economies of the participating countries unchanged? Or, as others believe, did such exchange constitute a true system, an interlocking and integrated market that affected the institutions and behavior of all participants, even those inhabiting smaller-scale communities in outlying regions?[1]

In using pearls to throw additional light on the question, the first order of business is to provide working definitions by which they can be classified for purposes of analysis. Natural denotes pearls produced without human intervention; cultured, those whose development is initiated by humans; substitutes are wholly artificial creations, made to be more affordable versions of the originals; and counterfeits are conscious acts of fraud, intended to deceive. The next thing to be said is that the borderlines between these categories are extremely porous. Cultured pearls are in fact by-products of natural processes manipulated in a way to increase production and reduce acquisition costs. And the relationship between substitutes and counterfeits is slipperier still. An artificial pearl might be presented to a sophisticated market as a cheaper replacement, while to the unwary it might be passed off as "real" and priced accordingly.

In addition, there is yet another layer of complexity to be considered, one that applies to a wide variety of commodities and collectibles. In modern times the quest for the authentic pervades the evaluation of all arts, crafts, antiquities, and natural treasures. Earlier ages, however, were more willing, even in the face of evidence that an object was fake, to embrace it as worthy, and in the course of time it might change categories, acquire an authenticity of its own, and attain a viable place in the market.[2] This categorical vagueness, as we shall see, was an asset allowing objects to gain acceptance, enter into and affect the economic sphere at all levels—local, regional, and continental.

As was true of prestige goods generally, pearls inspired the search for more affordable or accessible alternatives. The first indications of the production of alternatives are ancient. Button or blister pearls, carved from mother-of-pearl, are found in the fourth millennium BCE in Upper Egypt some time before real pearls appear in the archaeological record.[3] In this instance, the human use of substitutes is in evidence prior to use of the prototypes, an anomaly explained by the fragility of pearls.

In later centuries, the search for replacements takes on new and more sophisticated forms. Cultured pearls made by inserting a foreign substance into an oyster that then coats it with nacre was a technique known to the Chinese from the ninth century.[4] Although an undoubted technical achievement, cultured pearls were of limited economic significance in premodern times. Far more important were the artificial varieties. Although there are hints that the technique goes back in China to the late Han, the first recipes are two found in a seventh-century handbook of alchemy, both of which begin the process of fabrication with nacre.[5] And very soon thereafter, these or similar formulas were utilized in the Tang for the industrial production of artificial pearls to meet rising demand.[6] In the following centuries the Chinese continued to produce these for the less affluent. The Persian account of the Temürid embassy to the Ming court in 1419 makes a clear distinction between the artificial varieties (*mavārīd-hā-i darūghī*) worn by Chinese entertainers and "fine, large pearls" displayed by the elite.[7] The fact that the Chinese *zhu*, "pearl," is regularly prefixed with either of two characters pronounced *zhen*, "genuine" and "precious," tells us that the artificial variety enjoyed a prominent place in the domestic market.

The artificial pearls of China soon achieved a foothold in foreign markets as well. In the first half of the eleventh century al-Bīrūnī speaks of the growing suspicion in Islamic lands that many Chinese pearls were man-made.[8] At this point, it is obvious that merchants were attempting to pass them off as the real thing, with some success. Over time, however, they became accepted for what they were—well-crafted imitations. Their growing acceptance in foreign lands and the volume of their production is conveyed by the Russian merchant Afanasii Nikitin, who, while traveling in western India in 1475, was informed by locals that in South China (Chīn) "they make (*delaiut*) pearls of the highest quality, all at low prices."[9]

An early mention of artificial pearls originating outside China comes from the *Zhoushu*, completed in 636, which notes that Persia (Posi) produces "genuine pearls (*zhenzhu*) and artificial pearls (*lizhu*)," literally, "far from [real] pearls."[10] In Islamic times these were made of nacre, mercury, talc, and other ingredients, and according to al-Bīrūnī most were conscious forgeries.[11] That they, too, enjoyed a profitable market share throughout West Asia is indicated by an Arabic commercial manual of the ninth century, which explains that the artificial float in water, while the genuine sink.[12]

It seems likely as well that when artificial pearls penetrated Inner Asia, they met with a similar range of responses. Clearly, they were popular: throughout the western steppe in the pre-Mongolian era, paste glass pearls, loose and set in silver and gold jewelry, are regularly recovered from grave sites. This tells us that the substitutes were used by elites, not just commoners.[13] The vast majority of these were certainly imports from the sedentary world, but with the advent of the Mongolian Empire, many were made in the steppe by transported artisans. One of the local industries at Qara Qorum was the production of spherical and ellipsoidal white glass beads as substitutes for real pearls.[14]

But pearls were hardly alone in this regard; substitutes were sought for all precious and semiprecious stones. The skills to do so are closely tied to the jeweler's trade, in which the "enhancement" of precious stones was an intrinsic part of the craft, since the proper setting of a gem, its aesthetic context, was all important. And beyond this, their brilliance could be intensified by backing stones with other minerals or by drilling and the introduction of colorants.[15] Jewelers, in short, had a set of techniques, many of which were considered legitimate, to improve their product. But it is equally true that these same skills could be applied to the creation of substitutes, which began at a very early date. By the Eighteenth Dynasty (ca. 1570–1304 BCE) the Egyptians had learned to imitate lapis lazuli, a distant import, and later the Assyrians began to make paste versions of their favorite stone, the sapphire.[16] In the sixteenth century these ancient crafts were still very much alive, for European merchants commonly encountered "fictitious Jewels" of all kinds in the markets of the Islamic lands and the subcontinent, which, with due caution, they purchased as costume jewelry.[17] Most esteemed were those fabricated by South Indian lapidaries, who, in the judgment of early Portuguese observers, were greatly skilled at polishing and setting real gems and producing high-quality "false stones."[18]

While jewelers were major participants in the production of substitutes and counterfeits, the development and spread of "fictitious Jewels," like that of artificial pearls, is intimately connected to the practice of alchemy. In addition to its principal objectives, finding the elixir of life and turning base metals into gold, alchemists from China to the Mediterranean learned to fabricate artificial gems of every kind.[19] It is evident, moreover, that this, a secondary line of work, was soon taken up by others, lapidaries and entrepreneurs, who achieved considerable commercial success, since there are repeated warnings concerning the prevalence of fakes on the market. One of the first to raise warnings about the industry was Pliny, who says that dishonest manufacturers used glass, amber, and other materials to counterfeit beryl, opal, and many other stones on a large scale. For each of these he offers tests, of weight, hardness, and reflectivity, by which the natural gems can be distinguished from the artificial.[20] In the Middle Ages al-Bīrūnī sounded the same alarm and provided details on the manufacture of artificial gems in the Islamic world and India.[21] The active participation of alchemists in this trade is documented by the tenth-century Arab bibliographer al-Nadīm, who records that Isḥāq ibn Nūṣayr, a noted specialist on enamels and glassmaking, produced a volume entitled *The Making of Precious Pearls*.[22]

In early modern China forgeries of favored gems were also common, and the underlying industrial technologies diffused rapidly, in many cases through the medium of print.[23] Interestingly, as I discuss below, rapid diffusion seems to be characteristic of other industries engaged in the search for substitutes. In turn, this helps explain why their production and the problems they caused became so widespread so early, ultimately embracing the whole of Eurasia and covering every type of gem, including diamonds.[24]

Accurately reflecting conditions across the rest of Eurasia, concerns about counterfeits were very much alive in the late medieval West.[25] There were even suspicions about their use in the most elevated circles. When, for instance, the papacy presented the Il-qan envoy Rabban Sauma with a pair of pearled shoes in 1288, the Syriac account of his embassy is at pains to point out that they were "real."[26] And there was good reason for this caution and suspicion. From European merchant tolls of the same period it is evident that large amounts of false stones (*lapidum falcium*) were in circulation, some of sufficient quality to gain entry into royal collections.[27]

All this prompts questions about the true scope of alchemy's activities and objectives. The prevalence and prominence of counterfeit gems in the industry and commerce of the Mediterranean world, Joseph Needham has argued, is in all likelihood connected to the early development of glass in the region of Syria and the "imitative" goals and processes associated with alchemy in the Hellenistic period.[28] The undeniable importance of these techniques in the creation of false gems in western Eurasia in subsequent centuries requires some adjustment in our general perception of alchemy's place in history. While we are accustomed to accept alchemy as the forerunner of modern chemistry, it was more than that. What has been left out, or at least underappreciated by nonspecialists, is that much craft technology was encoded in alchemy as a means of protecting trade secrets, and it thus functioned as a substitute for copyright and patent law. This can be seen in ninth-century Coptic alchemy, which was largely concerned with finding cheaper replacements for expensive dyes like murex, and in the number of Muslim alchemists who wrote works on the same subject.[29]

Taken together, the accumulated evidence leaves the strong impression that such production was a common and profitable enterprise, which raises a further and intriguing question: Who had the larger market share, the dealers in real gems or the purveyors of substitutes and counterfeits? This is unanswerable in quantitative terms, but it is easy to believe the long-held assumption that much of the wealth and glitter associated with the ruling classes was produced with the aid of gold foil and fake gems. Deceptive practices of this kind are ancient, attested in the Mediterranean by the middle of the third millennium BCE.[30] And by late antiquity suspect goods circulated in sufficient quantity to attract attention in distant lands. Speaking of Daqin, the Hellenistic Orient, the *Hou Hanshu* comments that the "items of rare and exotic stones produced in this country are bogus wonders, for the most part not authentic and therefore not detailed [here]."[31] The author of this work, Fan Ye (398–445), is telling us that by his day there were far more artificial stones in circulation than real ones. But whatever the actual numbers involved, there is no doubt that the high demand for affordable substitutes stimulated the growth of local production centers throughout Eurasia, and that these eventually gave rise to the modern costume jewelry industry.

The ramifications of the search for replacements, so often stimulated by the circulation of foreign precocities, were profound and by no means limited to gems and pearls. While almost every expensive product generated such a search, there were different objectives and methods in doing so. In the case of gems, as we have seen, fakes intended to deceive were common. In the case of medicines the fakery was of a different kind. In the drug trade both the domestic and the international markets were afflicted with rampant deception and counterfeiting, and most commonly, as in the case of Chinese rhubarb, a favored stomach medicine in western Eurasia, the original product was extensively adulterated and diluted.[32] Replacements for manufactured goods, on the other hand, were fairly obvious cheaper imitations of the originals. In the manufacture of jewelry, for example, substitutes surely outnumbered counterfeits, since precious metals are difficult to imitate, and the techniques used to reduce production costs like gold foiling are immediately detectable.[33]

To illustrate the wide distribution and important consequences of these practices we can use two widely traveled Chinese-inspired luxury goods: chinaware, especially porcelain, and a textile known as *kimkhā* in the Islamic lands and *camoca* in Europe.

Starting in the early ʿAbbāsid period, Chinese decorative ware—ceramics, lacquerware, and porcelain—reached Iraq and Iran, and soon thereafter there is evidence of a developing connoisseurship.[34] Great amounts were imported, which had a pronounced effect on elite tastes and lifestyles. In subsequent centuries there were intensifying efforts to reproduce these goods domestically using local artisans and materials. The result was an upsurge in technical innovation and domestic production of substitute chinaware of every kind.[35]

Christian Georgia offers a helpful illustration of these developments. Here, imported Chinese ceramics of the Tang, Five Dynasties, and Song exercised a substantial influence on local potters, stimulating an industry that thrived between the eleventh and thirteenth centuries. And as is typical of such enterprises, local materials and regional techniques developed in Byzantium and Iran were also drawn upon and modified to produce replacements for Chinese-style ceramics, including the famous Tang-era polychrome glazed ware.[36]

Porcelain, first mentioned in Arabic sources in the mid-ninth century, attracted particular attention in the Islamic East. Attempts were made to penetrate its deeper secrets and to manufacture locally a comparable if not identical product. In this Muslim technicians achieved a measure of success. In some locales the efforts were well advanced by the Mongolian era. Li Zhichang in 1221 could note with approval that Samarqand produced "a porcelain like the *ding* ware of the Central Plain [China]," a type greatly admired during the Northern Song and Jin.[37] This ivory- or cream-colored ware retained a measure of popularity under the Mongols, for several well-used bowls and pots in this style have been recovered at Qara Qorum.[38]

The Chinggisids provided much additional impetus to simulate and update local manufactures of substitutes, since great amounts of Yuan porcelain were exported to markets from the Philippines to the Persian Gulf and the east coast of Africa.[39] Such influence was also projected overland. The Golden Horde offers helpful material on the distribution of these imitative industries in the steppe zone. Here, archaeological evidence of imported porcelain, Chinese and more rarely Korean, in the cities of the Volga basin has been found in strata dating to the fourteenth century. Also recovered was a porcelain-like vase with Chinese motifs and an inscription in Arabic letters that has plausibly been identified as the work of an Iranian master endeavoring to imitate the Chinese prototypes.[40] In this instance, imported originals and imported and locally made substitutes coexisted and competed in the same market, a situation that served to inspire new attempts at emulation.

In Iran such efforts continued into later centuries, meeting with considerable success, most interestingly in major cities and in small provincial towns.[41] Of course, not all efforts at duplication met with approval, and there is testimony as well to failures and fraud.[42] Still, the fascination with, and attempts to reproduce, Chinese blue and white porcelain spread throughout Afro-Eurasia. The appeals of porcelain were many and varied, and this explains why it found a welcome place and performed diverse functions over such a vast territory.[43]

But besides porcelain's utility and beauty, it possessed another quality greatly attractive to people of this earlier age, one that has received insufficient emphasis in recent scholarship. As the researches of Paul Pelliot established decades ago, the medieval European forms of the term, *porcelain, porcellana*, and the like, had as their primary meaning "cowry," a name transferred to porcelain because it was widely believed in the Christian and Islamic worlds that these shells were a vital ingredient in its manufacture. Of even greater importance, however, the accompanying myth that cowries and thus porcelain had the capacity to filter out impurities and neutralize poisons was also widely accepted.[44] And however inaccurate these opinions, we must also recognize that the reputation of porcelain as an effective antitoxin was nonetheless deserved, since it has fewer pits and cracks in which bacteria causing food poisoning can form. So, like many products of the Far East, porcelain was endowed with special life-saving powers, a selling point that further enhanced the demand for china cups and bowls in the Far West.

The multiple appeals of porcelain certainly inspired the many projects at duplication that culminated in the breakthrough made by the factories at Meissen.[45] Once again the interrogation of foreign luxuries and the search for accessible and affordable substitutes stimulated local innovation, production, and consumption that affected local and regional economies. But it is important to understand that it is not only the major breakthroughs that served as catalysts of economic activity; rather primitive efforts could as well. In discussing gourds (*kādū*) in his agricultural manual of 1309–10, Rashīd al-Dīn reports that in

Yazd and Iṣfahān "they paint them [the gourds] in the manner of chinaware (*ālāt-i khitā'ī*) and turn them into wine cups."[46] Because these products were clearly not authentic and had limited prestige value, their manufacture informs us that even low-end substitutes prompted by popular foreign luxury goods could attract the attention of the poorer classes and find a place in local economies and markets.

Our next case study, the textile called in Arabo-Persian *kimkhā, kamkhā, kimkhāb*, and *kamkhāb*, all plausibly derived from the Chinese *jinhua*, "golden flowers," was, at least initially, silk damask with designs woven in gold thread.[47] The textile is first mentioned in the fifth century CE as the covering for the head-dresses of Inner Asian women.[48] Down to the Mongolian era it is consistently described in Muslim sources as a Chinese product and import.[49] There is, however, firm evidence that its manufacture was also slowly moving westward. An anonymous Persian geography, *'Ajā'ib al-Dunyā* (The Wonders of the World), compiled in 1220 at the time of the first Mongolian incursions into Iran, reports that *kimkhā* was one of the important products of Baghdad and Tabriz.[50] And just a few years later it is noted as a native product (*tuchan*) of Iraq (Daqin) by Zhao Rugua under a variant name, *huajin*, "flowered brocade."[51]

While the introduction of locally produced *kimkhā* into the Islamic world precedes the Mongols, there is reason to believe that their arrival on the scene furthered its expansion. By the fourteenth century contemporaries report that high-quality *kimkhā* was being produced within the Il-qan realm generally and make reference to a new site, Nayshapūr/Nishapūr. Soon thereafter Ṣultāniyyah, Samarqand, and other locales in Turkistan are added to the list.[52] It is quite conceivable that Chinese weavers transported to Iran during the early empire may have had a hand in its spread, since we know that the Mongols regularly transferred technicians around their empire, including thousands of Muslim weavers forcibly sent to East Asia.[53]

These policies, in any event, point to another plausible pathway for this stimulus, one centered on Herat.[54] In 1221, following the city's initial occupation, the Mongols sent one thousand households of its weavers to Besh Baliq, the Uighur summer capital on the northern slope of the Tianshan. Here they entered a region in which textile production was a well-established branch of the domestic and commercial economy. In addition, this region was a true cross-road that regularly felt the influence of China and Iran on the local textile tradition.[55] Consequently, when in the late 1230s Ögödei ordered fifty or a hundred weavers sent back to Herat to help rebuild the damaged city, those who returned had been exposed to the Uighurs' syncretic decorative and manufacturing techniques for nearly two decades. Under these circumstances it would hardly be surprising if Herat served as a conduit of up-to-date information on textile manufacturing in the eastern half of Eurasia. It is also tempting to connect the introduction of *kimkhā* production in Nayshapur to stimulus from Herat, since both are located in the province of Khurāsān.

The volume of *kimkhā* produced in Islamic lands during the Mongolian era is unknown, but there is at least a hint of its high level. In his agricultural manual Rashīd al-Dīn details the large amounts of red dye (*qirmiz*) produced in Armenia and Azerbaijan for coloring the silk used in the manufacture of *kimkhā*.[56] Since this dye was long a staple in the textile industry of Iran and Transcaucasia, it seems safe to say that the production of *kimkhā* was widespread and competitive with other locally made fabrics.

More generally, the increasing demand for this textile is reflected in its extended commercial availability. In the Greek text of a Venetian treaty with Trebizond of 1364 there is a list of textiles, including one called *kulicarta*, a composite word derived from the Chinese *guli*, "firm," "durable," and *huaer*, "flower," plus the Mongolian possessive suffix *-tai*. The resulting formation, *goli quartai*, "durable flowered [silk stuff]," can be associated with the variant Chinese term *huajin*,"flowered brocade," since the Mongolian verb *quarla-* means "to embroider floral designs."[57] That the Mongolian name of this textile was known to European merchants operating out of Trebizond, with its active commercial ties to Iran, the Black Sea, and the Golden Horde, leaves the strong impression that a substantial demand for *kimkhā* existed throughout the western half of the empire.

Its growing acceptance in the Far West is also in evidence by the 1320s. Francesco Pegolotti records that *cammucca de seta* was sold in China and in Constantinople, Famagusta (in Cyprus), Messina, and Genoa and gives the prices for the Chinese variety in Genoese silver currency.[58] In addition, in the inventory of Marco Polo's property at the time of his death in 1324, five items of *chamocha* are listed, and three years later many colorfully figured *camocas* (kincob in English usage) were purchased for the coronation of Edward III.[59]

Given Marco Polo's connections and career we may fairly suspect that some or all his *camocas* were of Chinese manufacture, but by this time Chinese originals and Islamic imitations were no longer the only options available in Europe. Here a spin-off industry gradually emerged by creating a version of *kimkhā* adapted to local tastes and purchasing power. Indeed, this was a long-term trend in the West's textile manufacturing. As David Jacoby has shown, from antiquity through the Middle Ages expensive elite fashions in imported cloths were regularly imitated on the local level. Such downscaling entailed the blending of silk with less costly fibers, cheaper colorants (supplied by alchemists), and the replacement of woven by embroidered designs. These efforts not only made the latest styles available to lower-end markets, the cost-saving production methods tended to diffuse rapidly around the Mediterranean.[60] This kind of adjustment Jacoby has documented for Italy, where at the start of the fourteenth century *camocas* were produced in such quantities that they began to reduce the eastern imports and of such quality that local consumers had difficulty distinguishing between the two. And by the end of the century Italian-made *camocas* found a receptive market in the Islamic lands, formerly producers and exporters of their own substitute versions to Europe.[61]

The end result of this prolonged process was the emergence of variant forms of this textile type, all bearing the same name. Their divergence is reflected in modern classifications of *kimkhā,* which has been defined as brocade, campas, or damask (either single or multicolored), or simply as a Chinese silk. Most commonly, however, it is a richly patterned or decorated fabric whose base material is normally, but not exclusively, silk and which usually features floral designs brocaded or embroidered in gold or silver thread.[62]

Indeed, throughout Eurasia variant textile types slowly but continuously evolved, an evolution realized in incremental changes in decorative motifs, base materials, and weave structures that in combination and over time resulted in extensive adaptation and syncretism. Such variants, in other words, were constantly in the making.[63] And, as argued, on some occasions this was done quite consciously and at an accelerated rate in the continuing efforts of manufacturers and merchants to find lower-cost substitutes to meet changing demands in local and reginal markets.

The retention and widespread use of the label *kimkhā/camoca* was more than a matter of habit or tradition; it was also a marketing technique, what is now called a "branding strategy." Above all, it was a means of connecting a regionally made product with a foreign import of impeccable lineage, an image that was established and continually reinforced in the Islamic and Christian worlds by its circulation among elites at home and by its mention in descriptions of distant and glittering courts.[64]

At this time, there was no court in Eurasia so famed for its opulence as the Yuan, and here the textile enjoyed unquestioned preeminence, since only the highest-ranking officials were permitted to wear "attire [made] entirely of floral patterned gold brocade (*jinhua*)."[65] The luster of the Yuan court was in turn intimately tied to its control of China, universally acknowledged for the unrivaled excellence of its varied manufactures. This belief was expressed in a Muslim formula, taken over by the Christian West during the Mongolian era, that in the making of all things the Chinese had "two eyes," while all others were "one-eyed" or "blind," a usage that may have Chinese antecedents.[66] The specificity of the message and the uniformity of its transcontinental transmission provide convincing proof of the extent to which Europe viewed China through Muslim spectacles.

Several complementary hypotheses with wider historical applications are suggested by this data.

Downscaling could be applied to all kinds of products, and this explains why the type (but not the quality) of the objects available in regional and local markets so often paralleled those fashionable at court and among elites.[67]

In the absence of patent and copyright laws, stylistic and brand-name appropriation was common and regularly targeted popular foreign imports. In describing the manufactures of Gujarat under the Mughal emperor Akbar (r. 1556–1605), his secretary Abū'l Faẓl mentions matter-of-factly: "Imitations of stuffs from Turkey, Europe and Persia are also produced."[68] Clearly, he did not consider the practice unusual, dishonest, or new.

Substitutes and counterfeits of all kinds regularly entered the marketplace, and their presence there in numbers undermines the assumption that traditional long-distance trade, because it was largely in precocities directed at the upper strata of society, had no discernible effects on local economies. On the contrary, foreign models frequently created new regimes of consumption and stimulated the diffusion of new manufacturing technologies and new local production, and did so in leading sectors—costume jewelry, tableware, and textiles—which strongly supports the conclusion that the production of substitutes constituted a major component of the pre-machine-age industrial economy.

CHAPTER 12

By Land and by Sea

Long-distance merchants, the Polos among them, made regular use of land and sea routes, their decisions resting on a complex calculus involving weather, war, commercial possibilities, and government policies. And except for winds and weather, the other factors were always negotiable or potentially avoidable. So, for example, notwithstanding the traditional Chinese insistence that all individuals and missions must return home by their port of entry, whether inland or coastal, merchants managed to avoid such stipulations, selecting exit routes best suited to their immediate needs.[1] In this they were certainly aided by official corruption, but perhaps the more important ingredient in their success was the availability of up-to-date intelligence provided by ad hoc individualized news networks and by commercial postal agencies that moved information at rates of speed bureaucratic communication systems could not match.[2]

But, despite merchants' common use of both options, the relationship between maritime and overland trade has yet to receive the attention it deserves, a deficit attributable to several factors. Most important, there is a tendency to divorce the steppe from the sea. The general assumption that influences from the southern oceans did not reach Inner Asia is true for climatic forces, but not for commercial and cultural interactions.[3] The other and related difficulty is attributable to traditional academic divisions of labor in which steppe and maritime history are considered separate fields.

I do not mean to imply that no attention has been paid to their manifold interconnections; I mean rather that the number of studies devoted to overland or to maritime trade individually dwarfs that focused on their conjunctions. In recent decades quality studies on their interconnections that address a number of interrelated problems have appeared: the origins and destinations of natural products and finished goods entering and leaving maritime trade; the question of whether the volume of maritime and overland trade rises and falls in tandem or independently of each other; and the importance of exploring the multiple linkages between the regional economies of Eurasia, rather than simply comparing the structural characteristics of the European economy with that of Asia, comparisons that are often presented in a static, unduly homogenized fashion.[4] Among many other benefits, the further consideration of the patterns of intra-Asian trade will help identify the basic building blocks that enabled the Mongols to fashion a transcontinental network embracing both land and sea.

Without demonstrating and documenting these conjunctions in detail, the validity, nature, and dynamics of world systems, or at least Old World systems, cannot be determined. In pursuit of this goal, one of the basic issues is that of data and source material. There is, to begin with, a considerable body of information that directly documents the crucial connections between the two systems of transport. We know from literary and archaeological evidence that throughout the Middle Ages the major entrepôts of the Persian Gulf—Sīrāf, Kīsh, and Hormuz—were connected to the larger cities of Iran, Iraq, and the Levant by caravan routes, some of which were developed and funded by merchant princes with extensive maritime interests and commitments.[5]

Marco Polo's description of Curmos (Hormuz) gives a good sense of its distant and diverse connections: "And I tell you that all the merchants come there from all the different parts of Indie with their ships, bringing there all *spiceries* and other merchandise, that is precious stones and pearls and cloth of silk and gold and of other different colors and elephant tusks and many other wares, and in that city they sell them to many other men. There are merchants also of the city who then carry them through all the whole world, selling them to other merchant peoples."[6]

The Chinese, too, were well aware of these connections. In the early thirteenth century Zhao Rugua reports that annual camel caravans brought processed goods from inland to the Gulf, which were then off-loaded onto ships destined for Kīsh.[7] Speaking of Hormuz in the early fifteenth century, Ma Huan observes: "Foreign ships from every place and foreign merchants travelling by land all come to this country [Hormuz] to attend the market and trade."[8] Shortly thereafter, ʿAbd al-Razzāq Samarqandī, who passed through the port in 1442, provides another listing of the far-flung commercial ties of Hormuz. Most helpfully, he divides these into two categories: goods coming by sea from Southeast Asia, India, Ceylon, the Maldives, Arabia, and East Africa and those exchanged overland with Egypt, Syria, Rum, Transcaucasia, Iraq, Iran, Transoxania, Turkistan, the Qipchaq steppe, the Qalmaq land (Jungharia), and

North China.[9] Given its extensive and extended landward ties, it is hardly surprising that "plentiful" supplies of camels were available in the areas around Hormuz.[10]

There is, then, ample evidence that the interested parties on the ground and on the sea—local rulers, merchants, brokers, shippers, and caravanners—viewed and treated the two systems as complementary and interactive.

More general information on the commercial policies and political priorities of larger states leads to the same conclusion and confirms this had long been the case. As Nina Pigulevskaia recognized and documented decades ago, between the fourth and early sixth centuries the Byzantines and Sasanids engaged in an intense and protracted competition to control Chinese silk coming overland and by sea, and this entailed direct confrontations in Mesopotamia and the Caucasus, proxy wars in Abyssinia and the Red Sea, and the dispatch of diplomatic embassies deep into Asia.[11] Less dramatically but equally convincing, the Song, rightly considered the dominant economic power of its era, was actively engaged in and promoted both maritime and overland commerce.[12]

Beyond the information on institutions, infrastructure, and government policy, trade in maritime products can tell us much about the integration of the two systems. After all, ambergris, an excretion of the sperm whale, and musk, extracted from a gland of deer species found in Inner Asia, were both essential ingredients in perfume, a highly valued West Asian commercial specialty, and thus held to be gifts appropriately given together in princely presentations.[13] Also informative and persuasive is the case of cowry shells from the Indian Ocean, which were much admired in the Baltic region throughout the later Middle Ages as a form of bodily adornment.[14] And of greater consequence, these shells were used as currency in many parts of Afro-Eurasia, a topic discussed in a different context later in the chapter.

Of more immediacy, there is a surprising amount of information available on the movement of coral and pearls into the interior of Eurasia. These, the most visible of maritime products, offer guidance on the chronology and motives for the interconnections between the two commercial circuits.

The major source of high-quality coral was the central Mediterranean, a variety admired throughout antiquity and the Middle Ages for its rich red color.[15] A secondary source was the Red Sea, which gained increasing acceptance in later centuries.[16] Coral was also harvested off Ceylon, Malaya, China, and Japan; significantly, the redder hues were preferred in these regions as well, which strongly suggests that the coral of the Mediterranean determined the standards by which all others were valued.[17]

Long-distance maritime trade is clearly documented in the second century BCE when Mediterranean coral was exported to India, a lively traffic that continued into the Muslim era.[18] At this time it was sold by the branch, string, bag, and chest and traded throughout West and South Asia.[19] A good indication of the commodity's pan-Eurasian importance is that by Tang times the Chinese were well informed on the Mediterranean technique of harvesting coral using metal dragnets.[20]

While much of the traffic in coral moved west to east along the maritime routes, there was also a steady movement of the product northward. In the second century BCE, Mediterranean red coral with engraved Indic designs is found in Ai-Khanum, the Greco-Bactrian center in northern Afghanistan, and several centuries later pink coral beads are common in Khwārazm and neighboring regions.[21] The progress of Mediterranean coral inland continued, reaching Kashmir, Tibet, Khotan, and the Uighur and Tangut kingdoms during the Middle Ages.[22] From the chronology of its commercial expansion it is evident that its spread along maritime and overland routes was roughly contemporaneous, supporting the notion that the two systems were interactive and complementary from the first emergence of Eurasian exchange networks in the centuries just before the Common Era.

The Mongols, too, evinced an early and avid interest in coral. In 1222 Mongolian military officers in northern Afghanistan purchased from "people coming back from the west" fifty branches of coral that were certainly Mediterranean in origin.[23] And it appears likely that a red coral bead uncovered in Qara Qorum shares the same pedigree.[24] Later, under the Yuan much coral, Chinese *shanhu*, was used to seal precious objects, imperial documents, and religious texts.[25] According to an Italian document from about 1345, there was also a steady demand for Mediterranean coral in the Golden Horde; it was sold there by the *mena*, a Venetian weight equal to eight pounds, a unit of measure that implies sales in volume.[26]

In the postimperial period, when their purchasing power sharply declined, Mongols of both sexes turned from saltwater pearls to the far more affordable coral for use as personal adornment.[27] And even into these later centuries the red varieties retained their preeminence.[28]

The appeal of coral was manifold: like pearls, it too came from a strange, distant environment, possessed aesthetic, medicinal, and magical properties in the major cultural zones of Eurasia.[29] To these must be added its intimate ties to Buddhism; as one of the "seven treasures," often bracketed with *maṇi* pearls in Chinese sources, coral was an appropriate gift to and decoration for stupas, temples, and monasteries.[30] Wherever Buddhism spread, coral followed in its wake, and its sanctification only increased demand.

The same can be said of pearls; they too came by land and sea, and their strong religious associations added to their luster and value. The nomads' initial acquisition of pearls in quantity can in fact be located in areas close to Buddhism's birthplace, northern India, and dated to the early centuries of the new faith's development and expansion.

While it is understandable that Buddhism enhanced the spiritual and commercial value of pearls among the faithful, it is important to recognize that it did the same among non-Buddhists.[31]

Other world religions furthered and reinforced pearls sanctification. For Eastern Christians, pearls symbolized the articles of faith and decorated their most sacred objects; tales based on the biblical "pearl of great price" became in the Nestorian tradition the counterpart to the Holy Grail in the West.[32] In the easternmost outposts of Manichaeism, a Uighur text of the pre-Mongolian era makes reference to a *yenchüglüg monchuglar*, which, while translatable as "pearled necklace" or "pearled talisman," was most probably understood by contemporaries in both senses, as something attractive worn around the neck that possessed spiritual and protective powers.[33]

The penetration of pearls into the steppe zone is closely tied to the nomads' strong attachment to jewelry, a subject requiring additional consideration. The nomads' attraction to this form of adornment is easily explained. Four interlocking reasons underlay their preference. First, it was readily transportable. Second, of the wide array of positional goods displayed in sedentary societies and courts, jewelry was consequently the most easily accommodated to the nomads' mobile lifestyle. Third, because of their near-universal appeal, jewelry and gems served as an intercultural language that rapidly and accurately communicated information about individual and collective status, wealth, and power. Last, and often overlooked, jewelry was recyclable: the gems themselves could be removed and the precious metals melted down and new ornaments fashioned from the original materials. Few other culturally processed products are so amenable to reverse engineering.

This is not to say that the same tastes were shared by all. As a starting point for this discussion, it is important to realize that the boundaries separating regional and supraregional preferences in prestige goods are surprisingly ancient and extremely stable, enduring in some cases for millennia.[34] This is clearly documented in the history, geography, and typology of bodily adornment in eastern Eurasia, which indicate fundamental differences between the Chinese and their pastoral neighbors.[35] Whereas for the Chinese of the Shang and Zhou (ca. 1500–221 BCE) jade and copper were paramount in personal ornamentation, the people along the Inner Asian frontier very much favored gold or silver as symbols of rank and status. Most popular were gold earrings, attested archaeologically in Gansu and the Ordos, which have affinities with pieces from western Central Asia and Siberia dating to the mid-second millennium BCE. And while gold began to make inroads into China during the imperial period, jade always remained the supreme expression of beauty, value, wealth, and standing.

If we now view the culture history of western Eurasia in similar perspective, it is immediately evident that gold replaces jade in both its ornamental and its symbolic functions. Among other things, gold was equated with the sun and held to embody vital cosmological principles relating to light, indestructability, incorruptibility, longevity, value, and purity. Not surprisingly, gold was also associated with imperial governance and legitimacy, concepts that have a long and shared history among steppe people and their sedentary neighbors.

The same holds true for pearls. It is most suggestive that the several hundred pierced pearls, presumably for stringing necklaces, found in Susa and Pasargadae, from about the fourth century BCE, are associated with the Achaemenids, the first universal empire.[36] More certainly, pearl necklaces served as a royal emblem for Sasanid sovereigns depicted on the ceramics and metalware of the period.[37] These practices may well have influenced popular tastes in later centuries. In any case, during the Middle Ages Muslims preferred necklaces and rosaries, forms of jewelry in which pearls and rubies, their gems of choice, dominated the metalwork.[38] In time, such Western preferences spread to China. By the Tang there was also a limited range of gems used as ornaments on jewelry; here, not surprisingly, pearls shared the stage with jade to the virtual exclusion of other kinds.[39]

Consequently, despite their distant geographical location, the Mongols exhibited preferences in prestige goods that were consonant with those of the "West," not of China.[40] This consonance was itself a result of the spread across the steppe of select components of the material and spiritual culture of India, Iran, and the Near East, with which the nomads had ancient and productive exchanges.

Initially, the nomads' gold jewelry was not set with precious stones, and set only occasionally with imported lapis lazuli and turquoise.[41] In the western steppe in Scythian and Sarmatian times, jewelry, primarily necklaces and earrings made for pierced ears, was for the most part adorned with glass beads and colored and semiprecious stones.[42] This selection of raw materials is understandable, since the Ural Mountains, particularly their eastern slopes, have a high concentration of ores and minerals, including gold, and a variety of semiprecious stones used locally for toolmaking and adornment.[43]

In the eastern steppe of the period, styles were similar, mainly gold earrings, worn by both sexes, from which were suspended spherical, pearl-like beads, some made of mother-of-pearl.[44] In the succeeding Xiongnu era, from the third century BCE to the early centuries CE, there is again much archaeological evidence of beads made of diverse materials—amber, agate, faience, glass, and glass tinctured with gold. The latter, found across the steppe, is of special interest, since glass was an import from Syria, yet another indication that exchanges at this time were truly continental in scope and that West Asian styles and products regularly reached the eastern steppe. It is evident, too, from their context as grave goods, that these items had an expanding social range and a growing number of consumers, since they circulated among the middle and upper echelons of Xiongnu society.[45]

While archaeology clearly indicates the prevalence of colored stones and artificial beads in the early steppe, it also documents some notable exceptions. And significantly, these tend to be pearls. Among the Scythians, there is a pearl bracelet found in a female grave on the lower Dniester of the fourth century BCE, and, most spectacularly, among the Sarmatians a gold diadem from a grave at the mouth of the Don from the turn of the Common Era lavishly adorned with amethyst, garnets, and pearls.[46] In the east, among the Scythian antiquities collected in the Altai in the time of Peter the Great, there is a signet ring set with a single pearl.[47]

The slow, incremental transition to precious gems in the interior of Eurasia becomes increasingly visible with the Kushans, originally a nomadic people, who dominated Transoxania and northwestern India in the first centuries of the Common Era. Documentation for this can be found at Tillya Tepe, their royal tombs in northern Afghanistan, where much of the clothing and some of the jewelry are decorated with pearls. It has been suggested that this transformation of taste began when the invading Kushans plundered the treasuries of the Greco-Bactrian kingdoms.[48]

In the following centuries pearls and gemstones steadily spread into Inner Asia and the steppe, a period that coincides with the extension and intensification of trans-Eurasian exchange, now conventionally called the Silk Road. The literary sources mark their progress and their expanding functions. In 60 CE the Yuezhi commander fighting Han forces in the Tarim basin had at his disposal a substantial supply of loose pearls, now an important political currency, with which to attract allies.[49] Evidence that pearls and gems had become markers of royal status comes in the fifth and sixth centuries. At the height of their power in the 450s the notables of the European Huns wore many gems, and Attila himself was buried, in the words of Priscus, "with various precious stones and ornaments of various types [which are] the marks of royal glory." Most of these were acquired through plundering and diplomatic gifts, including, on one occasion, "Indian gems," a possible reference to pearls.[50]

In the East, the ruler of the Tu-yu-hun in the Qinghai region of northern Tibet wore pearls in his hair, while the queen of the Hephthalites in Transoxania wore a *boghta* adorned with multicolored pearls.[51] During the same period, the rulers of Gaochang in Turfan and of the Ruanruan in the eastern steppe sent as tributes/diplomatic gifts pearled images (*xiang*) to the court of the Tuoba, Inner Asian founders of the Northern Wei Dynasty (381–535).[52] Since the latter patronized Buddhism, this was a most appropriate presentation. At the same time, pearls had secular uses as well, for the Tuoba ruling elite advertised their status by the possession and ostentatious display of "fabulous pearls."[53]

Most helpfully, near Chang'an, in the sarcophagus of a young Sui princess buried in 608, there was found a necklace of twenty-eight pearls set in gold beads and a bracelet similarly adorned. On stylistic and technical grounds, both pieces of jewelry are of Byzantine or possibly Persian manufacture.[54] In either case, there is a strong presumption the pearls, too, have a western origin, that those harvested in the Gulf were now reaching Northeast Asia.

Additional assurance that western jewelry and pearls were moving overland can be found in the period of the Türk Qaghanate (552–744), the first nomadic empire to dominate the entire steppe. While the Turkic word for pearl, *yenchü* or *yünchü*, is of Chinese origin, which indicates an initial exposure to varieties from the East, the qaghanate's dominant role in trans-Eurasian exchange resulted in the ever-increasing influx of those from the West. One source, certainly, was diplomatic gifts. According to a Syriac text, the Byzantines opened their negotiations with the Türk, around 569, by giving their qaghan "many presents of gold, silver and pearls and splendid garments of kingship."[55] Reports in the Tang Dynastic Histories that Ho-sa-na (r. 603–11), a former ruler of the Western Türk, while in exile at the Tang court, offered the emperor Gaozu a large pearl (*da zhu*) in 618 again point in the same direction.[56]

Türk rulers entrusted the management of their extensive commercial dealings to Sogdian merchants who, from their home bases around Samarqand, formed a series of trading colonies that extended from Mongolia and North

China to the Crimea. And since control of transcontinental trade was the priority of Türk foreign policy, Sogdians were also made responsible for the conduct of interstate relations, a position that afforded them ample opportunity to pursue their own economic interests and to help shape the court culture of their patrons.[57]

Evidence for their interest and trafficking in pearls comes from diverse sources. As is well documented in art and archaeology, the Sogdians themselves were much enamored of pearls, which they called *mrγ'rt*, a word closely related to the Persian, Armenian, and Greek forms.[58] Statuary and wall paintings from Sogdia during the Türk era depict gods and humans decked with pearls set in earrings and necklaces and basted on clothing.[59] Moreover, Sogdian dancers, highly popular in Tang China, are depicted with pearled hats, and near Xi'an in a tomb of a Sogdian notable, most likely a successful merchant, the grave guardians wear pearl necklaces and earrings.[60] The latter, dated to 580, is thus just thirty years earlier than the grave of the Sui princess in Chang'an containing very similar jewelry.

Perhaps most significantly, archaeology provides evidence that the merchants and their nomadic sponsors shared common tastes in such matters: on the stone statues of Türk notables in the Altai during this period, some are wearing circular earrings from which hang pearl-shaped spheres that in design are the same as those depicted on notables in wall paintings at Penjikent and Afrasiab, Sogdian cultural centers near Samarqand.[61] Obviously, the merchants' own tastes provided a model for emergent nomadic elites, to whom they offered scaled-up, more expensive versions of the nomads' traditional adornments, thus encouraging demand for new positional goods that reached into the heart of the continent.

The Sogdians were able to exercise such far-reaching influence and create and supply new market demands for several reasons. By this point they had long experience in providing royal houses and imperial courts with prestige goods and could rightly claim authoritative knowledge on these matters. Next, although an inland people, they regularly went to sea in search of products and profits. Ṭabarī reports in 751/52 a Sogdian traveling in Oman, and the only plausible reason for his presence there is the acquisition of pearls, the country's sole export.[62] The Sogdians were also active in South China, Southeast Asia, and Ceylon, and from these locales they had access to the whole range of goods conveyed along the maritime routes.[63] The extent of their connections and commercial success is neatly summed up by the historian Narshakhī, writing in the mid-tenth century, who relates that the merchants of Baykand, a town on the western frontier of Sogdia, "traded with Chīn and the *sea* and became very wealthy."[64]

It is quite understandable, then, that Chinese in the seventh century mistakenly thought that there were locales in the Western Region that "produce[d] pearls."[65] This helps explain why the first attestation of the Turkic term for pearl comes in the Orkhon inscription of the early eighth century, where it is used in a toponym, Yenchü Ögöz, "Pearl River," to designate the middle course of the Sir Darya, a place name accurately reflected in the Zhenzhu He of the Tang sources.[66] Thus by the time of the Türk Qaghanate, pearls, the preeminent product of the sea, had become fully assimilated into the oasis culture of the Sogdians and the steppe culture of the nomads.

In the aftermath of the Qaghanate the traffic continues. In the western steppe and its hinterlands during the Khazar era, from the seventh to tenth centuries, various kinds of jewelry have been recovered from archaeological sites, particularly earrings. Made primarily of precious metals, they were adorned with semiprecious stones and with pearl-shaped objects of paste glass, cornelian, gold, and, occasionally, real pearls.[67]

Evidence for the increasing presence and popularity of pearls across Inner Eurasia takes several different forms. Their frequent visual representation, found on medallions, plates, elegant wood containers, and musical instruments, tells us that the treasures of the sea were regularly connected with imperial courts, local elites, and popular foreign entertainments.[68] The wide dispersal of these objects further solidified the appeal of pearls by underscoring their distant, royal, and fashionable associations.

The literary sources sustain this line of argument, providing additional examples of their extended circulation. In the far northwest, an ʿAbbāsid embassy of 922 presented to the ruler of the Volga Bulghars and his wife robes and bulk pearls.[69] And in the ninth to eleventh centuries, unnamed patrons from the Western Region donated twenty-one strings of pearls to a Buddhist monastery in Dunhuang, while 117 strings were sent to a private individual in Uighuristan, and still others were purchased by Qarakhanid rulers.[70] During the same period, the Uighurs of Gansu brought tribute pearls to the Song court. The fact that in 1004 they requested Chinese craftsmen "skilled in pearl inlaying" strongly suggests they had substantial supplies.[71] In the next century, Khotan and the Uighurs of Gansu and Turfan sent pearls and other tributes to the Qitan every three years.[72] Since it is most likely that Khotan and Turfan received their supplies from India and the Gulf, it's clear that western pearls had now entered the forests of Manchuria and the Volga-Kama region.

There is, then, good evidence for the accelerating inflow of pearls into Inner Asia. Several general considerations can be offered in support of this view, considerations that presage coming events. The importance of pearls in the political culture of the region expands and is consolidated. To cite one example, the ruling strata of the Turfan Uighurs, soon to become the chief sedentary advisers of the Chinggisids, coveted and competed for pearl earrings.[73] And pearls were still being used extensively for decoration and display in Buddhist societies.[74] The increasing influence they exercised in Inner Asia is tied to the reconfiguration of the Buddhist world. In consequence of its decline in India and continuing Muslim military pressure, there was an out-migration of monks and believers that strengthened the Buddhist presence in a bloc of states founded by the Uighurs, Tanguts, Qitans, and Jürchens. Thus, in the century before the Mongols, pearls from the southern seas, provided by well-developed delivery systems across Inner Asia and China, were abundant along the margins of the eastern steppe.[75]

Let me sum up the findings so far and set the stage for a discussion of how the Chinggisids' developed their intense interest in maritime trade.

The many pearl-shaped ornaments in possession of the nomads across the centuries clearly served as substitutes for the much-coveted real ones. To a surprising extent, many of these were locally made by homegrown or conscripted foreign artisans, which testifies to their great significance to these societies.[76]

The natural consequence of the preoccupation with, and production of, substitutes is obvious. Whenever real pearls became available, the transition was rapid and seamless; the nomads simply replaced the artificial beads on their jewelry with a natural bead, the pearl, which then took its place as the rightful partner of gold. Later Mongolian preferences were clearly an inherited tradition deeply embedded in the culture history of the steppe.

Because of their steady accumulation over many centuries, large quantities of pearls were in circulation in the interior of Eurasia by the beginning of the Mongolian Empire. This explains why Wu-gu-sun, a Jin envoy sent to Chinggis Qan in 1220, says in his travel report that the Western Region was "rich" in pearls.[77] It is hardly surprising that the Mongols' early campaigns in regions so distant from the sea nonetheless gathered a fine harvest. And, as already noted, even greater returns came during the second stage of the Mongol's conquests directed at the Islamic heartlands and the Southern Song. Yet despite all these massive hauls, the Mongols, ever eager for more, made careful advance preparations to tap directly into the principal sources of saltwater pearls.

FIGURE 3. Gold necklace with pearl-shaped beads, western steppe, circa fourth century BCE. University of Pennsylvania Museum of Archaeology and Anthropology.

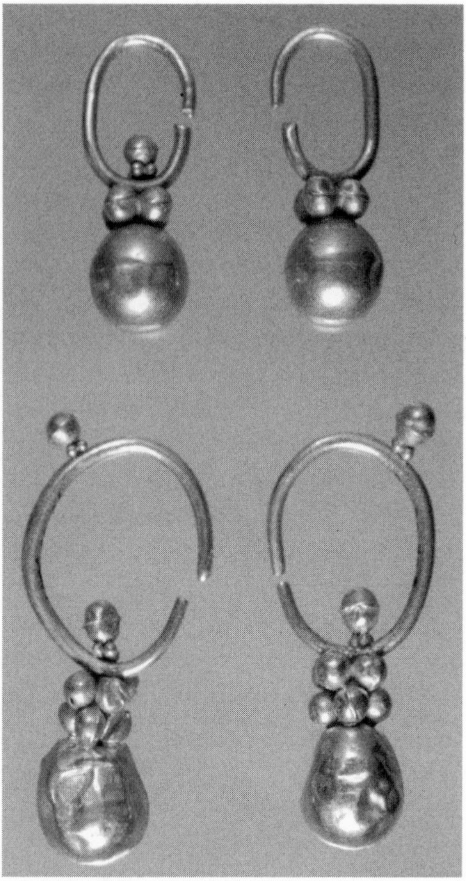

FIGURE 4. Gold earrings with pearl-shaped ornaments. northern Caucasus, circa eighth century CE. University of Pennsylvania. Museum of Archaeology and Anthropology.

Given the tendency to divorce the steppe from the sea, this subject has yet to be investigated in depth. What follows is a preliminary excursion, an attempt to establish the basic chronology, methods, and motives of the Mongols' *Drang nach Süden*. Although the Il-qans encountered a sea frontier somewhat earlier, this attempt is best realized by concentrating on the evolution of this enterprise in the eastern half of the empire, for here the stated intentions and follow-up actions of those responsible for its initiation and implementation are well documented.

We can start with the Mongols' early exposure to tropical products. Since such goods were already circulating in East Asia, the Mongols must have acquired a fair sampling during their campaigns against the Jin and Tanguts,

1205–34. This exposure surely provided their initial awareness of the vast and varied treasures to be had in the far south.

The first unmistakable evidence of plans to gain direct access to these lands is conveyed in the dispensations made to imperial princes following Möngke's enthronement in 1251. A clear idea of the scope of the Mongols' maritime ambitions emerges from the list of territories the new qaghan allotted his brother Qubilai. The fullest account is provided by Rashīd al-Dīn, who records that these included "the kingdoms of Khitāi (North China), Machīn (South China), Qarājāng (Yunnan/Dali Kingdom), Tangut, Tibet, Jūrchah (Manchuria), Sulangqah (Solonqa/northernmost Korea), Gūlī (Gaoli/Korea) and those parts of Hindustan that are contiguous to Khitāi and Machīn (Southeast Asia)."[78]

The passage presents several features of interest. Most strikingly, the list combines without distinction lands already under Chinggisid rule, Tangut and North China, with others yet to be conquered, Yunnan and the Southern Song. For assignments of this kind there was already firm precedent in Chinggis Qan's "bestowal" of unconquered lands west of the Urals to his son Jochi. In this and in later dispensations, Chinggisid princes were assigned the right and the solemn duty of conquering territories beyond the imperial frontiers. Further, and of equal significance, Qubilai's commission in the south was only partially fulfilled: while Yunnan and the Song ultimately fell to Mongolian arms, Southeast Asia, although repeatedly attacked, successfully avoided permanent occupation, an issue considered again in Chapter 14.

Rashīd al-Dīn's account of Möngke's dispensations is sustained by the Chinese sources, which detail the Mongols' efforts to bring these territories into the empire. In pursuit of this grand design, for which there was no precedent in steppe history, the Mongols wasted little time. By the fall of 1252 plans for a major assault on the Song were finalized. For strategic and logistical reasons the first stage concentrated on Yunnan, seat of the independent Dali kingdom. Qubilai commenced operations in early 1253, and by year's end its capital was taken, after which he returned north. His subordinate, Uriyangqadai, then took command of the campaign, which was nominally completed in 1257, although local resistance aided and abetted by the Song prevented the intended use of this region as a platform for launching further operations to the south.[79]

As an adjunct to their military thrusts southward, the Mongols also used "diplomacy" of a sort. The general nature of these efforts is accurately and succinctly characterized by Rashīd al-Dīn, who says that Qubilai "dispatched envoys by ship to most of the countries of the Indies (Hind) in order [to demand] they submit."[80] While uncompromising in tone, these commands, especially those directed at states beyond the Mongols' reach, can also be understood as invitations to enter into commercial exchange, which, reflecting long-standing Chinese usage, were regularly cast in the guise of tributary relationships, a practice whose possibilities were fully understood and regularly exploited by neighboring states and distant commercial interests.

For those nearer at hand, however, Mongolian diplomacy was always coupled with the very real possibility of invasion. This is well illustrated in the pressure the Mongols placed on Annam (North Vietnam) that began in 1257. Thereafter a series of military and naval operations followed that extended south into Champa and ended in costly defeats. In all cases these attempts, terminated with the death of Qubilai, were halted by the ever-present combination of stiff resistance, logistical problems, difficult terrain, and tropical disease.[81] And it was at these junctures that the Mongols regularly reverted to their particular brand of diplomacy. Fortunately, the basic details are recorded in Chinese and Vietnamese sources that together throw much light on the Mongols' commercial goals and the tactics employed to achieve them.[82] These can be conveniently presented in tabular form and chronological order.

1262. According to a Vietnamese source, Naṣīr al-Dīn, the first imperial agent (*darughachi*) sent to Annam to monitor and guide the affairs of the court, was well received but treated as a normal envoy, not an all-powerful viceroy, as part of ongoing attempts to elude the Mongols' embrace.[83] The reason a Muslim was selected for this assignment becomes intelligible only when a few years later the Chinese sources provide details of what the Mongols' expected from this reluctant client.

1263. In the face of persistent pressure, the ruler of Annam yielded to the least onerous of the Mongolian demands, delivering to Qubilai the first shipment of tribute goods—gum resins, fragrances, exotic hardwoods, elephant ivory, rhinoceros horn, and pearls.[84] Some of these were native to Vietnam, and some were imports from neighboring regions.[85] The Mongols' attraction to these tropical and semitropical products is confirmed institutionally by the establishment between 1263 and 1275 of manufacturing offices in North China specialized in the fabrication of items from these materials.[86]

1267. In addition to the standard demands for census data, tributes, troops, and hostages, this, the latest in a series of Qubilai's unfulfilled orders of submission to the Annam ruler, closes with the following stipulation: "Because your state has Muslim (Hui-hui) merchants, it is desired that you seek out and use those persons of the Western Region for [government] service."[87] The purpose behind this particular demand is self-evident and explains the earlier selection of a Muslim as *darughachi*.

1269. The basic dynamics of their relationship, characterized by Vietnamese evasion and Mongolian persistence, is fully displayed two years later when Qubilai again ordered his reluctant client to enlist Muslims advisers.[88] In this instance, the message is less specific about the pool of potential recruits, so long as they are merchants.

A more generalized picture of the geographical range, type of goods sought, and motives behind the Yuan court's commercial initiatives can be obtained from another set of imperial initiatives dating to the 1270s.

1272. Qubilai sent the Uighur, Yigmish, a high-ranking court official, "overseas" to Ba-la-ben (Palembang), and two years later he returned with its representatives, who presented precious gems (*zhenbao*) as tribute.[89] Since this exploratory mission took place about six years before the fall of the Song, the Mongols' access to the southern seas was limited to the recently seized ports on the eastern coast of China or by negotiated passage through Southeast Asia. In either case, such circuitous routing testifies to the Mongols' eagerness to penetrate maritime markets.

1273. The Yuan court dispatched envoys "with 100,000 ounces of gold to imperial prince Abaqa [in Iran] to purchase drugs (*yao*) from Ceylon (Shizi)."[90] Most certainly this huge investment was prompted by the belief of Christians and Muslims, including Rashīd al-Dīn, that the island was the original biblical paradise and thus hallowed ground offering potent medicinal plants and healing waters.[91] On this occasion Qubilai's envoys presumably traveled overland, for if by sea they would hardly have need for Il-qan mediation.

1279. After the Muslim merchants in Quanzhou, long affiliated with Song overseas trade, went over to the advancing Mongols, Qubilai issued a decree stating: "Of the various foreign states located on large and small islands to our southeast, all have in their hearts admiration [for us]. You [the Muslim merchants] may therefore proclaim our message to foreign ships that if they come to court with sincerity, we will show them favor and kindness. They may come and go [freely] and all may conduct their business as they please."[92]

Collectively, these data show that starting from 1251, the Mongolian leadership consistently pursued plans to participate actively in the commerce of the southern seas. While the Mongols invested much military and diplomatic effort toward this end, the long-term success of their strategy depended on the cooperation of Muslim merchant communities who dominated these networks and who were much attracted to Chinggisid courts. From this it follows that in pursuit of their maritime goals, the purchasing power of the Yuan always counted for more than their military power. The same can be said of the Il-qans and the Golden Horde; although neither had a navy, their buying power nonetheless enabled them to influence the decisions and behavior of merchants plying the waters off their shores.[93]

This leads to one final and obvious question: How did an inland people like the Mongols become so well informed on maritime affairs? There can be little doubt their initial source of information came from the large contingents of Muslim merchants in their service. The accumulation of commercial agents and advisers began in Chinggis Qan's day, and his immediate successors continually added to their ranks. The subsequent appointment of Muslims to positions of high authority in Sichuan and Yunnan and in the major Chinese ports constitutes a reward for services rendered and affirmation of the accuracy and utility of the maritime intelligence they provided the Mongols.[94]

But this is not the whole story. In the course of the push southward, the Mongols encountered, engaged, and incorporated a number of peoples and states with extensive experience managing the linkages between overland and maritime circuits. Most important were contacts with an arc of territory extending from southwestern China through Upper Burma into northeastern India, which served as the principal transitional zone connecting silk routes to sea routes.[95]

For the Mongols, the principal nexus was Yunnan, which had long functioned as such a transit point.[96] The region was controlled successively by two kingdoms founded by dynasties with Tibeto-Burman or Tai affinities, Nanzhao (748–937) and its successor, Dali (938–1257). Their centuries-long dominance of this transition zone and their intimate ties to the maritime world is clearly manifested in their monetary systems, based on extensive use of cowry shells.[97] The most commonly used of these, *Cypraea Moneta*, originating in the Maldive Islands, spread, starting in prehistoric times, overland through South India to Bengal and then to Southwest China and simultaneously by sea to Africa, mainland Southeast Asia, and the outlying islands.[98]

In Yunnan the use of cowries as the principal medium of exchange began in the ninth century under Nanzhao, whose main supply was still imported from the Maldives. Dali continued the practice and, following the Mongolian occupation in the mid-1250s, cowries, somewhat unexpectedly, retained their utility and value until finally displaced by Chinese currency in the early Qing.[99] The acceptance by the Yuan of cowry currency was itself recognition that the region's commercial connections and currency preferences facilitated their own ambitions in the southern seas.

Although the Chinggisids' intentions, methods, models, and sources of commercial intelligence are clear enough, the influence their policies exerted on the interactions between these circuits requires more extended treatment.

CHAPTER 13

Balance of Trade

One helpful way to approach the issue of balance of trade is to summarize the perspectives on long-term trends in the interactions of the two circuits advanced by historians focusing on maritime trade, and then compare these with patterns discernible during the Mongolian era. Such a procedure recommends itself for our inquiry about pearls because these scholars are more inclined to generalize and seek common perspectives on the origins and subsequent configurations of the two circuits.

Foremost among their findings is that the development of land and seaborne commerce was synchronous and synergic and that their coevolution was an ongoing process whose beginnings are found in deep antiquity. Already at the end of the second millennium BCE there is evidence that camel caravans carried incense from South Arabia to ports on the Mediterranean shore.[1] This can be viewed as one of the several regional precursors to the formation of a pan-Eurasian exchange network, which Philippe Beaujard views as entailing the emergence of both land and sea routes by the early centuries of the Common Era.[2]

K. N. Chaudhuri, characterizing the situation in the eighteenth century, argues that in combination large ocean-going vessels, small riverine craft, oxcarts, and camel caravans conveying both merchant princes and humble peddlers served to tie together transcontinental, regional, and local commercial networks. Although the volume of goods carried on land and sea routes varied over time, the two always remained connected and to a surprising extent coordinated.[3] One expression of this is found in the report from 1750 of an East India Company agent, who states that the timing of the merchant caravan from Basra to Aleppo "depends principally on the arrival of the ships from India."[4] While the vagaries of weather and politics often disrupted these schedules, there can be little doubt that efforts at coordination were of long standing.

The variability in the amount of goods carried by the two systems is of course the central question but one that is often beclouded by questionable assumptions. Chief among them is the pronounced tendency to ascribe any "decline" in overland trade to warfare, most especially to that initiated by expansive nomads. And when this occurs, it is further and almost automatically assumed that seaborne trade was the immediate beneficiary. Perceptions of this kind, however, need to be reconsidered from the perspective of steppe history and the systems of resource extraction that predominated there for several millennia.

This is necessary because one of the defining characteristics of the nomadic economy is that it is "non-autarchic." A number of factors account for this. Pastoral economies are subsistence oriented, their major resource, animals, is widely dispersed over large areas and is susceptible to the forces of nature—predators, epizootics, droughts, and blizzards. Consequently, steppe peoples were unable to support substantial and permanent political structures whose construction and maintenance required regular and substantial inputs, of both necessities and luxuries, from external, nonpastoral societies.[5]

These items, as previously enumerated, could be acquired by raiding, tributary arrangements, and trading. Trading was a particularly attractive option because it can be reasonably well controlled by leaders to secure a reliable supply of the positional goods essential for political mobilization. And, as an additional benefit, once they formed a viable state, nomadic rulers could then extract taxes from the transit trade and profits from investment partnerships with merchants. As a general proposition, then, steppe polities had a many-sided interest in, and generally sought to facilitate, commercial exchange.

The relationship between nomads and sedentaries was therefore far more variable and complex than the "heroic" and "epic" struggles stereotypically portrayed in traditional chronicles and tales, images, moreover, that have at times been accepted uncritically by modern schools of national (and nationalist) historiography. In the pre-Chinggisid era the relations between the Eastern Slavs and their nomadic neighbors, Khazars, Pechenegs, and Polovetsy/Qipchaqs, offer a good example of the misunderstandings involved. Though conventionally depicted as a series of military confrontations between hostile ethnic groups, one group identified exclusively with the steppe and the other with the sown, this warfare commonly involved coalitions composed of both nomads and sedentaries fighting similarly mixed alliances for various political and economic gains. Even more striking, their relations were often characterized by ongoing commercial exchange even in times of hostilities. This is the case because nomadic warfare did not have as its primary goal the curtailment of exchange with the outside world; rather, its intent was to force settled societies into such relationships.[6]

The continuity and intensity of the desire for trade, so apparent during the subsequent Mongolian period, was, moreover, still characteristic of the postimperial age, circa 1400–1800, when nomadic formations across the steppe were smaller in scale and differed substantially in their level of political development. Yet despite these differences, all exhibited a profound interest in regular trade relations with sedentary economies. For this purpose all had the necessary institutions and the personnel, drawn mainly from the ranks of Muslim merchants, to seek out and conduct such exchanges, sometimes at great distances. In the mid-seventeenth century, for example, the Altan Qans, a very minor polity in northwestern Mongolia, actively sought Moscovy's aid in establishing commercial connections with the Ottomans and Ṣafāvids thousands of kilometers away.[7]

This is not to say that nomads did not succumb to short-term greed leading to attacks on commercial centers and caravans. But while this occurred, we should also bear in mind that countervailing long-term political interests always favored the restoration of relations with merchant communities and exchange with the outside world. Such predation was not, then, a result of some innate urge to despoil, but one facet of the nomads' multisided relationship with nonpastoral societies.

The Mongols' treatment of merchants, collectively and individually, accurately mirrors the basic priorities of steppe peoples. In the midst of the campaign in Afghanistan, as already noted, Mongolian military officers *bought* coral from merchants when they were in a position to seize what they wanted. Their restrained behavior, of course, sent a welcoming message to commercial interests everywhere, one moreover that stood in stark contrast to the behavior of the Khwārazmians at Uṭrār in 1218, when they killed the merchant envoys (mainly fellow Muslims) sent by Chinggis Qan and seized his trade caravan.[8] In later decades Mongolian rulers continued to pursue such accommodating policies, going out of their way to present themselves as reliable partners of the merchant community, providing them with capital and paying off in full large commercial debts incurred by predecessors.[9]

Granted that steppe polities regularly pursued trade in times of peace and war, this still leaves open the question of the extent to which internal and external conflicts affected the frequency and routing of economic exchange during the Mongolian Empire. Such an inquiry is made necessary by the fact that even during those periods when the steppe zone was dominated by a single nomadic power there were still periods of disturbance and delay, since such empires were inevitably accompanied by rebellions, succession disputes, and civil war. The "Mongolian Peace," like all others, was never complete.

In the absence of contemporary records on the relative volume and value of traffic carried in the two circuits, the best alternative is a sampling of available data on the temporal and geographical patterns of contact between Chinggisid courts, which can be used as proxies in an effort to construct a generalized picture of the relationship between the overland and maritime circuits. While any form of contact tells us something about the state of travel and communications, the arrival of embassies, though nominally diplomatic or political in purpose, constitutes a particularly useful diagnostic tool, since these were regularly accompanied by "trade delegations" composed of court and private merchants. As to the total number of missions involved, the standard narrative sources record far more than those cited below; the limiting factor here is that in a large majority of cases it is not possible to determine their routing.

We begin the survey in the 1250s, generally considered the heyday of the empire.

Between 1254 and 1255 Het'um, king of Lesser Armenia (Cilicia), passed through the Il-qan lands, the Golden Horde, and the Chaghadai Qanate on his way to Qara Qorum and after an audience with Möngke returned home without incident.[10]

In 1259 Chang De, envoy of Möngke to Hülegü, reached Iran by way of Turkistan, again without any recorded difficulties.[11]

During the early 1260s, the elder Polos on their first trip east engaged in profitable trade throughout the Volga basin; prevented from returning home by the outbreak of war between the Il-qans and the Golden Horde, they spent three years in Bukhara and then made an unplanned journey to North China in the train of an envoy of Qubilai coming back from Hülegü's court. After a stay of several years, the Polos returned overland to Europe in 1269 as the emperor's personal emissaries to the papacy.[12]

In the middle of the same decade, Rabban Sauma, a Nestorian Christian monk, departed North China intending a pilgrimage to the Holy Lands. He reached Iran in 1266 after delays in the vicinity of Khotan and Kashghar occasioned by conflict between the forces of Qubilai and those of Qaidu (d. 1301), a descendant of Ögödei and leader (in Yuan eyes) of "rebellious" Chinggisid princes in Inner Asia during the latter decades of thirteenth century.[13]

Tekechüq, an envoy from Qubilai, reached Azerbaijan in 1270 after escaping capture by Boraq, the Chaghadai qan, an ally of Qaidu. In response, the Il-qans quickly mounted a military campaign against Qaidu, setting off new hostilities.[14]

The following year, 1271, the Polos, now accompanied by the young Marco, began their second trip to China, arriving at Qubilai's court circa 1275. While no major difficulties are mentioned in the rather sketchy account of their overland trip, its very length hints that they encountered some form of hindrance connected with ongoing princely strife.[15]

In 1276 a wealthy Eastern Christian merchant in the company of a Uighur envoy sent by the Il-qans to the Yuan court safely returned to Iran.[16] Since they reentered Il-qan territory through Khurāsān, they traveled overland.

At the very end of 1285, two Yuan envoys, ʿIsā the Interpreter and Bolad Aqa, a high-ranking Mongolian official, reached Iran following a perilous journey across Central Asia. Early the next year they started back by the same route; encountering "rebellion," Bolad was forced to return to Iran, while ʿIsā, braving "slings and arrows," successfully reached China after a year full of dangers and adventures.[17]

In the next decade, as the Chinggisid civil war intensified and became generalized, there is a noticeable shift to seaborne communications. Because of the mounting dangers, Qubilai chose this option when sending a promised bride to the il-qan Arghun. She was accompanied by a large embassy that included the Polos; they departed China in 1290/91 and arrived in Iran in 1293/94.[18]

The Il-qans responded similarly to the spreading hostilities. Ghazan dispatched a large, multipurpose embassy to the Yuan that left in 1298 and returned nine years later, traveling both legs by sea. The length of time involved was the result of many misadventures, including a disastrous shipwreck.[19]

Conditions inland improved dramatically by 1304, when envoys of Temür Qaghan, Qubilai's successor, and of Chabar, the son of Qaidu, arrived in Iran to finalize a general settlement among the Chinggisid princes.[20] That they came overland is guaranteed by the participation of the representatives of Chabar, whose home territory was in the Ili River valley.

Peace restored, the il-qan Öljeitü in 1305 hastened to announce the good tidings to the "international community" in a missive to Philip the Fair of France in which he makes a special point of declaring that all the postal relay stations (*jamud*) are now reconnected, thus restoring secure land communications throughout the empire.[21]

In 1306 another distinguished embassy from the Yuan court came overland to Iran. Since this mission, like its immediate predecessor, served as an occasion for reciprocal gift giving on a grand scale, much wealth was exchanged.[22] It is tempting as well to assume that both missions were accompanied by court merchants.

Peace came to an end in 1316 when general hostilities broke out in Inner Asia, a development that presumably hindered overland passage for several years.

Sometime before 1326, general peace was restored, for in the course of this year the il-qan Abū Saʿīd on four separate occasions sent western horses and single-humped camels to the Yuan.[23] Given the nature of his presentations, it seems a fair surmise they went by land.

Most certainly the land routes were open by this time. In October 1326 the Yuan court dispatched a mission to the Chaghadai Qanate, Golden Horde, and Il-qans to announce the bestowal of a prestige title on Chuban, the chief minister of the il-qan Abū Saʿīd, which arrived in Azerbaijan in November 1327.[24] Taken together, distances covered during the outward mission, a bare minimum of sixty-eight hundred kilometers, and the time in which it was accomplished, thirteen months, argues that efficient transportation and safe travel conditions prevailed across the empire.[25]

This grand diplomatic tour by a single embassy was an event of great symbolic significance, a statement of unity. It was followed by another prestigious set of embassies, dispatched in 1330. On this occasion, the Yuan emperor separately and simultaneously sent high-ranking imperial princes on individual missions to the other qanates.[26] Those directed to the Chaghadaid and Jochid courts without question traveled by land, and it is likely his princely envoy to the Il-qans did as well.

In 1336 Özbeg, ruler of the Golden Horde, sent an envoy to the Yuan court requesting the proceeds from the Jochids' allotted territories in North China, needed to provide funds for the maintenance of their military post (*junzhan*). The envoy added somewhat plaintively that the "metropolitan authorities" (the Yuan central government) did not assume responsibility for keeping the system in working order.[27]

In 1353, another Golden Horde ruler, Jani-Beg, sent "a great tent" of elegant Byzantine cloth to the Yuan.[28] This, apparently, is the last mission sent by another Chinggisid court to Dadu.

The two Jochid missions introduce yet another important variable in gauging the impact of warfare on overland exchange and its maritime repercussions—the availability of alternative routing. There were in reality a number of "silk roads" and "fur roads" crisscrossing the interior of Eurasia. One of the most important and least appreciated of these was first described in detail, around 1340, by the Arabic encyclopedist/geographer al-ʿUmarī, whose data come from Muslim merchant informants. This road extended from Dadu to Qara Qorum, then to the middle Yenisei, the borderland between the Yuan and the Golden Horde, then across southern Siberia, through the Bashkir lands to Jūlmān (the Kama River) in Volga Bulgharia.[29] From here, of course, there were long-standing caravan and river connections with the lower Volga and Crimea and thence to the Caspian, Black, and Mediterranean seas.

The question of when the Siberian route was first opened cannot be answered with certainty. It is most likely, however, that it emerged through a process of accretion in consequence of the conquest by the Mongols of southern Siberia, begun in 1208, and their preparations for the invasion of Central Asia in 1219. A line of communication connecting a number of preexisting local and regional routes with the Mongolian homeland was an essential accompaniment to these operations. And since the conquest of the forest zone on both sides of the Urals was under the control of the Jochids, the progressive extension of the Siberian road westward can be viewed as a natural adjunct to the formation of the Golden Horde.

The first certain evidence of its active use dates to 1221, when the Daoist adept Changchun visited Chinggis Qan in the Western Region. During the outward leg of the journey, Li Zhichang reports, they encountered at the Öröngö River just west of the Yenisei a recently built road, postal riders (*yiqi*), and a supply of remounts. It is evident that the road in question was fairly substantial, for the party were conveyed to their audience on wagons drawn by teams of oxen.[30]

The next references come from the 1270s and '80s. Marco Polo relates that under King Conci (Qonichi), the Jochid prince whose domain included central Siberia, there was a series of postal relay stations in the forest zone serviced, according to season, by horses and dogsleds. To the north of these stations in the "Land of Darkness," the subarctic, there were "hamlets" established as collection points for furs, a major source of income for the Princes of the Left Hand.[31] Although the Venetian never visited the region in person, his information is consistent with the report of Rashīd al-Dīn, confirmed by Chinese records, that in 1280 there was considerable commercial activity extending from the Yenisei Qirghiz land to the plain of Barghu east of Baikal, in the hands of Muslim merchants who brought northern products to the Yuan court. The name of a well-connected merchant in Dadu, ʿUmar Qirqīzī, indicates a long association with, and perhaps even a base of operations on, the Yenisei.[32] Such bases certainly existed, for there is archaeological evidence of several Muslim settlements and cemeteries in this region during the Mongolian era.[33]

In evaluating the historical position of the forest road, it is useful to consider later Russian experience in Siberia. Once the Russians penetrated beyond the Urals in the early seventeenth century, they began to fashion their own version of this post, and the modes of transport used by them, a mix of riding horses and sleds, is in general accord with Marco Polo's information.[34] This raises the additional question of whether there were other continuities mediated by the Qanate of Sibir, a successor state of the Golden Horde. We know definitely that Moscovy systematically assimilated the Mongolian postal system west of the Urals and very likely continued the practice in Siberia. At the very least, it is safe to say that the Russian post closely followed the route utilized by the Chinggisids and, further, that east-west trade routes intersecting those in the steppe zone were a recurrent feature of Siberian history.

This excursion deep into the northern forests has seemingly taken us far from maritime matters and the southern seas. As the discussion below documents, however, the Siberian post does in fact have a direct bearing on the central theme of this chapter—the interrelationships between seaborne communication networks with those located deep within the continent. The crucial data come in two letters sent from Dadu by the Franciscan friar John of Monte Corvino to church authorities in the West.

In the first, directed to the papacy in 1305, he speaks of the urgent need for additional missionaries and then makes the following remarks on the routes by which they can best reach North China:

> I report that the way by the land of Cothay [Toqta, r. 1291–1312], the emperor of the Northern Tartars [the Golden Horde], is safer and more secure, so that, traveling with envoys, they [the missionaries] might be able to arrive within five or six months. But the other route is the most long and perilous since it involves two sea voyages, the first of which is about the distance between Acre to the province of Provence, but the second is like the distance between Acre and England and, it may happen that the journey is scarcely completed in two years. But the first [route] was not safe for a long time on account of the wars and for twelve years I have not received news of the Roman Curia, and of our Order and the state of the West.[35]

In the second letter, sent in 1306 to officials of the Franciscan Order resident in Iran, the friar makes reference to his own use of the Siberian post:

> Wherefore I now notify you that last year at the beginning of January, I sent letters by a friend of ours who was among the companions of the Lord Chaan Cothay who came to the Lord Chaan of Cathay [China], to the Father Vicar and the brethren of the province of Gazaria [the Crimea], informing them briefly of my present situation and circumstances. In this letter I asked the Vicar to send on copies of it to you, and now I find from reliable men who have come to the Lord Chaan of Cathay with envoys of the aforesaid Lord Cothay that my letter has reached you and that the same messenger who carried it afterwards came from the city of Sarai to Tauris [Tabriz].[36]

A number of these statements call for comment. In the first place, the Friar John is well aware of the importance of "traveling with envoys," since it was the practice of the Mongols to provide free transportation, lodging, and food to all persons authorized to use their postal system. In consequence, merchants and other travelers always tried to associate themselves with official missions and succeeded in doing so with great regularity. Next, the extended geographical range of these interconnected postal services, reaching from Dadu through Siberia to Sarai, the Crimea, and Iran, is graphically illustrated and confirmed by John's own experience; the very fact that the letters found their way into the Vatican archives provides irrefutable proof that the Siberian post delivered.

Most interesting, however, is the assertion by the friar that there was greater speed and security along the Siberian road than along the sea lanes. On this particular matter it may well be that his views were "adjusted," made compatible with his self-interest as a resident of Dadu, the eastern terminus of the northernmost land route. In making claims of this sort John was hardly alone; like many other missionaries before and after, he prepared reports to ecclesiastical authorities carefully calculated to elicit a positive response to his pressing needs and, in this instance, one that depicted travel on his preferred line of communication to Europe in a most favorable light. Still, while we need not take his assessment of travel times and security at face value, the more important point is that there was in the first decade of the fourteenth century a heavily trafficked postal and commercial road well known to Muslim merchants running across southern Siberia.

The existence of alternatives deserves special attention because the disruption of one land route is often interpreted to mean the cessation of *all* trade rather than its shift to another route. It is quite natural, of course, to think of these "roads" and "routes" in terms of modern transportation systems that are stable, fixed in place, but those actually traversed by caravans were sometimes little more than a "direction of march," to use Owen Lattimore's apt phrase.[37] In reality, a number of options were generally available, which ranged from heavily used built roads usually in the vicinity of imperial centers through frequently traveled branch routes to less desirable backups held in reserve for emergencies. The backups, typically reverted to in times of political turmoil, were longer and more difficult but nonetheless viable alternatives to the primary routes. And when disturbances became prolonged, new roads were sometimes opened by states and private entrepreneurs to attract trade from troubled neighbors. Such disturbances might even be manufactured to "channel" trade elsewhere for greater control and a greater share of the profits. Indeed, creating such disturbances was a very common tactic, one utilized by ancient empires, medieval nomads, and early modern European mariners.[38]

Given the undeniable and intimate connections between economic and diplomatic exchange in this era, it is equally important to recognize that there was a surprising amount of flexibility in the organization, operation, and routing of the imperial post, a characteristic that closely mirrors that of commercial roads. As one example, recently documented by Hosung Shim, when Qaidu and his allies increased pressure on the northwestern frontier of the Yuan in the early 1280s, Qubilai responded by building an alternative post along the southern rim of the Tarim that allowed continued, albeit more limited, communications with the Il-qans. In large part, this is explained by Shim's further finding that contrary to long-held assumptions, my own included, the Chinggisid post did not, at least in its entirety, consist of fixed routes with permanently staffed relay stations. These prevailed around major political centers, in some densely populated regions, and at threatened frontiers, but in the heart of the continent and the steppe there was no such infrastructure; in these boundless tracks settled and nomadic communities supplied remounts and provisions as the need arose.[39]

The capacity to operate successfully on this ad hoc basis is nicely illustrated by an incident in 1389 when a minor Mongolian prince at the command of the Ming court improvised a *jam* to transport supplies to his surrendering followers.[40] In this we have an example of a system hastily organized to meet a temporary need, which offers good evidence that the institution, so identified with periods of empire, was part of the nomads' standard logistical repertoire even in periods marked by political disintegration. The Mongolian post had considerable adaptive potential that was frequently tested and realized.

There is, then, every reason to believe that while overland commercial and diplomatic communication was at times reduced in volume, these systems were characterized by substantial resiliency and flexibility. Consequently, disruptions were sporadic and of limited duration, and most important, did not result in permanent or decisive shifts of trade from land to sea routes. And in this connection, the clear warnings of Friar John of Monte Corvino, the travails experienced by Ghazan's embassy to China (1298–1307), and the naval confrontations between Kīsh and Hormuz are welcome reminders that dangers and delays were hardly a monopoly of the overland routes. This also means that merchants engaged in long-distance exchange, whether on land or sea, had to deal with delays and diversions as a normal and accepted part of doing business in these markets.

This is not to argue that maritime trade did not increase and prosper in the period from the late thirteenth to early fifteenth centuries. As a result of conflicts among the independent qanates the sea lanes acquired new and vital strategic functions; these may have served to heighten, but certainly did not create, the appreciation the Mongols had of the commercial possibilities of these connections or the economic importance of their sea frontiers.[41] Rather, the flourishing of the seaborne trade during this period is best understood as a result of the conjunction of two key factors. Most important, its success rested on its own firm foundations, the volume and value of commercial traffic built up in the centuries before the Mongols; consequently, its prosperity was not achieved by default, by the sudden rush of commercial traffic from disabled inland routes to secure sea lanes.[42] To this, of course, must be added the Mongols' intense interest in trade generally and in maritime products particularly. And these interests are clearly articulated several decades before the troubles in Inner Asia turned the sea routes into a strategic asset for the allied regimes in China and Iran.

A useful picture of the general characteristics, vigorous state, and attractive powers of this trade can be obtained by looking at the Il-qans' maritime interests and commitments in the early fourteenth century. We can start with a closer examination of Ghazan's economic mission to the Yuan of 1298. The first thing to be noted is that the types of exchange are varied and quite similar to those found on land—a combination of princely presentations, proceeds from allotted lands in North China, commercial ventures of private merchants, and government trade capitalized by the royal treasury. As regards government trade, the scale of the court's investment is most impressive, amounting in this instance to "ten *tūmān* of gold dinars."[43] Since the *tūmān* was an accounting unit of ten thousand coins it is evident that the Il-qan court was heavily engaged in this trade. A further and even more striking measure of involvement comes from a report, dating to 1311, which states that great quantities of Egyptian and

North and South Chinese wares whose combined value was placed at one hundred *tūmān* of dinars were destroyed in a fire at Baghdad.[44]

Besides providing general guidance on the volume of the commercial traffic at this time, the incident also affirms that the Il-qans enjoyed regular dealings with networks reaching from the East China Sea to the eastern Mediterranean. The size and diversity of these exchanges did not go unnoticed by contemporaries. The court historian Qāshānī offers a detailed picture of the riches, routing, means of transport, and origins of the trade goods available in Iran during the 1320s. He writes that the rarities of the farthest Chīn and Māchīn and the goods of India are found at Maʿbar together with the wealth of the Persian Gulf and the ornaments, perfumes, and dyes of Iraq, Khurāsān, Byzantium (Rūm), and Europe (Farang). He is careful to point out as well that all these wondrous wares reached Maʿbar and Iran "on great ships, that is to say on junks (*jung*)."[45] His observations strongly support the view that the high point of the Indian Ocean trade came in the Yuan and early Ming, or, to situate this in the context of Islamic history, during the Il-qan and early Temürid periods.

To close this discussion of the fluctuations in trade carried in the two systems, several other variables deserve consideration. Because of intrinsic properties, some products traveled better on a particular circuit. Under the Yuan, porcelain, given its weight and susceptibility to breakage, went mainly by sea from Chinese ports to India and Arabia.[46] In the post-Mongolian period, on the other hand, large quantities of Chinese rhubarb came through Siberia and Central Asia in the hands of Muslim merchants (Bukhartsy).[47] In this instance, these routes were preferred because it was thought rhubarb deteriorated in sea air, a notion no doubt encouraged by overland merchants.[48]

Most important, we must not lose sight of the actions and the reactions of the merchants themselves. Some of these changes in routing can be connected with long-term economic cycles, fiscal policies of governments, and collective decisions of merchants. As Keelong So has shown, it is these latter forces working in conjunction that best explain the fall off in maritime trade in the last decades of the Song.[49] And, of courses, it is the intrusion of the Mongols, the most expansive of all the nomads, that best explains its rapid recovery in the last decades of the thirteenth century, a revival that was accompanied and symbolized by a massive influx of imported pearls from the southern seas, an influx noted by sources from across the entire continent.[50]

CHAPTER 14

Sea Frontiers

Of the nomadic empires, that formed by the Mongols was the first and only one with extensive sea frontiers. Indeed, Chinggisid domains fronted on and interacted with three bodies of water. For our ends, it will be profitable to briefly describe and compare their natural, demographic, and historical characteristics to better understand the efforts by the Mongols to tap into and exploit their maritime products and commercial traffic.

In East Asia the Yuan had a coastline of some eighteen thousand kilometers, one of the longest sea frontiers in history.[1] The climate, at least along the southern littoral, ranged from subtropical to tropical. The population was extremely dense and diverse, consisting of numerous indigenous people, Han Chinese, and foreign-merchant communities. Agricultural productivity, measured by the standards of the Middle Ages, was very high. This is evidenced by extensive crop specialization and by the prevalence of early ripening rice, yielding in some areas three harvests per year.

The Mongols' sea frontier on the Persian Gulf, by contrast, was far shorter, and its shoreline was composed mainly of deserts, semideserts, and salt marshes. The climate, noted for its extreme heat and humidity, was by regional reputation extremely undesirable. Along all its shores population density was low, and on its northern littoral it was a mixture of Arabs, Persians, and Iranian-speaking pastoralists. Local agricultural production was limited, and food often had to be imported. The shortage of essential resources is underscored by the pressing need of Kīsh for water, which, despite extensive collection and conservation measures, had to be augmented by supplies brought from the mainland at great expense.

The Black Sea, approximately twice the size of the Gulf, has a moderate and variable climate; the southward-facing valleys of the Crimean Peninsula enjoy

Mediterranean-like conditions capable of sustaining a prosperous viniculture. Since before the Common Era, the Crimea and the lands to its north with rich black soil have been major exporters of grain to the south. The population, as on the other two sea frontiers, was mixed, composed of many in-migrating groups seeking sanctuary and commercial opportunity—Greeks, Jews, Goths, Armenians, and others.[2]

But beyond their decided differences, the three frontiers shared a common feature: all contained multiple centers of long-distance maritime trade with highly developed commercial cultures and institutions.

In East Asia, the primary social dynamic in Guangzhou (Canton) and other ports was the intensification of interaction between foreign merchant communities with the indigenous populations and increasing numbers of Han immigrants. And while their relationships sometimes generated tension and conflict, they also resulted in mutually beneficial political alliances and economic associations.[3] Under the Tang and Song, the number of these merchants became so large that the Chinese established officially sanctioned semiautonomous ghettoes for foreigners (*fanfang*) in the major ports of the south.[4]

At the same time, the growth of Chinese diaspora communities on mainland Southeast Asia and outlying islands further solidified and extended these networks in the centuries preceding the Mongols.[5] The reaction of these interlocking networks to these invaders is most revealing. When the last Song emperor fled Quanzhou in 1276, the commercial elite of the city were already making preparations for its peaceable submission to the Mongols, negotiations that were finalized in the following year. The major player in this transition was Pu Shougeng. He and his family, Muslim immigrants from the Western Region, had deep roots in Fujian and enjoyed wide support among the local Chinese political and military leadership. As the maritime trade commissioner (*shiboshi*) Pu also had close ties to the foreign merchants; the latter, consisting mainly of Arabs, Persians, and Indians, were numerous, wealthy, and equally inclined to come to terms with the new regime.[6]

Their calculations were quite correct; as soon as the Mongols defeated the Song in 1279 and occupied the coastal provinces, the Yuan court began to encourage the rapid build-up of foreign merchants, especially Muslims, in the southern provinces. Many of these came by sea from West and South Asia, but some of the leading administrative appointees, such as Sayyid Ajall and Bahā al-Dīn Qunduzī, were natives of inland regions, Turkestan and Khurāsān. In all cases the court allowed these communities a measure of internal autonomy and extensive rights of travel, including regular contact with their homelands. Their privileged status in the south was institutionalized and advertised by their inclusion in the ranks of the *semuren*, "sundry category people," West and Central Asians who received preferential treatment in appointment to official posts during the Yuan. In consequence, the families of Pu Shougeng and his many associates continued, as under the Song, to exercise great influence on formulation and implementation of commercial policy on behalf of their new masters.[7]

These policies had the desired effect of facilitating the successful takeover of Song networks and the cooperation of additional merchant diasporas in the southern seas.[8] At the same time, they made preparations to profit from this influx of merchants and merchandise. The first Yuan Maritime Trade Office (*sibosi*) was established in Quanzhou in 1277, and by 1294 the number had risen to seven. The subsequent and frequent changes in the administration of the ports and the jurisdiction of their trade offices reflect the competitions of merchant cliques and their supporters at court. These ongoing contests are expressed in the central government's introduction of new trade regulations and their futile attempts to impose a state monopoly over maritime commerce.[9]

In West Asia the Mongols' awareness and attraction to the wealth of the Gulf can be dated to about 1230, some twenty-five years before the arrival of Hülegü. Initially they obtained access to the maritime resources through the mediation of a number of local rulers and merchant princes in the south of Iran. The first were the Qutlughshāhs, a recently formed dynasty of Qara-Qitan origin in Kirmān who joined the Mongols in 1221–22 shortly after they arrived on the scene. Next were the Salghurids, a line of Turkmen *atabegs* in Fārs, who, following a brief period of Khwārazmian dominance in the mid-1220s, willingly turned to the advancing Mongols. Their ruler Abū Bakr Qutlugh (r. 1231–60) submitted in 1231, dispatching his brother to Ögödei, who accepted their pledge of fixed annual tributes. Not surprisingly, since Abū Bakr had just reasserted his influence in Bahrain, Kīsh, and Hormuz, pearls formed a part of these payments.[10]

Because the relationships between the qaghans in Mongolia and their proxies in the Gulf were so attenuated, they are also rather indistinct. The basic features, however, are recoverable. Local ruling houses were left in place under the distant authority of Chinggisid governors-general headquartered in Khurāsān who, so far as we know, never visited either region. For their part, the clients dutifully paid tributes, accepted the posting of imperial agents (*darughachin*) at their courts, and renewed their patents of investiture with Ögödei and his immediate successors.[11] Though recognizing Chinggisid authority and fulfilling the obligations placed upon them, their rulers nevertheless retained substantial internal autonomy and freedom of action in dealings with other trade emporiums and pearling stations in the Gulf and neighboring seas.

The extent of their independence becomes even more apparent with the division of the empire and the formation of the Il-qan regime centered in Azerbaijan. During the 1250s the two clients in the south contended for commercial predominance throughout the Gulf by means of their own proxies in Kīsh and Hormuz. These proxies in their turn used their liquid wealth in coin and pearls to maintain substantial naval forces and a large measure of independence from their nominal masters. In an effort to circumvent these second- and third-hand methods of control, Hülegü and his successor, Abaqa, sent personal agents, mainly Mongols, to Fārs and Kirmān to ensure the full and prompt delivery of stipulated tributes. When this failed to produce the desired results the Il-qans then changed tactics in the 1270s, farming out the taxes and general administration of these districts to court-affiliated Muslim merchants. But this, too, produced disappointing returns, for by this time communications with the south were greatly hampered by raids of the Lurs and the Nīgadurīs, the latter a confederation of freebooters composed of Mongols, Indians, and others. In consequence, the rulers of Fārs and Kirmān acquired even greater autonomy, minting coins in their own names and according to their own standards of weight and purity.[12]

The next and decisive shift in policy occurred in 1292 when the il-qan, Geikhatu, changed tactics yet again, this time farming out the taxes of Fārs and the Gulf for four years to a true insider in the region, Shaikh al-Islam Jāmal al-Dīn Ibrahīm, the ruler of Kīsh. In return for this concession, made necessary by the near depletion of the royal treasuries, the shaikh provided the court with an immediate cash infusion amounting to one million *tūmān*. In this way a merchant prince based on a small desolate island became the chief tax collector and chief creditor of the Il-qan regime.

Jāmal al-Dīn, who had accumulated a vast fortune in the China trade and whose family business had "branch offices" on the western coast of India, used his resources and connections to ingratiate himself with Geikhatu's successor, Ghazan. In 1296 the shaikh had an audience with the new il-qan, who showered him with precious gifts and appointed him, over opposition, chief tax farmer for all the Gulf and southern Iraq. He exercised this office until 1302, at which point he fell from favor, and his activities were restricted to Kīsh and a few other islands. Although he and his descendants continued to serve Ghazan's successor, Öljeitü (r. 1304–16), in a limited capacity, the princes of Hormuz, the longtime rivals of Kīsh, now became the il-qan's chief representatives in the Gulf.[13]

While some later sources leave the impression that major pearling centers like Oman and Kīsh were under direct Il-qan administrative authority, this was never the case.[14] The most immediate access of the Mongols to the trade and treasures of the Gulf was a consequence of their successive agreements with resident merchant princes, which reduced the previous tangled chain of intermediaries to a single agent. But even this measure of control was achieved only some thirty years after the formation of the Il-qan regime. This, of course, stands in sharp contrast with the situation in East Asia, where the Yuan began to assert effective administrative control over their sea frontier in 1277, two years before direct military occupation. Furthermore, there was no equivalent Il-qan military presence along the Gulf, and so far as is known the Il-qan armies never undertook large-scale operations in this extremely hostile environment.

The nomads' commercial connections with the Black Sea frontier can be traced back in the written and archaeological record to Scythian times. Throughout most of its history, in the region from North Caucasia across the coastline of the Black Sea to the Balkan Peninsula political authority was typically fragmented. With the notable exception of the Bosporan kingdom (ca. 438 BCE–370 CE), this is true as well of the Crimea. Following this extended period of relative stability, political authority was generally dispersed among a patchwork of city-states and commercial and ethnoreligious communities. In some measure, this was a result of the peninsula's unique geopolitical position; the Black Sea is the only one of the three sea frontiers with a land power to its south and, somewhat intermittently, one or occasionally two to its north that regularly competed for influence throughout the region. Most commonly, however, the objective of these competitions was not military control over the entire peninsula or its hinterlands but the possession of outposts and enclaves for trade and intelligence gathering. As a result, these struggles often served to perpetuate or magnify the fragmentation, since their rivalries resulted in loose and uneasy forms of joint rule, the exercise of which necessitated the cultivation and appeasement of various local commercial interests, clients, and proxies; such a pattern is clearly visible in the tenth-century struggles of Byzantium and the Khazars for influence in the peninsula.[15]

In the centuries before the Mongols, maritime trade within the Byzantine sphere of influence was characterized by concessions to foreign merchant communities that included general trading rights, territorial enclaves providing a measure of self-governance, reasonable and stable tariff rates, and special courts to adjudicate personal and commercial disputes between people of different ethnic and religious affiliations. Similar arrangements were found in cities along the northern shore of the Black Sea and on the lower Volga, the center of nomadic states in the western steppe in the later Middle Ages. The institutionalized tolerance of ethnic and confessional diversity prevalent here is attributable to the desire of the principals, international merchants, investors, and customers to benefit from this commercial traffic, a habit of mind fully consonant with the attitudes of nomadic elites, for whom the continued inflow of natural and cultural commodities was essential to their political economy. Already in the mid-tenth century there was such a court at Itil, the Khazar capital on the Volga delta, composed of seven arbitrators, two each for the Jews, Muslims, and Christians and one "idolater" for the pagans, to adjudicate intercommunal conflicts.[16]

The pattern of arrangements the Golden Horde encountered on their sea frontier thus had a lengthy history and a recognized legitimacy rooted in their proven utility in the conduct of trade between overland and maritime circuits. The arrival of the Mongols did little to disturb this; following brief interruptions occasioned by active military operations in 1223 and 1236–41, the Black Sea trade rapidly revived. The only discernible change was that the share of the proceeds formally paid to Qipchaq leaders now went to the Jochids.[17]

The consolidation of Chinggisid rule in the western steppe in the following decades witnessed a notable increase in Italian participation in this commerce, further testimony to the attractiveness of Mongolian markets.[18] Under concessions granted by the Golden Horde, the Italians received the usual package of rights accorded foreign traders, including semiautonomous *comptoirs*, "factories" or "trading posts." Given the prevailing geopolitical arrangements, the Italians had to acquire their access to Black Sea markets through separate agreements with two powers, the recently restored Byzantine Empire and the recently established Golden Horde. Their acquisition of these trading privileges was cumulative and protracted. In 1261 the Byzantines allowed the Genoese access to the Black Sea through the Straits. Several years later the Golden Horde qan, Berke (r. 1257–66), and his successor, Möngke Temür (r. 1266–80), granted the Genoese a concession at Caffa in the Crimea. At this same time the Byzantines also granted the Venetians the privilege of free passage through the straits. The Venetians' position in Tana on the lower Don was first officially recognized by the Golden Horde in 1322 and reaffirmed in 1332. These agreements, although marked by recurrent crises, conflict, and adjudication, remained in place until Temür's assault on the Golden Horde in the 1390s, after which the situation slowly deteriorated, as Tatar elites, now converts to Islam, were less inclined to form commercial partnerships with Europeans.[19]

Beyond the institutional continuities, there is also a noticeable constancy in the directionality of the trade and the products exchanged. Under the Mongols, as in previous centuries, northern goods, natural products primarily of animal origin—furs, wax, honey, isinglass, and slaves—came south in return for finished goods—textiles, coinage, gems, pearls, and other *spezierie*—sent north. This, of course, contrasts sharply with the trade patterns found along the Chinese coast and in the Gulf, where the northern hinterlands also brought many processed goods to ports in the south.

Next, we need to examine the evolution of these three frontiers in an even broader comparative framework. It is well to begin with the term "frontier," to which various and seemingly contradictory meanings have been attached. Sometimes it has been defined as a fixed, precisely demarcated border line between established states and jurisdictions, at other times as ever-changing zones of transition whose primary characteristic is their openness, permeability, and cultural diversity. Indeed, it is the latter conceptualization of frontiers that makes them so interesting to historians and so useful to the present inquiry.

What follows is an attempt to compare the political economies found along the continent's steppe frontiers with those on its maritime littoral. And despite the distortions and overgeneralizations that inevitably accompany such an enterprise, the result can still be productive in framing new questions and advancing tentative answers. The comparative framework selected for my purposes, which focus on state formation, the geographical mobility of frontier populations and their military potential is designed to elucidate the interconnections between the steppe and the sea.

As a point of departure we can examine the question in the context of Chinese history. In a pioneering investigation Hugh Clark argued that the sea frontier differed from its inland counterpart in several significant ways: it was nonexpansionary, and in this zone the Chinese authorities exercised greater control over the social and economic relations between the Han population and the foreign communities in their midst.[20] These are valid points, but in a wider perspective there are also notable similarities.

Viewed cartographically, the two frontiers appear at first glance to be quite distinct. That on the inland has variable environments, fingers of the steppe that penetrate the agricultural zone, extensions of deserts and semideserts into the steppe and isolated patches of tundra in elevated regions of the forest and the steppe. The sea, on the other hand, appears to be clearly distinguishable from the mainland, but this is misleading, for there are gradients, transition zones, here as well, estuaries that bring oceanic environments and resources well inland and off-shore islands that are extensions of the mainland modified by intense interaction with the sea.

This environmental variation offers options for settlement and exploitation that require and reward human flexibility. On the inland frontiers pastoral, agricultural, and hunting-gathering activities are typically combined, allowing communities and polities to utilize different environments seasonally and to make longer-term commitments to one branch of their domestic economy over another. Moreover, such was their flexibility that shifts, once made, could later be reversed under pressure of changing ecological or political circumstances. The same holds true of many coastal zones, where agricultural production and maritime extraction industries can be pursued seasonally, and over time one may become favored over the other.

Because of their transportation capabilities and logistical skills, the populations on both frontiers were extremely mobile and flexible and could, when advantageous, engage in trading, raiding, smuggling, or the sale of military services, activities that readily merged into one another. For the nomads, this was made possible by substantially lower military costs, since their heavy investment in horses and weapons greatly aided pastoral production, while at the same time it increased their capacity to extract goods from the sown by force or threat of force.[21] And for many coastal people their investment in boats and weapons had the same consequence, allowing them, in varying combinations, to engage in piracy and raiding as well as the secure transportation of others' commercial goods, all of which is well exemplified in the ever-changing occupations of the Malays, the quintessential "nomads of the sea."[22] Consequently, for the mobile populations on these two frontiers, unlike those societies with a firm commitment to intensive agriculture, the perennial question of balancing civil and military spending, of beating swords into plowshares, rarely if ever arose.

While similarities in their political economies are many, there is one very basic difference between the two frontiers, exhibited in the pattern of state formation. The major locus of these endeavors in East Asia was the North China Plain; here Inner Asians and Chinese competed and collaborated in this recurrent process, which resulted in formations ranging in size from small, ephemeral border regimes to large regional states to transcontinental empires.[23] Of the latter type, there were no close equivalents in the southern seas.

Maritime peoples did of course form states, but on a different scale. The territory under the control of Palembang (Srīvijaya), a major commercial center in the centuries before the Mongols, comprised only the lower course of the Musi River in southern Sumatra. And after the Mongols, Aceh on the northern tip of the island also achieved commercial success with an equally small home base, as did its near neighbors and competitors, Sumadra and Pasai.[24] Trading states of this approximate size and commercial reach, sometimes called "trading empires," are quite common—Phoenicia and Venice being the prime examples in the Mediterranean world.

Of more relevance here is the island of Vân-dôn off Haiphong, which flourished as a pearling, trade, and smuggling center between the twelfth and fifteenth centuries. The port's emergence, in tandem with several similar emporiums, can be seen as part of a larger process, the intensification of coastal trade in China and Southeast Asia that entailed the interaction of indigenous peoples with one another and with major mainland states, the Ly and Trân dynasties in Vietnam and the Song, particularly following its relocation to the south in 1126. Shortly thereafter, Vân Dôn became a flourishing regional center with commercial ties to Java and China. Its resiliency is evidenced by the fact that even when occupied in succession by the Vietnamese and the Mongols in the course of their naval confrontations, the island was always able to reestablish its freedom of action.[25] Kīsh and Hormuz, in terms of their size and staying power, can therefore be viewed as typical historical formations, close analogues of other maritime states of the age.

Positions of dominance in the regional networks across the southern seas were achieved mainly by economic and organizational means and only in part by naval force. A brief recapitulation of the Mongols' various maritime ventures and misadventures will show the limits of naval influence. From the plentiful documentation available, it is clear that as part of their operations against the Southern Song, the Yuan were forced to invest in a "big navy." To this end they instituted major shipbuilding programs, systematically impressed Chinese and Korean sailors and then employed this force aggressively.[26] A creditable case can be made that the larger aim of their repeated military and naval assaults on Annam and Champa was to impose direct Mongolian political control over the eastern section of the maritime circuit, thereby replicating in some measure the domination of transcontinental routes, or, perhaps more accurately, the arrangements they implemented on the South China coast.[27] Their demands that Chinese-style Maritime Trade Offices (*shibosi*) be established on mainland Southeast Asia and their insistence that the ruler of Annam form a "coalition government" with Muslim merchants, both unrealized, strongly support this hypothesis.

Exactly how and when the idea of asserting direct control over the maritime circuit arose is unknown. As a matter of conjecture, it may be that this was not part of the Mongols' original grand design in the south, and that it was only the increasing naval power Qubilai had at his disposal that suggested such an enterprise. In any event, the abject failure of his forward policy provides convincing proof that naval domination of even a sizable section of the maritime routes, much less the whole, was simply unobtainable. The interlocking spheres of influence making up the maritime circuit remained regional, variable, contested, and, like those on land, prone to disturbance, delay, and diversion. The perception that the sea lanes were somehow more peaceable and secure is a by-product of our sources, particularly narrative histories and works on statecraft, which tend to focus on inland frontiers; this preoccupation is perfectly understandable, for the only serious threats to the integrity or the very existence of major sedentary states came from steppe people, not sea people. In this respect, maritime frontiers were indeed nonexpansionary.

In explaining the success and staying power of these smaller-scale maritime polities, we need to consider their own particular set of strengths. Under extreme pressure, sea peoples, like nomads, could decamp, move on, taking much of their property with them. Since their wealth was for the most part in *spezierie*, valuable and portable trade goods, and since they owned or had access to shipping, it was difficult for land-based powers to seize their highly liquid assets. In the end, it was usually more profitable to come to terms by accommodating their basic economic interests and recognizing their autonomy.

The freedom of action enjoyed by maritime commercial centers was further underwritten by their structural peculiarities. The trade networks of the Indian Ocean were characterized by extended horizontal interdependence of long-distance merchants, an interdependence that of necessity cut across linguistic, ethnic, and religious divides.[28] In many cases, therefore, transactions entailed an intricate web of exchanges in which empires, city-states, diffuse ethnic-confessional diasporas, and private individuals all had a hand. Such integration could only be built up slowly by individuals, families, and syndicates over a number of years or generations. The same is true for the vertical organization required for harvesting maritime products like pearls. Here, as already discussed, a hierarchy of specialists from divers to brokers had to be mobilized and brought together in remote and often barren places, a task that demanded extensive local knowledge and local connections that again could only be fashioned over time.

Under these circumstances, great powers, even those with navies, could not just step in and dictate an entirely new set of terms. This is forcefully illustrated in the Gulf, where merchant princes enjoyed substantial independence. Here the struggle for supremacy between Kīsh and Hormuz that began in the eleventh century continued unabated during the Mongolian period. To a surprising extent the Il-qans, like their predecessors, were merely observers of these commercial and naval competitions and simply accepted the results and made deals with the winner.

The other common and critical characteristic of the three frontiers is their ethnic diversity, which was both a by-product of and a profound influence on the historical development of maritime commerce. And this diversity is central to explaining the successful integration of the two circuits.

Most fundamentally, communities of long-distance merchants with common economic interests and commercial techniques were present and active on inland and maritime frontiers, and many had experience on both. The skill set needed to deal with the diversity encountered on one frontier could be applied to the other. These skills, it is important to recognize, were honed not only in dealings with fellow merchants of different backgrounds but also with an even more disparate collection of producers, brokers, carriers, and customers.

The same diversity was a crucial ingredient in the development of commercial conventions and institutions, which tended to become increasingly homogenized or "internationalized" in the course of the Middle Ages. That those used in commercial exchange on land and on sea were virtually identical provides further confirmation that the two systems evolved together. Among these were various types of partnership known from the Mediterranean to China in which the investor provides money or goods and the merchant his business skills, and the two share the profits at agreed-upon ratios.[29] Sometimes viewed solely as a means of avoiding loans and therefore the sin of usury, such agreements also provided the agent with the flexibility and autonomy essential in the conduct of long-distance commercial ventures that might take years to complete. Without doubt, the merchants themselves were the primary agents in this transcontinental diffusion.

From host countries, this diversity elicited efforts to minimize conflict by various institutional means. In the west, as we have seen, the practice was firmly in place under the Khazars, and in China it first emerged under the Tang.[30] In both instances it was the presence of large foreign merchant communities that provided a powerful stimulus for the elaboration of this legal machinery. And while these courts and their procedures took on varied forms, their basic aims and functions were nonetheless similar.

Closely related to the emergence of separate jurisdictions is the question of how merchants were accommodated while traveling or resident in foreign lands. In China, the influx of non-Han merchants led to the creation of foreign quarters, which were granted a degree of internal autonomy. Analogous institutions were also encountered by the Italians in the Black Sea. The practice there had deep roots in the Mediterranean, one that found its most mature and widespread form in the *funduq*, the merchants' hostels of the Islamic world. Certainly, the *fanfang*, *funduq*, and *comptoir* are functionally equivalent, if not identical, institutions designed in each case to enable governments to facilitate trade, reduce conflict, and monitor and control foreigners in their domains; this may be the consequence of convergence or diffusion, but in either case it is evident that all these responses were generated by sectarian and ethnic differences. The resulting institutions invite and certainly deserve detailed comparative treatment.[31]

From a chronological perspective, the appearance of these institutions in the course of the ninth and tenth centuries and their increased visibility in the thirteenth and fourteenth offer, in my view, an accurate index of the intensity of the ethnic encounters and long-distance exchange that characterize these two eras. Moreover, since these institutions arose and flourished in seaports as well as inland cities again testifies to the common history of the two circuits.

With this conceptualization of frontier dynamics in mind, we can better gauge the extent to which the Chinggisids adapted to the traditions of maritime commerce and the extent to which they were able to influence them. In considering this matter, one major commonality of the Mongolian approach to the maritime world stands out: as a direct consequence of their extended experience with overland commerce and its conventions, the Mongols were predisposed and preadapted to accommodate similar merchant interests and practices encountered along all three sea frontiers.[32] On the China coast the transition was almost seamless; here the Mongols rapidly took over the Song arrangements without significant change. Other Chinggisids did the same, albeit at a slower pace and with more contention in the Gulf and the Black Sea.

Examination of how the Mongols adapted to their sea frontiers leads us back to the relative contributions of military might and purchasing power to their success. In this instance, their ability to acquire maritime resources was owed overwhelmingly to their commercial strength, more specifically their attractiveness to foreign merchants, whose positive image of the Mongols was conditioned by their rulers' business-friendly policies and by their unbridled consumerism. Convincing proof of this assertion follows from the fact that merchants could not be forcibly drafted and transported like military recruits or artisans. By the very nature of their profession they had to operate as free agents, "to come and go" unhindered, as Qubilai publicly proclaimed. As a result, the innumerable merchants congregating at Chinggisid camps, courts, and ports were all "volunteers," drawn there by the prospect of brisk sales, elevated prices, and capital investments.

Conclusion

Given the immense size of their holdings, how did the Mongols extract and channel desired goods such as pearls from such distant and diverse climes?

In the far north, the Chinggisids revived and extended older trade and tributary relationships between peoples of the forest and those of the tundra. In this case, subjugated populations with long experience on the forest-tundra frontier served as their intermediaries in the quest for furs, white gyrfalcons, riverine pearls, and other northern goods.

In the steppe zone, the Mongols had no need for intermediaries or advisers. Here they successfully reconfigured its nomadic inhabitants, thereby mobilizing the military resources of the steppe, its manpower and horsepower, essential for the success of their imperial enterprise.

In the agricultural lands to the south of the steppe, they attracted, co-opted, and compelled native and imported bureaucrats, local ruling houses, and international merchants to help them identify and extract human and material resources from these complex societies. This was made possible by the progressive buildup in the centuries preceding the Mongols of pools of intermediaries in North China, Turkistan, and Khurāsān accustomed and willing to assist polities of Inner Asian origin to govern sedentary populations.

The extension of Mongolian influence into the maritime realm was for the nomads a new departure and a new challenge. The attempt by the Mongols to impose direct administrative control over Southeast Asia and assert naval dominance in surrounding waters met with repeated defeats. The defeats, of course, are best remembered, and these have tended to overshadow their many peaceable maritime successes. The successes were made possible by their possession of the Chinese coastline with its many facilities, which placed at their disposal the requisite maritime resources to participate actively in the commercial life of the southern seas. As Gang Deng has forcefully argued, judged by the range of activity, shipbuilding technology, navigational aids, and travel literature, China's maritime achievements climaxed in the Southern Song-Yuan era and not, as is commonly asserted, in the voyages of Zheng He in the early Ming.[1]

In selecting the specialist personnel for service in an environment that was completely alien to the nomads, the Mongols had several options. The Chinese could supply some of the personnel, but the Chinggisids gave preference to the Muslims, and for good reason: they not only had numerous and growing enclaves in China, Southeast Asia, and India but also had crucial ties to the Persian Gulf, the Red Sea, and the eastern Mediterranean. And in wedding together Chinese nautical technology with Muslim commercial networks the Mongols brought about the Golden Age of commerce in the southern seas.

Unlike their intermediaries in the northern forests and the agricultural zones of the empire who were charged with the administration of territories and control of subject populations, those in the southern seas were charged with finding ways to join, penetrate, and gain access to preexisting exchange networks. The Mongols are famous for establishing and operating an extensive land-based communications system, the imperial post, but it is far less appreciated that in later decades they successfully piggy-backed on an equally extensive maritime communications system created and operated by others, principally Indian-Buddhist and Muslim merchants skilled in cross-cultural commerce.[2]

As a result of these manifold connections, Chinggisid courts functioned as giant magnets attracting merchants and merchandise from every quarter of the Old World. The most common explanation for this achievement is that the empire created a "peace" facilitating the long-distance circulation of commercial and cultural wares. This, to be sure, is part of the answer, but on an even more fundamental level it is also true that the very act of forming such a vast nomadic imperium required the massive accumulation and redistribution of positional goods, a process that promoted new regimes of consumption on a truly continental scale. Under these conditions, it is hardly surprising that overland and seaborne trade flourished simultaneously, forming a dynamic exchange system moving commodities east and west, north and south, including a vast quantity of pearls. With these, the Chinggisids put on elaborate displays to demonstrate their reach and riches, to surround themselves with an aura of royal glory and, of course, to manufacture good fortune.

ABBREVIATIONS AND PRIMARY SOURCES

Abū'l Faẓl, *AA*	Abū'l Faẓl. *The Aʿīn-i Akbārī*. Trans. H. Blochmann. Reprint Delhi: Low Price Publications, 2006, 3 vols.
Abū'l Faẓl, *AN*	Abū'l Faẓl. *Akbar Nama*. Trans. Henry Beveridge. Reprint Delhi: Atlantic, 1989. Vol. I.
Abū'l Fidā	Abū'l Fidā. *The Memoirs of a Syrian Prince*. Trans. P. M. Holt. Wiesbaden: Franz Steiner, 1983.
ʿA-D	Smirnova, L. P., trans. *ʿAjāʾib al-dunyā*. Moscow: Nauka, 1993.
Al-Ahrī	Al-Ahrī, Abū Bakr. *Taʾrīkh-i Shaikh Uwais: An Important Source for the History of Adharbaījan*. Trans. H. B. Van Loon. The Hague: Mouton, 1954.
AM	Baladouni, Vahe, and Margaret Makepeace, eds. *Armenian Merchants of the Seventeenth and Early Eighteenth Century: English East India Company Sources*. Philadelphia: American Philosophical Society, 1998.
Ammianus	*Ammianus Marcellinus*. Trans. John C. Rolf. Loeb Classical Library. Cambridge, Mass.: Harvard University Press, 1958.
Ananias	Hewson, Robert, trans. *The Geography of Ananias of Širak: The Long and Short Recensions*. Wiesbaden: Reichert, 1992.
Arrian, *Ind.*	Arrian. *The History of Alexander and Indica*. Trans. P. A. Brunt. Loeb Classical Library. Cambridge, Mass.: Harvard University Press, 1989.
Al-Bākuwī	Al-Bākuwī, ʿAbd al-Rashīd. *Kitāb takhlis al-athir va ʿajāʾib al-malik al-qahār.* Trans. Z. M. Buniatov. Moscow: Nauka, 1971.

Bar Hebraeus	Bar Hebraeus. *The Chronography of Gregory Abū'l Faraj.* Trans. Ernest A. Wallis Budge. London: Oxford University Press, 1932. Vol. I.
Barbosa	Dames, Mansel Longworth, trans. *The Book of Duarte Barbosa.* 1918. Reprint Millwood, N.Y.: Kraus Reprint, 1967. 2 vols.
Bayhaqī/B	Bosworth, C. E., trans. *The History of Beyhaqi.* Cambridge, Mass.: Distributed by Harvard University Press, 2011. Vol. II.
Bayhaqī/F	Bayhaqī, Abū'l Fażl. *Tarīkh-i Bayhaqī.* Ed. ʿAlī Akbar Fayyaż. Tehran: Ferdowsi University Press, 1996.
Bell	Bell, John. *A Journey from St. Petersburg to Pekin, 1719–22.* Edinburgh: At the University Press, 1965.
Benjamin of Tudela	Adler, Marcus Nathan, trans. *The Itinerary of Benjamin of Tudela.* 1907. Reprint Malibu, Calif.: Pangloss Press, 1987.
Bernier	Bernier, François. *Travels in the Mogul Empire, A.D. 1656–1668.* 2nd ed. Oxford: Oxford University Press, 1934.
BF/D	Danīsh-pazhūh, Muḥammad Tāqī, ed. *Baḥr al-favāʿid.* Tehran: BNTK, 1966.
BF/M	Meisami, Julie Scott, trans. *The Sea of Precious Virtues (Baḥr al-favāʿid): A Medieval Islamic Mirror for Princes.* Salt Lake City: University of Utah Press, 1991.
BGR	al-Qaddūmī, Ghāda al-Ḥijjāwī, trans. *Book of Gifts and Rarities.* Cambridge, Mass.: Harvard University Press, 1996.
Al-Bīrūnī/B	Al-Biruni, Abu-r-Rakhan ibn Akhmed. *Sobranie svedenii dlia poznaiia dragotsennosti (Mineralogiia).* Trans. A. M. Beletnitskii. Moscow: Izdatel'stvo akademii nauk SSSR, 1963.
Al-Bīrūnī/K	Krenkow, Fritz, trans. "The Chapter on Pearls in the Book on Precious Stones by al-Bērūnī," pt. I. *Islamic Culture* (1941) 15: 399-421; pt. II (1942) 16: 21–36.
Al-Bīrūnī/S	Sachau, Edward C., trans. *Alberuni's India.* Reprint Delhi: Low Price Publications, 1989. 2 vols.
BS	*Beishi.* Beijing: Zhongguo shuju, 1983.

Carpini — Carpini, Friar Giovanni Di Plano. *The Story of the Mongols Whom We Call the Tartars*. Trans. Erik Hildinger. Boston: Branden, 1996.

Chardin — Chardin, John. *Travels in Persia, 1673–77*. 1927. Reprint New York: Dover, 1988.

Chaucer — *Canterbury Tales*. In Walter W. Skeat, ed., *The Complete Works of Geoffrey Chaucer*. Oxford: Clarendon Press, 1894. Vol. IV.

Cheng Jufu — Cheng Jufu. *Cheng xuelou wenji*. Taipei: Yuandai zhenben wenji, 1970.

Clavijo — Clavijo, Ruy Gonzales de. *Embassy to Tamerlane, 1403–6*. Trans. Guy Le Strange. London: Routledge, 1928.

CMS — Birell, Anne, trans. *The Classic of Mountains and Seas*. London: Penguin, 1999.

CP — Thackston, W. M., trans. *A Century of Princes: Sources on Timurid History and Art*. Cambridge, Mass.: Agha Khan Program for Islamic Architecture, 1989.

ČT — Sagaster, Klaus, ed. and trans. *Die Weisse Geschichte (Čaγan Teüke)*. Wiesbaden: Otto Harrassowitz, 1976.

CWT — Yule, Sir Henry, trans. *Cathay and the Way Thither, Being a Collection of Medieval Notices of China*. 1866. Reprint Taipei: Ch'eng-wen, 1966. 4 vols. in 2.

Darmasvāmin — Roerich, George, trans. *Biography of Darmasvāmin, a Tibetan Monk Pilgrim*. Patna: K. P. Jayaswal Research Institute, 1959.

Dasxuranc'i — Dasxuranc'i, Movsēs, *The History of the Caucasian Albanians*. Trans. C. J. F. Dowsett. London: Oxford University Press, 1961.

Al-Dawādārī — Ibn al-Dawādarī. *Kranz al-durar wa jāmi' al-ghurar*. Ed. Ulrich Haarmann. Cairo: Mafba'at 'Isā al-bābī al-Halabī wa shirkahū, 1971. Vol. VIII.

Dom. — Pouncy, Carolyn Johnston, trans. *The Domostroi: Rules for Russian Households in the Time of Ivan the Terrible*. Ithaca, N.Y.: Cornell University Press, 1994.

Drasxanakertc'i — Draskhanakerttsi, Iovannes. *Istoriia Armenii*. Trans. M. O. Dardinian-Melikian. Yerevan: Izdatel'stvo Sovetakan Grokh, 1986.

DRI	Carruthers, Douglas, ed. *The Desert Route to India, Being the Journals of Four Travellers*. London: Printed for the Hakluyt Society, 1929.
Dunaysarī	Dunaysarī, Shams al-Dīn Muḥammad. *Navādir al-tabādur li-tuḥfat al-bahādur*. Ed. Iraj Afshār and Muḥammad Tāqī Danīsh-pazhūh. Tehran: Pizhūhishgāh-i ʿulum-i insānī va mutālaʿāt-i farhangī, 2008.
Ełishē	Ełishē. *History of Vardan and the Armenian War*. Trans. Robert W. Thomson. Cambridge, Mass.: Harvard University Press, 1982.
Ennin	Reischauer, Edwin O., trans. *Ennin's Diary: The Record of a Pilgimage to China in Search of the Law*. New York: Ronald, 1955.
ESMH	Schuh, Dieter, trans. *Erlasse und Sendschreiben mongolischer Herrscher für tibetische Geistliche*. St. Augustin: VGH, 1977.
EVTRP	Morgan, E. Delmar, and C. H. Coote, eds. *Early Voyages and Travels to Russia and Persia by Anthony Jenkinson and Other Englishmen*. 1886. Reprint New York: Burt Franklin, 1963. 2 vols.
Fan Chengda	Hargett, James M., trans. *On the Road in Twelfth Century China: The Travel Diaries of Fan Chengda (1126–1193)*. Stuttgart: Franz Steiner, 1989.
Faxian	*Faxian zhuan jiaozhu*. Beijing: Zhonghua shuju, 2008.
Faxian/L	Legge, James, trans. *A Record of Buddhist Kingdoms: Being an Account by the Chinese Monk Fa-Hein of Travels in India and Ceylon*. 1886. Reprint New Delhi: Munshiran Manoharlal, 1991.
FCH	Blockley, R. C., trans. *The Fragmentary Classicising Historians of the Later Roman Empire*. Vol. II, *Text, Translation and Historiographical Notes*. Liverpool: Francis Cairns, 1983.
Fletcher	Fletcher, Giles. *Of the Russe Commonwealth*. Ed. Richard Pipes and John V. Fine, Jr. Cambridge Mass.: Harvard University Press, 1966.
Fryer	Fryer, John. *A New Account of East India and Persia, Being Nine Years' Travels, 1672–1681*. Ed. William Crooke. 1909. Reprint Millwood, N.Y.: Kraus Reprint, 1967. 3 vols.

GC	Vivian, Katherine, trans. *The Georgian Chronicle: The Period of Giorgi Lasha*. Amsterdam: Adolf M. Hakkert, 1991.
GLR	Sørensen, Per K., trans. *A Fourteenth Century Tibetan Historical Work: rGyal-rabs gsal-bai me-loṅ*. Copenhagen: Akademisk, 1986.
GOT	Tekin, Talât, trans. *A Grammar of Orkhon Turkic*. Uralic and Altaic Series 69. Bloomington: Indiana Aniversity Publications, 1968.
Grigor of Akancʿ	Blake, Robert P., and Richard N. Frye, trans. "History of the Nation of Archers (The Mongols) by Grigor of Akancʿ." *Harvard Journal of Asiatic Studies* (1949) 12: 269–399.
Ḥ-ʿA	Minorsky, V., trans. *Ḥudūd al-ʿAlum*. 2nd ed. London: Luzac, 1970.
Ḥafiẓ-i Abrū/B	Ḥāfiẓ-i Abrū. *Ẓayl jāmiʿ al-tavārīkh-i Rashīdī*. Ed. K. Bayānī. Salsatat-i instishārāt-i aṣar millī, no. 88. Tehran: Anjuman-i Athar, 1971.
Ḥāfiẓ-i Abrū/M	Maitra, K. M., trans. *A Persian Embassy to China, Being an Extract from Zubatu't Tawarikh of Hafiz Abru*. Reprint New York: Paragon, 1970.
HCGVC	Perfecky, George A., trans. *The Hypatian Codex,* vol. II, *The Galician-Volynian Chronicle*. Munich: Wilhelm Fink, 1973.
Hetʿum	Hayton. *La flor des istoires de la terre d'Orient. Recueil des historiens des croisades, documents arméniens*. Paris: Imprimerie nationale, 1906. Vol II.
Hetʿum/B	Boyle, John A., trans. "The Journey of Hetʿum I, King of Lesser Armenia to the Court of the Great Khan Möngke." *Central Asiatic Journal* (1964) 9: 175–89.
Hex.	Golden, Peter B., ed. *The King's Dictionary: The Rasūlid Hexaglot, Fourteenth Century Vocabularies in Arabic, Persian, Turkic, Greek, Armenian and Mongol*. Leiden: Brill, 2000.
HG	Brosset, M., trans. *Histoire de la Géorgie,* pt. 1, *Histoire ancienne jusqu'en 1469 de JC.* St. Petersburg: Académie des sciences, 1850.
HHS	Fan Ye. *Hou Hanshu*. Beijing: Zhonghua shuju, 1973.

HI	Elliot, H. M., and John Dawson, trans. *The History of India as Told by Its Own Historians: The Muhammadan Period*. 1867. Reprint New York: AMS Press, 1966. Vol. III.
Huan Kuan	Huan Kuan. *Yantie lun jiaozhu*. Beijing: Zhonghua shuju, 1992. 2 vols.
HYYY	Mostaert, Antoine, trans., and Igor de Rachewiltz, ed. *Le matérial du Houa i i iu de Houng-ou (1389)*. Brussels: Institut belge des hautes études chinois, 1977–95. 2 vols.
Ibn ʿArabshāh	Ibn Arabshah, Ahmed. *Tamerlane or Timur the Great Amir*. Trans. J. H. Sanders. Reprint Lahore: Progressive Books, n.d.
Ibn Baṭṭuṭah	Gibb, H. A. R., trans. *The Travels of Ibn Baṭṭuṭa*. Cambridge: Cambridge University Press for the Hakluyt Society, 1958–94. 4 vols.
Ibn Faḍlān	Ibn Faḍlān. *Mission to the Volga*. Trans. James E. Montgomery. In *TATB*.
Ibn Jubayr	Ibn Jobair. *Voyages*. Trans. Maurice Gaudefroy-Demombynes. Paris: Librairie orientaliste Paul Guenther, 1949–65. 4 vols.
Ibn Khaldūn	Ibn Khaldūn. *The Muqaddimah: An Introduction to History*. Trans. Franz Rosenthal. New York: Pantheon, 1958. 3 vols.
Ibn Riḍwān/D	Dols, Michael W., trans. *Medieval Islamic Medicine: Ibn Riḍwān's "On the Prevention of Bodily Ills in Egypt."* Berkeley: University of California Press, 1984.
Ibn Riḍwān/G	Grand'Henry, Jacques, trans. *Le livre de la méthode du médecin de ʿAlī b Riḍwān (998–1067)*. Louvain-la-Neuve: Université catholique de Louvain, Institut orientaliste, 1979–84. 2 vols.
Ibrāhīm	Ibrāhīm, Muḥammad ibn. *The Ship of Sulaiman*. Trans. John O'Kane. New York: Columbia University Press, 1972.
Isadore	Schoff, Wilfred H., trans. *Parthian Stations by Isadore of Charax*. Reprint Chicago: Ares, 1989.
Jāḥiẓ	Pellat, Charles, trans. "Ǧāḥiẓiana I: Le *Kitāb al-tabaṣṣur bi-l Tiǧara* attribué à Ǧāḥiẓ." *Arabica* (1955) 2: 153–65.

JS	Rogers, Michael C., trans. *The Chronicle of Fu Chien* [from the *Jinshu*]: *A Case Study in Exemplar History*. Berkeley: University of California Press, 1968.
JTS	*Jiu Tangshu*. Beijing: Zhonghua shuju, 1975.
Juvaynī/B	Juvaynī, ʿAtā-Malik. *The History of the World Conqueror*. Trans. John Andrew Boyle. Cambridge, Mass.: Harvard University Press, 1958. 2 vols.
Juvaynī/Q	Juvaynī, ʿAtā-Malik. *Ta'rīkh-i Jahāngushā*. Ed. Mirzā Muḥammad Qazvīnī. London: Luzac, 1912–37. 3 vols.
Jūzjānī/L	Jūzjānī. *Ṭabaqāt-i nāṣirī*. Ed. W. Nassau Lees. Bibliotheca Indica 44. Calcutta: College Press, 1864.
Jūzjānī/R	Jūzjānī, *Ṭabaqāt-i nāṣirī*. Trans. H. G. Raverty. Reprint New Delhi: Oriental Book Reprint, 1970. 2 vols.
KDA	Chunakova, O. M., trans. *Kniga Deianii Ardashir syna Papaka*. Moscow: Nauka, 1987.
Khiṭā'ī	Khiṭā'ī, ʿAlī Akbar. *Khiṭā'ī-nāmah*. Ed. Iraj Afshār. Tehran: Asian Cultural Documentation Center for UNESCO, 1979.
Khorezmi	Khorezmi. *Mukhäbbät-name*. Trans. E. N. Nadzhip. Moscow: Izdatel'stvo Vostochnoi literatury, 1961.
KI	*Kazanskaia istoriia*. In *Pamiatniki literatury drevnei Rus: Seredina XVI veka*. Moscow: Khudozhestvennaia literatura, 1985.
Kirakos/B	Boyle, John Andrew, trans. "Kirakos of Ganjak on the Mongols." *Central Asiatic Journal* (1963) 8: 199–214.
Kirakos/Kh	Kirakos Gandzaketsi. *Istoriia Armenii*. Trans. L. A. Khanlarian. Moscow: Nauka, 1976.
LAÖPB	Mostaert, Antoine, and Francis W. Cleaves, trans. and eds. *Les lettres de 1289 et 1305 des Ilkhan Aryun et Öljeitü à Philippe le Bel*. Cambridge, Mass.: Harvard University Press, 1962.
Li Zhichang	Li Zhichang. *Xiyu ji*. In *MGSL*.
Li Zhichang/W	Li Chih-ch'ang. *The Travels of an Alchemist*. Trans. Arthur Waley. London: Routledge and Kegan Paul, 1963.
Linschoten	Linschoten, John Huyghen van. *The Voyage to the East Indies*. Ed. Arthur Coke Burnell and P. A. Tiele. London: Hakluyt Society Publications, 1985, 2 vols.

LKA Strong, John S., trans. *The Legend of King Aśoka*. Princeton: Princeton University Press, 1983.

LMJT Goitein, S. D., trans. *Letters of Medieval Jewish Traders*. Princeton: Princeton University Press, 1973.

LS *Liaoshi*. Beijing: Zhonghua shuju, 1974.

Ma Huan Ma Huan. *Ying-yai sheng-lan: The Overall Survey of the Oceans' Shores*. Trans. J. V. G. Mills. Cambridge: For the Hakluyt Society, 1970.

Mandeville Mosely, C. W. R. D., trans. *Travels of Sir John Mandeville*. New York: Penguin, 1983.

Al-Maqrīzī Al-Maqrīzī, Aḥmad. *Kitāb al-sulūk li ma'rifat duwal al-mulūk*. Ed. M. M. Ziyādah. Cairo: Lajnal al-ta'ilif wa al-tarjamah wa al-nashr, 1956–73. 4 vols. in 12 pts.

Marco Polo Marco Polo. *The Description of the World*. Trans. A. C. Moule and Paul Pelliot. London: Routledge, 1938. Vol. I.

Menander Blockley, R. C., trans. *The History of Menander the Guardsman*. Liverpool: Francis Cairns, 1985.

MGSL Wang Guowei, ed. *Menggu shiliao sizhang*. Taipei: Zhenzhong shuju, 1975.

Mīrzā Ḥaydar Mirza Muhammad Haidar. *A History of the Mughals of Central Asia*. Trans. E. Denison Ross. Reprint New York: Praeger, 1970.

MKK Budge, Ernest A. Wallis, trans. *The Monks of Kūblāi Khān*. London: Religious Tract Society, 1928.

MM Dawson, Christopher, ed. *The Mongol Mission: Narratives and Letters of the Franciscan Missionaries in Mongolia and China in the Thirteenth and Fourteenth Centuries*. New York: Sheed and Ward, 1955.

MMR Di Cosmo, Nicola, and Dalizhabu Bao, trans. *Manchu-Mongol Relations on the Eve of the Qing Conquest: A Documentary History*. Leiden: Brill, 2003.

MREAS Bretschneider, Emil, trans. *Medieval Researches from East Asiatic Sources*. London: Routledge and Kegan Paul, 1967. 2 vols.

MS *Mingshi*. Beijing: Zhonghua shuju, 1974.

MTMW Lopez, Robert S., and Irving W. Raymond, trans. *Medieval Trade in the Mediterranean World*. New York: Columbia University Press, 1990.

Mufaḍḍal/B — Moufazzal, Ibn Abil-Faza'il. *Histroire des Sultans Mamelouks*. Trans. E. Blochet. Patrologia orientales, XII, fasc. 3, no. 59. Reprint Turnout: Brepols, 1982.

Mufaḍḍal/K — Kortantamer, Samira, trans. *Ägypten und Syria zwischen 1317 und 1341 in der Chronik des Mufaḍḍal b. Abī l-Faḍā'il.* Freiburg: Klaus Schwarz, 1973.

Al-Nadīm — Dodge, Bayard, trans. *The Fihrist of al-Nadim: A Tenth Century Survey of Muslim Culture*. New York: Columbia University Press, 1970. 2 vols.

Narshakhī — Narshakhī. *The History of Bukhara*. Trans. Richard N. Frye. Cambridge, Mass.: Medieval Academy of America, 1954.

Al-Nasawī — Al-Nasawī, Muḥammad. *Sīrat al-Ṣulṭān Jalāl-Dīn Mankubirtī*. Ed. H. Hamdī. Cairo: Dār al-fikr al-ʿArabī, 1953.

NC — Zenkovsky, Serge A., and Betty Jean Zenkovsky, trans. *The Nikonian Chronicle*. Princeton: Kingston and Darwin Press, 1984–89. 5 vols.

Nikitin — Nikitin, Afanasii. *Khozhdenie za tri moria*. 2nd ed. Moscow: Izdatel'stvo akademii nauk SSSR, 1958.

NITP — Grey, C., trans. *A Narrative of Italian Travels in Persia*. London: Hakluyt Society, 1875.

Niẓām al-Mulk — Niẓām al-Mulk. *Siyāsat nāmah*. Ed. ʿAbbās Iqbāl. Tehran: Intishārāt-i asātīr, 1990.

Niẓāmī — Nizami Ganjavi. *The Haft Paykar: A Medieval Persian Romance*. Trans. Julie Scott Meisami. Oxford: Oxford University Press, 1995.

Olearius — Baron, Samuel H., trans. *The Travels of Olearius in Seventeenth-Century Russia*. Stanford: Stanford University Press, 1967.

Pegolotti — Pegolotti, Francesco Balducci. *La Practica della Mercatura*. Ed. Allan Evans. Cambridge, Mass.: Medieval Academy of America, 1936.

Peng and Xu — Peng Daya and Xu Ting. *Heida shilue*. In *MGSL*.

Pliny — Pliny, *Natural History*. Trans. H. Rockham and W. H. S. Jones. Loeb Classical Library. Cambridge, Mass.: Harvard University Press, 1960–67.

PME — Casson, Lionel, trans. *The Periplus Maris Erythraei*. Princeton: Princeton University Press, 1989.

Possevino — Graham, Hugh E., trans. *The Moscovia of Antonio Possevino.* University of Pittsburgh Series in Russian and East European Studies, no. 1. Pittsburgh: University Center for International Studies, 1977.

PR — Elverskog, Johan, trans. *The Pearl Rosary: Mongol Historiography in Early Nineteenth Century Ordos*. Publications of the Mongolia Society, Occasional Paper no. 26. Bloomington, 2007.

PRDK — Demidova, N. F., and V. S. Miasnikov, eds. *Pervye russkie diplomaty v Kitae*. Moscow: Izdatel'stvo Nauka, 1966.

Procopius, *HW* — Procopius. *History of the Wars*. Trans. H. B. Dewing. Loeb Classical Library. London: Heinemann, 2001.

PSRL — *Polnoe sobranie russkikh letopisei*. Vol. II, *Ipat'evskaia letopis.* Moscow: Iazyki russkoi kul'tury, 1998.

Qāshānī/A — Qāshānī, Abū al-Qasīm. *ʿArā'is al-javāhir va nafā'is al-aṭā'ib*. Ed. Iraj Afshār. Tehran: al-Maʿī, 2007.

Qāshānī/H — Qāshānī, Abū al-Qasīm. *Ta'rīkh-i Ūljaytū*. Ed. M. Hambly, Tehran: BTNK, 1969.

Qazvīnī, *NQ* — Qazvīnī, Ḥamd-Allāh Mustawfī. *The Geographical Part of the Nuzhāt al- Qulūb*. Trans. Guy Le Strange. London: Luzac, 1919.

Qazvīnī, *ZSNQ* — Qazvīnī, Ḥamd-Allāh Mustawfī. *The Zoological Section of the Nuzhāt al-Qulūb*. Trans. J. Stephenson. London: Royal Asiatic Society, 1928.

Quan Heng — Quan Heng. *Gengshen waishi*. Taipei: Guangwen shuju, 1968.

Quintus Curtius — Quintus Curtius. *History of Alexander*. Trans. John C. Rolfe. Loeb Classical Library. Cambridge, Mass.: Harvard University Press, 1946.

Rashīd/B — Rashīd al-Dīn. *The Successors of Genghis Khan*. Trans. John Andrew Boyle. New York: Columbia University Press. 1971.

Rashīd/D — Rashīd al-Dīn. *Savāniḥ al-afkār-i Rashīdī*. Ed. M. T. Dānish-pazhūh. Tehran: Instishārāt-i kitābkhānah-i markazī va markaz-i asnad, 1979.

Rashīd/J — Jahn, Karl, trans. *Die Indiengeschichte der Rašīd ad-Dīn*. Vienna: Herman Böhlaus, 1980.

Rashīd/K — Rashīd al-Dīn. *Jāmiʿ al-tavārīkh*. Ed. B. Karīmī. Tehran: Eqbal, 1959. 2 vols.

Rashīd/M — Martinez, A. P., trans. "The Third Portion of the Story of Gāzān Xān in Rašhīdu'd-Dīn's *Ta'rīx-e mobārak-e Gāzānī*," pt. I. *Archivum Eurasiae Medii Aevi* (1986–87) 6: 41–127; pt. II (1992–94) 8: 99–206.

Rashīd/S — Rashīd al-Dīn. *Athār va aḥyā*. Ed. M. Sutūdah and Iraj Afshār. Tehran: University Press, 1989.

Rashīd/Q — Raschid-Eldin. *Histoire des Mongols de la Perse*. Trans. Étienne Quartremère. Reprint Amsterdam: Oriental Press, 1968.

RBK — Berry, Loyd E., and Robert O. Crummy, eds. *Rude and Barbarous Kingdom: Russia in the Accounts of Sixteenth Century English Voyagers.* Madison: University of Wisconsin Press, 1968.

RCS — Dmytryshyn, Basil, et al., trans. *Russia's Conquest of Siberia*, vol. I, *A Documentary Record, 1558–1700*. Portland, Ore.: Western Imprints, 1985.

Remezov — Remezov, Semen Ul'ianovich. *Istoriia sibirskaia.* In *Pamiatniki literatury drevnei Rusi, XVII vek*, bk. II. Moscow: Khudozhestvennaia literatura, 1989.

RMO — Slesarchuk, G. I., ed. *Russko-mongolskie otnosheniia, 1654–1685: Sbornik dokumentov.* Moscow: Vostochnoi literatury RAN, 1996.

Roe — Foster, William, ed. *The Embassy of Sir Thomas Roe to the Court of the Great Mogul, 1615–1619*. Reprint Nendeln: Kraus Reprint, 1967. 2 vols.

RTC — Majeska, George P., trans. *Russian Travelers to Constantinople in the Fourteenth and Fifteenth Centuries*. Washington, D.C.: Dumbarton Oaks, 1984.

Rubruck — Jackson, Peter, trans., and David Morgan, ed. *The Mission of Friar William of Rubruck*. London: Hakluyt Society, 1990.

Rust'haveli — Rust'haveli, Shot'ha. *The Man in the Panther's Skin*. Trans. Marjory Scott Wardrop. London: Luzac, 1966.

Al-Sābi' — Al-Sābi', Hilāl. *Rusūm dār al-khilāfah: The Rules and Regulations of the 'Abbāsid Court*. Trans. Elie A. Salem. Beirut: American University of Beirut, 1977.

Al-Samarqandī — Levey, Martin, and Noury al-Khaledy, trans. *The Medical Formulary of al-Samarqandī*. Philadelphia: University of Pennsylvania Press, 1967.

Sayf	Sayf ibn Muḥammad ibn Yaʿqūb al-Havarī. *Taʾrīkh nāmah-i Harāt*. Ed. M. Ṣiddīqī. Calcutta: Baptist University Press, 1944.
SBM	Budge, Ernest A. Wallis, trans. *The Syriac Book of Medicines: Syrian Anatomy, Pathology and Therapeutics in the Early Middle Ages*. Reprint Amsterdam: APA-Philo Press, 1976. Vol. II.
SCBM	Xu Mengxin, comp. *Sanchao beimeng huibian*. Shanghai: Guji chubanshe, 2008.
Schiltberger	Telfer, J. Buchan, trans. *The Bondage and Travels of Johann Schiltberger.* London: Hakluyt Society, 1878.
SH	de Rachewiltz, Igor, trans. *The Secret History of the Mongols: A Mongolian Epic Chronicle of the Thirteenth Century*. Leiden: Brill, 2004. 2 vols.
Shao Yuanping	Shao Yuanping. *Yuanshi leibian.* Taipei: Guangwen shuju, 1968.
Al-Sīrāfī	Al-Shīrāfī, Abū Zayd. *Accounts of China and India.* Trans. Tim Mackintosh-Smith. In *TATB*.
Sima Guang	de Crespigney, Rafe, trans. *To Establish Peace: Being the Chronicle of the Later Han for the Years 189–220 as Recorded in Chapters 59 to 69 of the Zizhi tongjian of Sima Guang.* Canberra: Faculty of Asian Studies, Australian National University, 1996. 2 vols.
SJV	Kane, Daniel, trans. *The Sino-Jurchen Vocabulary of the Bureau of Interpreters*. Indiana University Uralic and Altaic Series, 153. Bloomington: Research Institute for Inner Asian Studies, 1989.
SMOIZO	Tizengauzen, V. G., trans. *Sbornik materialy otnosiashchikhsia k istorii Zolotoi Ordy*, vol. II, *Izvlecheniia iz persidskikh sochinenii*. Moscow: Izdatel'stvo Akademii Nauk SSSR, 1941.
Song Yingxing	Sung Ying-sing. *Tien-kung-kai-wu: Exploitation of the Works of Nature*. Taipei: China Academy, 1980.
SPKB	Dmitriev, L. A., and O. P. Likhacheva, eds. *Skazaniia o kulikovskoi bitve*. Leningrad: Nauka, 1982.
SWQZL	*Shengwu qinzheng lu*. In *MGSL*.
Al-Ṭabarī	*The History of al-Ṭabarī.* Trans. various hands. Albany: State University of New York Press, 1985–99. 39 vols.

Tacitus, *Agr.* — Tacitus. *Agricola, Germania, Dialogus*. Trans. M. Hutton. Loeb Classical Library. Cambridge, Mass.: Harvard University Press, 1970.

Tao Zongyi — Tao Zongyi. *Nancun chuogeng lu*. Beijing: Zhonghua shuju, 2004.

TATB — Kennedy, Philip F., and Shawkat M. Toorawa, trans. *Two Arabic Travel Books*. New York: New York University Press, 2014.

Teixeira — Sinclair, William F., trans. *The Travels of Pedro Teixeira.* London: Hakluyt Society, 1902.

TGPM — Howes, Robert Craig, trans. *The Testaments of the Grand Princes of Moscow*. Ithaca, N.Y.: Cornell University Press, 1967.

Thaʿālibī — Bosworth, C. E., trans. *The Book of Curious and Entertaining Information: The Laṭāʾif al-maʿārif of Thaʿālibī*. Edinburgh: University of Edinburgh Press, 1968.

Theophanes — Turtledove, Harry, trans. *The Chronicle of Theophanes.* Philadelphia: University of Pennsylvania Press, 1982.

Theophylact — Whitby, Michael, and Mary Whitby, trans. *The History of Theophylact Simocatta*. Oxford: Clarendon Press, 1988.

THPN — Mair, Victor H., trans. *Tun-huang Popular Narratives*. Cambridge: Cambridge University Press, 1983.

TLT — Thomas, F. W., trans. *Tibetan Literary Texts and Documents Concerning Turkistan*. London: Luzac, 1951–55. Vols. II–III.

TMC — Hartwell, Robert M., trans. *Tribute Missions to China, 960–1126*. Philadelphia: 1983.

TTK — Emmerick, R. E., trans. *Tibetan Texts Concerning Khotan*. London: Oxford University Press, 1967.

TTP — Alderly, Lord Stanley, ed. *Travels to Tana and Persia by Josafa Barbaro and Ambrogio Contarini*. London: Hakluyt Society Publications, 1873.

TTT — Bang, W., and A. von Gabain. "Türkische Turfan Texte," vol. II, "Manichaica." *Sitzungsberichte der Preussische Akademie der Wissenschaften, Phil.-Hist. Klasse* (1929) 22: 411–29.

Ṭūsī/B — Boyle, John Andrew, trans. "The Death of the Last *ʿAbbāsid Caliph*: A Contemporary Muslim Account." *Journal of Semitic Studies* (1961) 6: 145–61.

Ṭūsī/M — Minorsky, Vladimir, trans. "Naṣīr al-Dīn Ṭūsī on Finance." In his *Iranica: Twenty Articles.* Hertford: Stephen Austin, 1964.

TYH — Molé, Gabriella, trans. *The T'u-yü-hun from the Northern Wei to the Time of the Five Dynasties*. Rome: Istituto Italiano per il Medio ed Estremo Oriente, 1970.

TZTG — *Tongzhi tiaoge*. Hangzhou: Zhejiang guji chubanshe, 1986.

UE — Mackerras, Colin, trans. *The Uighur Empire According to the T'ang Dynastic Histories.* Canberra: Australian National University, 1972.

Al-ʿUmarī/L — Al-ʿUmarī, ibn Fazl Allāh. *Das mongolische Weltreich: Al-ʿUmarī's Darstellung der mongolischen Reiche in seinem Werke Masālik al-abṣār fī Mamālik al-amṣār*. Trans. Klaus Lech. Wiesbaden: Otto Harrassowitz, 1968.

Al-ʿUmarī/S — Spies, Otto, trans. *Ibn Faḍlallāh al-ʿOmarī's Bericht über Indien in seinem Werke Masālik al-abṣār fī mamālik al-amṣār*. Leipzig: Otto Harrassowitz, 1943.

Vaṣṣāf — Vaṣṣāf, ʿAbd Allāh ibn Faḍl Allāh. *Ta'rīkh-i Vaṣṣāf.* Reprint Tehran: Ibn-i Sina, 1959.

VSMY — Ligeti, Louis, trans. "Un vocabulaire sino-mongol des Yuan: Le *Tche-Yuan yi-yu.*" *Acta Orientalia Academiae Scientiarum Hungarica* (1990) 44: 259–77.

Wang Shidian — Wang Shidian. *Mishu zhi.* Taipei: Weiwen dushu banshe, 1976.

XTS — *Xin Tangshu*. Beijing: Zhonghua shuju, 1975.

Xuanzang — Xuanzang. *Da Tang xiyu ji jiaozhu*. Beijing: Zhonghua shuju, 2008, 2 vols.

Xuanzang/B — Hiuen Tsiang. *Si-yu-ki: Buddhist Records of the Western World*. Trans. Samuel Beal. Reprint Delhi: Oriental Books Reprint, 1969. 2 vols.

Yang Xuanzhi — Yang Hsüan-chih. *A Record of Buddhist Monasteries in Lo-yang*. Trans. Yi-t'ung Wang. Princeton: Princeton University Press, 1984.

Yang Yu — Yang Yu. *Shanju Xinhua.* Zhi bu zu zhai congshu ed.

Yazdī	Yazdī, Sharaf al-Dīn ʿAlī. *Zafar-nāmah*. Ed. M. ʿAbbāsī. Tehran: Chāp-i rangin, 1957. 2 vols.
YCS	Armstrong, Terence, ed. *Yermak's Campaign in Siberia: A Selection of Documents*. Trans. Tatiana Minorsky and David Wileman. London: Hakluyt Society, 1975.
YDBH	Cai Meibiao, ed. *Yuandai baihua bei jilu*. Beijing: Kexue chubanshe, 1955.
Ye Longli	Ye Longli. *Qidan guoji*. Shanghai: Guji chubanshe, 1985.
Yelu Chucai	de Rachewiltz, Igor, trans. "The *Hsi-yu lu* by Yeh-lü Ch'u-ts'ai." *Monumenta Serica* (1962) 21: 1–128.
YS	*Yuanshi*. Beijing: Zhonghua shuju, 1978.
Yūsuf	Yūsuf Khaṣṣ Ḥājib. *Wisdom of Royal Glory (Kutadgu Bilig): A Turko-Islamic Mirror for Princes*. Trans. Robert Dankoff. Chicago: University of Chicago Press, 1983.
YWL	Su Tianjue, comp. *Yuan wẹnlei*. Taipei: Shijie shuju yingxing, 1967.
Al-ẓāhir	Ibn ʿAbd al-ẓāhir, Muḥyī al-Dīn. *Tashrīf al-ayyām wa al-ʿuṣur fī sīrāt al-Malik al-Manṣūr.* Ed. Murād Kāmil. Cairo: al-Sharikah al-ʿArabiyāh lil-tibāʾah wa al-nashr, 1961.
Zhao Hong	Zhao Hong. *Mengda beilu*. In *MGSL*.
Zhao Rugua	Zhao Rugua. *Zhufan zhi jiaoshi.* Beijing: Zhonghua shuju, 1996.
Zhao Rugua/H	Chau Ju-kua. *His Work on the Chinese and Arab Trade in the Twelfth and Thirteenth Centuries, Entitled Chu-fan-chi*. Trans. Friedrich Hirth and W. W. Rockhill. Reprint Taipei: Literature House, 1965.
Zhou Mi	Zhou Mi. *Guixin zazhi.* Beijing: Zhonghua shuju, 1988.
ZS	Miller, Roy Andrew, trans. *Accounts of Western Nations in the History of the Northern Chou* [*Zhoushu*]. Berkeley: University of California Press, 1959.

NOTES

INTRODUCTION

1. I have used the standard scholarly transliterations of Mongolian and Turkic names—Chinggis Qan, Qubilai, and others—since there are no established popular forms.

2. Marco Polo, 231; and CWT, II, 228–29.

3. Khazanov 1994, 231 ff.

4. "Southern seas" collectively designates the South China Sea, Indian Ocean, Persian Gulf, the Arabian Sea, and the Red Sea.

5. Shaffer 1994, 1–21.

6. Cf. Abalahin 2011, 683–88.

7. Christian 2000, 7 ff.

8. Schneider 1977, 20–29.

CHAPTER 1

1. My treatment of the natural properties of pearls is based on Landman et al. 2001, 123–61.

2. Donkin 1998, 44–50.

3. Renfrew 1988, 143–44 and 158–62.

4. Maquet 1993, 30–40.

5. Pliny, XXXVII.204; *Qur'ān*, *Sura* 55.22–33; and al-Sīrāfī, 124–25.

6. Theophylact, IV.16.22; al-Bīrūnī/K, pt. I, 412–13; Rust'haveli, v. 16 and 836; Nīẓāmī, v. 4.72, 8.23, 32.411 and 33.144; *CP*, 139; *THPN*, 124; al-Nadīm, II, 856; Yūsuf, 160, 183, 207, 223, 253, and 258; and Khorezmi 36 and 76 (v. 112).

7. Goitein 1967–93, IV, 26; Nīẓāmī, v. 45.210; and Serruys 1967, 254.

8. Jāḥiẓ, 155–56; Gode 1957, 130–33; Clunas 1991, 33; and Needham 1959, 648 and 669.

9. Pliny, IX.112–15 and Jāḥiẓ, 155–56.

10. Al-Bīrūnī/K, pt. I, 403–6, and pt. II, 21, 23 and 32–33; Qāshānī/A, 92–100; and Fryer, II, 363–64 and 367.

11. *BS*, ch. 97, 3222, and al-Bīrūnī/K, pt. I, 414–17, and pt. II, 24. See also *ZS*, 13 and 74 (15b); Yang Xuanzhi, 226; *LS*, ch. 12, 134; and Wittfogel and Feng 1949, 259.

12. The comments of Quintas Curtius, IX.i.29–30, are typical.

13. Zhao Rugua, 204, and Zhao Rugua/H, 230.

14. *BGR*, §§ 93 and 346, and al-Bīrūnī/B, 144.

15. *BGR*, §§ 18, 22, 29, 93, 112, 116, 150, 194, 218, 224, 252, 333 and 398; Qāshānī/A, 92; Ma Huan, 155; and Barbosa, I, 55, 81, and 93–94.

16. Al-Bīrūnī/B, 143–44; *HG*, 560–61; and Behrens-Abouseif 2014, 56–57.

17. *BGR*, § 22; Ibn Baṭṭuṭah, III, 683; and *PR*, 54 and 116 (18v3).

18. *YS*, ch. 180, 4160, and *MREAS*, I, 161–62.

19. Al-Bīrūnī/K, pt. II, 24; Ibn Khaldūn, I, 367; and Mokri 1960, 390–95.

20. Morony 1984, 50, and Behrens-Abouseif 2014, 128.

21. Al-Bīrūnī/B, 133–35, and al-Bīrūnī/S, I, 211.

22. For the distribution of species, see Landman et al. 2001, 54, 56, and 132 Donkin 1998, 29–35.

23. Ye Longli, ch. 26, 246; Vorob'ev 1975, 89; Vorob'ev 1983, 19, 27, 29, 62, and 90; James 1888, 14 and 282; Schlesinger 2017, 60, 65–64, and 68–74; and Hosie 1904, 166–67.

24. Marco Polo, 357, and Enoki 1957, 28 and 30–32.

25. Schafer 1967, 160–62, and Schafer 1970, 8–10 and 12.

26. Donkin 1998, 195–98; Huan Kuan, I, 29; and Anonymous 1914, 184–86.

27. Yang Xuanzhi, 205; Zhao Rugua, 50, 55, and 141; Zhao Rugua/H, 71, 77, and 160; and *H-'A*, 57.

28. Marco Polo, 365.

29. Ray 1998, 14, 17–19, 22, and 41; Raman 1991, 131; and Donkin 1998, 57–65.

30. Pliny, VI.89; *PME*, 85, 87, and 89; Ananias, 75a and 76; al-Sīrāfī, 24–25 and 112–13; and *H-'A*, 61 and 86.

31. Zhao Rugua, 67 and 76; Zhao Rugua/H, 88 and 96; Marco Polo, 381; *CWT*, II, 172; Rashīd/J, 37 and 41 and 335r and 336v; Qazvīnī, *NQ*, 224; al-Bākuwī, 18; Ibrahīm, 168; and Fryer, I, 129.

32. Isadore, 11; *PME*, 71; Arrian, *Ind*., 38.3; Ananias, 72; Barbosa, I, 81; and Fryer, II, 191 and 364–65.

33. *Ḥ-'A*, 58 and 127; *'A-D*, 57 and 358; Qazvīnī, *NQ*, 130 and 136; and Schiltberger, 45 and 164.

34. *PME*, 73 (36); Tha'ālabī, 132; *'A-D*, 224, 232, 520, and 525; Zhao Rugua, 90 and 108; Zhao Rugua/H, 116, 133, and 134; and 'Umarī/L, 97 and 156.

35. Nikitin, 24 and 84; al-Sīrāfī, 130–31; al-Bākuwī, 24–25; Teixeira, 173; Barbosa, I, 82 and 93–94; Chardin, 166; and Sykes 1902, 241.

36. *Ḥ-'A*, 147; *'A-D*, 57 and 348; and Qazvīnī, *NQ*, 226.

37. *PME*, 73 (36); Zhao Rugua, 203–4; Zhao Rugua/H, 229; Marco Polo, 383–84 and 402; and *CWT*, II, 146.

38. Ananias, 75a and 76; Marco Polo, 381; and *CWT*, II, 172 and III, 231 ff.

39. Pliny, IX.106; Jāḥiẓ, 156 and 160; Niẓāmī, v. 11.7 and 25.64; Qazvīnī, *NQ*, 226; Ibrāhīm, 168–69; Teixeira, 179; and Fryer, II, 365, and III, 9.

40. *YS*, ch. 63, 1571; and *MREAS*, II, 129–30.

41. Tacitus, *Agr*., 12.5; Ammianus, XXIII.6.88; Harada 1971, 72–73; Serruys 1967, 206–7; Holmes 1934, 198–99; and Cammann 1950, 60.

42. See al-Bīrūnī/B, 41; and *RBK*, 305.

43. Tao Zongyi, ch. 20, 243.

44. Wang 2011, 104–10.

45. Laufer 1915a, 55–71; Schafer 1963, 237–39; Nadeliaev et al.1969, 336; and Eitel 1976, 96 and 110–11.

46. *BS*, ch. 97, 3228 and 3239.

47. Song Yingxing, 440, and *YS*, ch. 23, 519–20.

48. Rockhill 1916, pt. II, 270–71; Song Yingxing, 440–41; *BGR*, §§ 106, 112, and 218; al-Bīrūnī/B, 142-51; and Procopius, *HW*, I.iv.16

49. *KDA*, 58, 80, and 127; and al-Bīrūnī/K, pt. II, 23.

50. Procopius, *HW*, I.iv.16.

51. Eberhard 1968, 381–82.

52. Al-Bīrūnī/B, 49, 73, and 81; and Yūsuf, 207.

53. *THPN*, 163; Huan Kuan, I, 42, and II, 438; and Song Yingxing, 437.

54. Pliny, IX.106; Arrian, *Ind.*, 8.13; and Gonda 1991, 32, 61, 77, and 130.

55. *King Henry V*, IV.i.280.

56. Pegolotti, 24; and *CWT*, III, 157.

57. Theophylact, IV.3.13; Yang Xuanzhi, 157; Yūsuf, 46 and 214; and ʿUmarī/S, 3 and 29, text, and 19 and 55, trans.

58. *SH*, §§ 238, 248, 252, 260, 265, 272, 273, and 279; and Cleaves 1959, 45 and 61.

59. Chaucer, 63 (v.2161).

CHAPTER 2

1. The best introduction is Donkin 1998, 119–32 and 157–65.

2. Even the well informed naturalist Song Yingxing, 438, was badly misled.

3. Bowen 1951a, 161–80; Bowen 1951b, 395–400; Rentz 1951, 397–402; and Mokri 1960, 381–88.

4. Al-Bīrūnī/K, pt. II, 27; Ibn Baṭuṭṭah, II, 407–9; Schafer 1967, 52–53 and 85–86; and Schafer 1970, 58 and 68.

5. Al-Bīrūnī/B, 136–42; Ibn Jubayr, I, 79; Zhao Rugua, 204; Zhao Rugua/H, 229–30; Shao Yuanping, ch. 42, 53a; *MREAS*, I, 145; Marco Polo, 381; Ibn Baṭṭuṭah, II, 407–9; Teixeira, 177–79; and Chardin, 166.

6. Song Yingxing, 438–41; and Needham 1971, 668–69.

7. Schafer 1967, 161; and Needham 1971, 669–74.

8. Kunz and Stevenson 1908, 343 ff.; Ibn Baṭṭuṭah, II, 848; and Rockwell 1915, pt. III, 387.

9. *BGR*, §§ 150 and 167. For examples of traditional instruments, see Landman et al. 2001, plate on 155.

10. Al-Bīrūnī/K, pt. II, 29–32.

11. *BGR*, § 29; and al-Bīrūnī/K, pt. II, 28.

12. Pegolotti, 138; Yazdī, II, 427; and *CP*, 93.

13. Landman et al. 2001, 18, 51–52, and 104; al-Bīrūnī/K, pt. II, 28–29; and Kunz and Stevenson 1908, 378–80, 383, 385, and 394.

14. Laufer 1915a, 27–35 and 38–40; Laufer 1919, 521; Maenchen-Helfen 1950, 187–88; Wheatley 1961, 113–14; Schafer 1963, 221; and Benn 2002, 104.

15. Yazdī, II, 429; and *CS*, 94.

16. Abū'l Faẓl/, I, 15–16.

17. *XTS*, ch. 170, 5169; and Moriyasu 2012, 32 and 57.

18. Goitein 1967–93, I, 99; Henning 1943–46, 465–69; Ibn Khaldūn, III, 432; and Abū'l Faẓl/, I, 16.

19. Marco Polo, 100; Bautier 1970, 284; Clavijo, 160–61; Ibn Arabshāh, 309; *TTP*, 79; and *NITP*, 173.

CHAPTER 3

1. *YS*, ch. 1, 18, and ch. 150, 3556; and *SH*, § 252.

2. Rashīd/K, I, 338.

3. Juvaynī/Q, I, 102, and Juvaynī/B, I, 129. Cf. Rashīd/K, I, 375.

4. Ibn Baṭṭūṭah, II, 571 and 573. Cf. the comments of Kirakos/Kh, 155, 156, and 163.

5. Grigor of Akancʿ, 337 and 343.

6. Shao Yuanping, ch. 42, 52b; and *MREAS*, I, 139–40.

7. Kirakos/Kh, 230; *HG*, 549–50; *ʿA-D*, 185 and 493; and Marco Polo, 101–2.

8. Cf. *CP*, 232–34, on the sack of Herat in 1507.

9. Dasxurancʿi, 95; Theophanes 140; *HGGVC*, 75–76 and 111–12; *PSRL*, II, 844 and 926–27; *NC*, III, 246, IV, 78, 86, and 163, and V, 5, 98, 280, and 285.

10. *HGGVC*, 47; *PSRL*, II, 781–82; and *NC*, II, 319, and IV, 8.

11. *HG*, 542. See also Rubruck, 174.

12. *SH*, § 238.

13. Rockstein 1972, 48; Ledyard 1963, 234–35; and *SH*, § 274.

14. *HG*, 520.

15. *YS*, ch. 209, 4635 and 4639; Vaṣṣāf, 22; and *HI*, III, 28.

16. *YS*, ch. 13, 264.

17. *BGR*, §§ 1, 5, 29, and 73; Sima Guang, I, 261; al-Bīrūnī/B, 65–66; al-Ẓāhir, 117; and Theophanes, 36.

18. YS, ch. 13, 264, and ch. 29, 645; Bar Hebraeus, 467–68; *CWT*, III, 232; and Ibn Baṭṭuṭah, IV, 774.

19. *YS*, ch. 15, 307, ch. 29, 662, ch. 24, 550, and ch. 30, 677; and Ḥāfiẓ-i Abrū/B, 115.

20. Vaṣṣāf, 401.

21. Eberhard 1941, 231; Wheatley 1961, 89–90; Gode 1957, 129–34; and Fryer, II, 365.

22. Pliny, XXXIV.163; and Ma Huan, 129.

23. Zhao Rugua, 35–36; Zhao Rugua/H, 61; Ma Huan, 136, 141, 143, and 165; Serjeant 1970, 203–4; and Yule and Burnell 1903, 63–64 and 189–90.

24. Lach 1965, 368.

25. Jacoby 2006, 195; Lopez 1943, 177–80; Lopez 1952, 74–75; and *MTMW*, 283.

26. *YS*, ch. 210, 4670.

27. Lambourn 2003, 220–24, 234–36, and 239–40.

28. Juvaynī/Q, I, 180; and Juvaynī/B, I, 224.

29. *YS*, ch. 3, 47.

30. Beaujard 2005, 411–59, direct quotes from 411 and 446.

31. Rashīd/K, I, 642; Rashīd/B, 278; and Pelliot 1959–73, II, 834–35.

32. Rashīd/J, 35–40 and 334v–336r.

33. Labib 1970, 211; and Bautier 1970, 314 and 319.

34. Martinez 2008–9, 193–95; and Martinez 2010, 64–68.

35. Chaudhuri 1985, 53 and 190–91; and Chen 1992, 191–94.

36. Ṭūsī/M, 72; *YS*, ch. 94, 2377; and Schurmann 1956, 152. Cf. also Huan Kuan, I, 78.

37. Zhao Rugua, 204; and Zhao Rugua/H, 230.

38. Benjamin of Tudela, 119; and Marco Polo, 381–83.

39. Serjeant 1970, 197.

40. Barbosa, II, 120 ff. See comments of Lach 1965, 236, 271–72, 408–9, and 433–34.

41. Faxian, 125; Faxian/L, 101; Xuanzang, II, 883; Xuanzang/B, II, 251; *CWT*, II, 171–72; Barbosa, I, 81–82, and II, 122–24; and Teixeira, 179.

42. Rockhill 1915, pt. III, 386–87, and pt. IV, 465.

43. Ma Huan, 128. Cf. Donkin 1998, 161.

44. Ibn Baṭṭuṭah, II, 403.

45. Tampoe 1989, 113–16 and 127–29.
46. Schafer 1952, 155–65; and Schafer 1970, 22.
47. Ye Longli, ch. 10, 102, and ch. 22, 213; *LS*, ch. 60, 929; Wittfogel and Feng 1949, 176; Vorob'ev 1975, 99–101; and Vorob'ev 1983, 237.
48. *SCBM*, 20 (ch. 3, 10a); and Shiba 1983, 98 and 103.
49. *YS*, ch. 88, 2227, and ch. 94, 2378 and 2380; Schurmann 1956, 153, and 156; and Farquhar 1990, 84.
50. Marco Polo, 273; and Pelliot 1959–73, II, 727–30.
51. *YS*, ch. 94, 2378; and Schurmann 1956, 153.
52. *YS*, ch. 26, 581, ch. 27, 603, ch. 39, 839, and ch. 40, 854; and Farquhar 1990, 381.
53. Clark 1991, 128–29.
54. *YS*, ch. 17, 362, and ch. 202, 4521.
55. *YS*, ch. 94, 2401–2; Schurmann 1956, 224 and 230–31; and Dars 1992, 221–27.
56. *YS*, ch. 143, 3413.
57. Kirakos/Kh, 221; *YWL*, ch. 57, 17a; *YS*, ch. 94, 2397–40, and ch. 146, 3460–61; Schurmann, 1956, 217–19; and Rashīd/K, II, 1041 and 1047–48.
58. Marco Polo, 351.
59. *YS*, ch. 94, 2401; Schurmann 1956, 230; and Hartwell 1988, 30 and 35.
60. Kirakos/Kh, 193.
61. Pegolotti, 28; and Martinez 1995–97, 229 and 251, n. 46.
62. Martinez 1998–99, 118–19.
63. Sen 2003, 154.
64. Al-Bīrūnī/B, 154 and 172; Zhao Rugua, 204; Zhao Rugua/H, 230; Teixeira, 179; and Roe, II, 423 and 439.
65. Schafer 1967, 36 and 77.

CHAPTER 4

1. Sayf, 650; Ḥāfiẓ Abrū/B, 124; and Yazdī, I, 203.
2. MacKenzie 1971, 36 and 120.
3. *BGR*, §§ 83, 86, 237 and 378.
4. Nadeliaev et al. 1969, 195.
5. *BGR*, §§ 67, 73, 81, 139, and 159; and Yazdī, I, 292–93, 538, and 558.
6. Eitel 1976, 148; and Donkin 1998, 178–79.
7. Bosson 1961, 80–92; Serruys 1975, 133–40, esp. 134; and *PR*, 21 and 92 (lv12–2r1).
8. Schafer 1965, 142–43.
9. Fan Chengda, 153.
10. *YS*, ch. 118, 2922.
11. *YS*, ch. 35,781–82 and 783, ch. 39, 834, ch. 36, 803, ch. 45, 948, ch. 119, 2948, ch. 123, 3021, ch. 128, 3135, and ch. 202, 4528.
12. *YS*, ch. 134, 3249–50; Moule 1930, 228–29; and Cheng Jufu, ch. 5, 4b and 5b.
13. Cleaves 1949, 36, 61, and 90.
14. Chardin, 165.
15. Ṭabarī, XXX, 251; *GBR*, § 25; and La Vaissière 2002, 329 and n. 108.
16. Bayhaqī/ F, 538; and Bayhaqī/B, 70.
17. Wilkinson 2013, 757.

18. For detailed analysis, see Hartwell 1988, 23 and n. 15, 28, 37–38, and 59 and n. 251.

19. *BGR*, § 1.

20. Vaṣṣāf, 336.

21. Qāshānī/H, 109, 156–63, and 182–83, esp. 161–62; and Aubin 1953, 100–101.

22. Qazvīnī, *NQ*, 118 and 135.

23. *YS*, ch. 78, 1938.

24. *TZTG*, ch. 9, 135.

25. Endicott-West 1989a, 13–14.

26. *YS*, ch. 13, 263.

27. *YS*, ch. 15, 319.

28. *YS*, ch. 16, 342.

29. Zhou Mi, 193.

30. Farquhar 1990, 444 and n. 7.

31. *YS*, ch. 99, 2536; and Hsiao 1978, 108.

32. Rashīd/K, II, 1057 and 1060; and Rashīd/M, pt. II, 135–39 and 154–55 and n. 67.

33. *TLT*, II, 381 (H1) and III, 161; and *TTK*, 84 (55), 143 and 145.

34. Marco Polo, 240.

35. *YS*, ch.3, 45.

36. *SH*, §§ 278 and 279; *YS*, ch. 99, 2532; Hsiao 1978, 102; Rashīd/K, I, 649; Rashīd/B, 288; and Farquhar 1990, 37.

37. Sima Guang, II, 408; Yang Xuanzhi, 193; Yarshater 1983, 407; al-Bīrūnī/B, 142 and 146; and *TTP*, 56, 57 and 60.

38. Al-Sīrāfī, 44-45; Niẓām al-Mulk, 99; *BGR*, §§ 14, 302, 377, 378, and 380; Horst 1964, 22–23; Rashīd/K, I, 237; Ibn Khaldūn, I, 366 and 368; Rust'haveli, vv. 1142, 1145, and 1155; and *TTP*, 42.

39. Barker 1969, 13 and 443–45 and Nicols 1988, 296-316. For another example, see Bar Hebraeus, 219.

40. Hartwell 1988, 20–81, esp. 28, 35, 37–38, 59, 60, and 63.

41. Juvaynī/Q, I, 164, and III, 95; Juvaynī/B, I, 207, and II, 611; and Marco Polo, 208 and 210.

42. Juvaynī/Q, I, 174; and Juvaynī/B, I, 218.

43. Menander, 121.

44. Carpini, 110.

45. For such a claim, see Rashīd/K, II, 971.

46. The only major pool of lapidaries beyond their reach was in South India and Ceylon. See Lach 1965, 345, 374, and 403.

47. Carpini, 111–12; and Olschki 1946, 28 ff.

48. On the mobilization of artisans in Armenia, see Kirakos/Kh, 221, and Babaian 1969, 239 ff.

49. *YS*, ch. 98, 2514; and Hsiao 1978, 80.

50. Litvinskii, ed., 1995, 10–11 and 35; Beletnitskii et al., eds., 1973, 81–89 and 288; and *'A-D*, 177, 184, 487, and 492–93.

51. *YS*, ch. 120, 2964.

52. Juvaynī/Q, I, 165; and Juvaynī/B, I, 208.

53. *YWL*, ch. 42, 16b–17a; Tao Zongyi, ch. 21, 261; *YS*, ch. 15, 308, ch. 16, 342, ch. 38, 826; ch. 88, 2225–26, and ch. 89, 2266; and Farquhar 1990, 82–83 and 321.

54. Feel 1965, 288–93; and Ṭūṣī/B, 160.

55. Gernet 1962, 87–88; and Tao Zongyi, ch. 12, 149.

56. Rybakov 1948, 141–73 and 237–45; Ioannisyan 1990, 300 and 302; and Noonan 1991, 107–11 and 129–31.

57. *PSRL*, II, 843, and *HGGVC*, 76–77; and Tikhomirov 1959, 75–76 for terminology.

58. See Fyodotov-Davydov 1984, 19, 21, 53, 156, 173, 179-80, 190-93 and 232. For Yuan practice, see Allsen 1997, 32.

59. Fyodotov-Davydov 1984, 181–84 and 190–93; and Kramarovsky 1992, 191–200.

60. *TZTG*, ch. 4, 60–61.

61. Khazanov 2015, 40–41.

62. Toynbee 1934–54, II, 317–19, and III, 22; and Bóna 1990, 113–17.

63. Dasxuranc'i, 104.

64. Pelliot 1928, 110–12.

65. Juvaynī/Q, I, 164, and III, 87–88; and Juvaynī/B, I, 207, and II, 605–66.

66. *YS*, ch. 90, 2275; and Farquhar 1990, 90–91, 95, 176–78, 307, 322, 329, and 334–35.

67. Tikhonov 1966, 54; and Nadeliaev et al. 1969, 17 and 582.

68. Fasmer 1967, II, 160.

69. *YS*, ch. 3, 46; Rashīd/K, I, 669; and Rashīd/B, 315.

70. Rashīd/K, II, 848.

71. Rashīd/K, II, 1091.

72. Rashīd/K, II, 978–79 and 1078; and Rashīd/M, pt. I, 58–61, and pt. II, 161–62.

73. Rashīd/K, II, 1091–92.

74. For Islamic norms, see Yusūf, 131.

75. *YS*, ch. 146, 3457.

76. *YS*, ch. 89, 2251.

77. Juvaynī/Q, III, 88; and Juvaynī/B, II, 606. Cf. Rashīd/K, I, 599 and Rashīd/B, 222.

78. Marco Polo, 239–40. On his nomenclature, cf. *MTMW*, 325.

79. *YS*, ch. 17, 364 and 371.

80. *YS*, ch. 170, 3988.

81. Rashīd/K, I, 678–79; and Rashīd/B, 330.

82. For another example, see *YS*, ch. 24, 537.

83. *YS*, ch. 175, 4077.

84. *YS*, ch. 33, 732, and ch. 35, 779.

85. Rashīd/K, I, 654–55, and Rashīd/B, 293–94. Cf. Elverskog 2010, 227 ff.

86. Cf. Endicott-West 1989b, 144–45 and 149–52.

87. Franke 1967, 202–8.

88. See, for example, Liu 2008, 138–40.

CHAPTER 5

1. *SH*, § 274 and *YS*, ch. 78, 1938. A later Mongolian usage, *jinjü*, derives from *zhenzhu*. Lessing 1973, 1058; and Kara 1965, 11.

2. Ligeti 1990, 271 and 55a; and *Hex.*, 303 (205C11).

3. Clauson 1966, 33–34.

4. *SCBM*, 17 (ch. 3, 3a.)

5. *BS*, ch. 97, 3222.

6. *YS*, ch.17, 364, and 371.

7. *YS*, ch. 16, 352.

8. Steingass 1970, 501; Khoury 1996, 26; and Rentz 1951, 397.

9. Rashīd/K, II, 765.

10. Goitein 1967–93, IV, 213–15.

11. Elikhana 2010, 43–44, and fig. 4e.

12. Juvaynī/Q, I, 174; Juvaynī/B, I, 218; Rashīd/K, I, 656; and Rashīd/B, 296.

13. al-Dawādārī, 265.

14. Boyer 1952, 92–100, and 123–25.

15. Rashīd/K, I, 385–86 and 433.

16. *YS*, ch. 180, 4160–61; *MREAS*, I, 161–62; Rashīd/K, II, 765; and Mufaḍḍal/B, 460.

17. Ibn Arabshāh, 319.

18. Bar Hebraeus, 434.

19. *YS*, ch. 78, 1942 and 1943, and ch. 105, 2680; and *TZTG*, ch. 9, 135 and 136.

20. Sakip Sabanci Müzesi 2006, 470–73, count from pl. 349. Cf. Mostaert 1927, 149.

21. Porada 1969, 187, pl. 53 and 211–13; Rose 2001, 45; Ṭabarī, V, 237–38; *ZS*, 15 and 74 (15b); Ye Longli, ch. 23, 225; and Abū'l Fidā, 81.

22. Detailed treatment in Boyer 1953, 17–92 and 103–21, esp. 109.

23. Roux and Massé 1976, 28–57, esp. 29–33, 38–40, and 45–53.

24. Zhao Hong, 424; Rubruck, 89; Marco Polo, 556; Ibn Baṭṭuṭah, II, 485; Olschki 1960, 106; and Jacoby 2006, 203.

25. *CWT*, I, 222.

26. Sakip Sabanci Müzesi 2006, 476, count from pl. 353; and *BGR*, § 13.

27. Theophylact, IV.3.7; Draskhanakertc'i, 153; and *BGR*, §§ 159–60.

28. *SH*, § 255.

29. Mandeville, 155.

30. *YS*, ch. 78, 1930 and 1931.

31. For examples, see *BS*, ch. 97, 3222; *MKK*, 191; and *EVTRP*, I, 4 and 132.

32. Juvaynī/Q, I, 208–9; Juvaynī/B, I, 254; *YS*, ch. 12, 255, ch. 23, 525, ch. 32, 715, and ch. 138, 3346.

33. Marco Polo, 221 and 225; and *CWT*, II, 224–25. *Bezants* are Byzantine coins.

34. Vaṣṣāf, 399; and *SMOIZO*, 84.

35. *YS*, ch. 27, 611, ch. 78, 1938; ch. 139, 3352, ch. 146, 3466, and ch. 207, 4599; and Pelliot 1930, 264–65 and n. 2.

36. Tao Zongyi, ch. 2, 25.

37. *YS*, ch. 36, 801, ch. 42, 900, and ch. 128, 3134.

38. Cleaves 1951, 31, 55, and 70; and *YS*, ch. 27, 603, and ch. 41, 871.

39. So and Bunker 1995, 77–84 and 161–74. Cf. Kessler 1993, 49–50 and 79, figs. 26–27 and 36.

40. Ełishe, 187; and Abū'l Fidā, 68 and 81.

41. Kovaleskaia 1979, 5–6 and 49–51; and Kubarev 1984, 29–39.

42. *YS*, ch. 13, 267, and ch. 205, 4579; Rashīd/K, I, 659 and II, 981; Rashīd/B, 300-301; and Mufaḍḍal/B, 460–61. See further Allsen 1987, 18–19, 48–49, and 54–55.

43. *YS*, ch. 78, 1931, 1932, and 1934.

44. *BGR*, § 263. Cf. the comments of Ṣābī', 67.

45. On pearl mesh, see Kunz and Stevenson 1908, 445.

46. Cleaves 1953, 254–59, esp. 256; Doerfer 1963, 239–41; Fan Chengda, 147; and Vorob'ev 1972, 85 and 87.

47. *YS*, ch. 99, 2527; and Hsiao 1978, 96.

48. *YS*, ch. 13, 270, 273, and 280, ch. 17, 366 and 375, ch. 18, 388, ch. 19, 409 and 412, ch. 34, 767, ch. 43, 910, ch. 46, 964, ch. 61, 1484, ch. 98, 2508, ch. 123, 3032, ch. 131, 3185, ch. 133, 3229, ch. 135, 3281, ch. 151, 3578, ch. 165, 3879, ch. 178, 4133 and 4134, and ch. 203, 4545; Marco Polo, 203–4; and Hsiao 1978, 73.

49. Yang Yu, 41b.

50. Quintus Curtius, VIII.ix.24; *THPN,* 145; *JS*, 149–50; *BGR*, §§ 73, 178, 198, 213, 222, 257, 373, 403, 408, and 409; al-Bīrūnī/B, 149; Zhao Rugua, 81; Zhao Rugua/H, 103; Behrens-Abouseif 2014, 44 and 162; *CP*, 314; and Bernier, 471–72.

51. Al-Bīrūnī/B, 27–28.

52. *YS*, ch. 3, 50, ch. 79, 1958, and ch. 120, 2964.

53. Carpini, 111–12; Pelliot 1973, 64–65; Juvaynī/Q, I, 193; Juvaynī/B I, 237; Qāshānī/H, 47; *YS*, ch. 78, 1944, 1945, 1946, 1947, 1948, 1949, 1950, 1951, 1952, and 1953; Marco Polo, 479; Mufaḍḍal/B, 459–60; and Andrews 1999, I, 561.

54. Marco Polo, 222.

55. *YS*, ch. 10, 267.

56. Rashīd/K, II, 743. My italics.

57. *ESMH*, 97, 98, 99, 116, and 118; and *YS*, ch. 29, 646.

58. Yang Yu, 15a.

59. *YS*, ch. 77, 1926.

60. Gordon 2001b, 1–19. For examples, see Dasxuranc῾i, 111, 116, 128, and 130.

61. *YS*, ch. 118, 2923, ch. 138, 3330, and 3331. Cf. ch. 32, 715.

62. *YS*, ch. 120, 2956, ch. 169, 3971, and ch. 174, 4061.

63. *YS*, ch. 162, 3796 and 3798–99.

64. *YS*, ch. 32, 721.

65. *YS*, ch. 121, 2976, and ch. 122, 3008.

66. Juvaynī/Q, I, 180; and Juvaynī/B, I, 224–25.

67. Juvaynī/Q, I, 189–90; and Juvaynī/B, I, 234. For other such bestowals, see *YS*, ch. 18, 390, ch. 21, 451, ch. 32, 715, ch. 117, 2908, ch. 120, 2957, ch. 128, 3136, and ch. 133, 3224. Cf. also *BGR*, § 66; Ibn Baṭṭuṭah, III, 678; and *CP*, 25.

68. Vaṣṣāf, 331.

CHAPTER 6

1. Li Zhichang, 281–82; and Li Zhichang/W, 71.

2. See Dale 2015, 186–206.

3. Zhao Hong, 441 and 455.

4. Ye Longli, ch. 21, 205.

5. *SCBM* 17 (ch. 3, 4a); and Rashīd/K, I, 192 for quote.

6. *SH*, § 133; *SWQZL*, 44; and Pelliot and Hambis 1951, 191–92 and 202–3.

7. On continuities see Khazanov 2016, 171–88; and Allsen 1997, 69–70.

8. Jūzjānī/L, 336; and Jūzjānī/R, II, 966.

9. *YS*, ch. 2, 39–40.

10. Juvaynī/Q, I, 24; and Juvaynī/B, I, 33.

11. Carpini, 41.

12. Rashīd/K, II, 1080–81.

13. *MTMW*, 99.

14. Rashīd/K, II, 1056; and Rashīd/M, pt. II, 128–30.

15. Yang Yu, ch. 19a; *YS*, ch. 21, 449, ch. 119, 2945, and ch. 139, 3353.

16. Rashīd/K, I, 650–51, 653, and 655–56; and Rashīd/B, 289–90, 293 and 295–96.

17. *YS*, ch. 12, 241.

18. *BF*/M, 150–52.

19. Rashīd/K, II, 792.

20. Yang Yu, 54a.

21. Quan Heng, 32b.

22. *MS*, ch. 2, 24; and Dardess 1978, 9–10.

23. Yü 1967, 172, 177, 178, 182, 192, 193, and 199–201; Shiba 1983, 96; and Pliny, XXXVII.12–18.

24. Huan Kuan, I, 29 and 235.

25. *YS*, ch. 78, 1942.

26. Herskowitz 1951, 544–46 and 560.

27. See, for example, Juvaynī/Q, I, 147 and Juvaynī/B, I, 186.

28. Clavijo, 258–60.

29. Peng and Xu, 479; Grigor of Akancʿ, 289; Bar Hebraeus, 352; and Hetʿum, 148–49.

30. Juvaynī/Q, I, 15; and Juvaynī/B, I, 21–22.

CHAPTER 7

1. Juvaynī/Q, I, 174; and Juvaynī/B, I, 218.

2. Juvaynī/Q, I, 189; Juvaynī/B, I, 233–34; *YS*, ch.142, 3406; Wittfogel and Feng 1949, 276; Clauson 1971, 176 (r15–16), 178, and 182; Yazdī, II, 435, 441, and 442; Clavijo, 248; and *CP*, 95–96, 98, and 99.

3. For examples, see *BGR*, §§ 111 and 116; Ibn Arabshāh, 220–21; and *Dom.*, 233. Cf. Kunz and Stevenson 1908, 304–7.

4. Rashīd/K, I, 169–70.

5. Rashīd/K, I, 172.

6. Rashīd/K, I, 178.

7. Rashīd/K, I, 219.

8. Rashīd/K, I, 214.

9. Al-Bīrūnī/B, 17; and *CP*, 20 and 101.

10. Jāḥiẓ, 156; and *BGR*, §§ 160, 224, and 333.

11. *SH* §§ 17–22.

12. Kirakos/B, 203; and Kirakos/Kh, 173.

13. Woods 1990, 85–125; Abū'l Faẓl, *AN*, 37–39, 178–83, 190, and 353; and *CP*, 15 and n. 12 and 101.

14. Golden 1992, 120.

15. Pakhomov 1970, 133.

16. Zhukovskaia 1988, 76–77 and 158–60. Cf. Lubsangjab 1980, 41–43.

17. *YS*, ch. 119, 2929.

18. *SH*, § 202; Rashīd/K, I, 307; and *SWQZL*, 147; and Pelliot 1959–73, II, 860–61.

19. Skrynnikova 1992–93, 51–59.

20. *YWL*, ch. 57, 12a. My italics.
21. Marco Polo, 186–88 and 222–23. Cf. *CWT*, II, 239, and Serruys 1974, 1–15.
22. Bar Hebraeus, 453, 466, and 480; and *MKK*, 250–51.
23. Vaṣṣāf, 399; and *SMOIZO*, 84.
24. *YS*, ch.155, 3656.
25. *YDBH*, 29, 34, and 35.
26. *YS*, ch. 209, 4635.
27. Gerritsen 2012, 241–73, esp. 250–53, 258–59, and 263–66.
28. Mufaḍḍal/B, 459; *CT*, 81–82, 105, 107, and 193 ff.; and Rubruck, 73.
29. For examples, see Yūsuf, 139, and Yelu Chucai, 22 and 115 (3a).
30. Briant 1982, 451–56.

CHAPTER 8

1. Bokshchanin 1968, 143, 150, 164, and 165–66.
2. Ma Huan, 170 and 172; and *MS*, ch. 326, 8453.
3. *MS*, ch. 66, 1621, 1622, 1624, and 1626, and ch. 67, 1644.
4. *MS*, ch. 66, 1615, 1618, 1626, 1627, 1628, and 1630, and ch. 67, 1637, 1642, 1643, 1644, 1645, 1646, 1649, 1650, and 1652.
5. *MS*, ch. 66, 1611–12, 1623, 1624, and 1625.
6. Serruys 1967, 207 and 253.
7. *PRDK*, 132–33 and 136.
8. Schlesinger 2017, 34, 47 and 69-70; Lessing 1973, 776; Kane 1989, 351; Rozycki 1994, 201 and Tsintsius 1975-77, I, 601 and II, 160-61.
9. *MMR*, 56 and 59.
10. Schesinger 2017, 25–26 and 28–29.
11. Yazdī, I, 236.
12. Clavijo, 220, 227–28, 254, 258–59, and 269–70; Ibn Arabshāh, 216; and Andrews 1999, II, 950–51, 962, 965, 987, 1030–31, 1124, and 1227.
13. Clavijo, 270.
14. *BGR*, §§ 215 and 408.
15. Balard 1978, I, 350, and II, 720.
16. Ciocîltan 2012, 114–39. Cf. Berendei and Veinstein 1976, 117 and 123–24; and Bautier 1970, 314.
17. Bratianu 1929, 244; Pegolotti, 24; and *CWT*, III, 158.
18. Balard 1978, I, 405.
19. For other cases, see Ashtor 1983, 68, and Roe, II, 507.
20. Jenkins 1988, 29-42; and Fyodotov-Davydov 1984, 191–92.
21. Ḥāfiẓ-i Abrū/B, 229 and 134–35; and al-Ahrī, 78–79 and 178–79.
22. Bautier 1970, 316; and *MTMW*, 282 and 284.
23. *SPKB*, 12, 72, 136, and 197; and *NC*, III, 303.
24. *YCS*, 50 and 150; and Remezov, 556.
25. Róna-Tas 1982, 152. On the wide diffusion of the term, see *SJV*, 350 (#1067); Tsintsius 1975-77, I, 601; and Krippes 1992, 103.
26. For examples, see Sreznevskii 1989, I/2, 855.

27. *NC*, III, 23, 59, 67, 105, and 303, IV, 14–15, and V, 14.

28. Pelenski 1974, 109–10; Jenkins 1988, 32–35; Kramarovsky 1992, 191–200; and Noonan 1983, 217.

29. *TGPM*, 117, 118, 182, 183, and 185.

30. *TGPM*, 124, 129, 132, 153, 199–200, 216, 223, and 297.

31. Fasmer 1967, IV, 155.

32. *KI*, 340.

33. *KI*, 526, 528, 534, and 544. On *bisar* as "pearl," see *Slovar* 1975–, I, 185, and Vasmer 1967, I, 168.

34. *KI*, 546.

35. Bushkevich 1980, 61–62 and 155; Willan 1968, 53, 57 and 249; *EVTRP*, I, 115; Fletcher, 43v–44; and *RBK*, 275.

36. *NC*, V, 172–73.

37. Fletcher, 58v and 113v–115; *EVTRP*, I, 33 and 39–40; and Olearius, 127–29.

38. *EVTRP*, II, 360 and 366; and Possevino, 47.

39. See Donkin 1998, 250–54, on pearls in Byzantium; and Pelenski 1979, 93–109 on the historiographical debate.

40. For this usage, see *Slovar* 1975–, XIII, 64.

41. Poluboiarinova 1978, 8–18.

42. On the etymologies, see *Slovar* 1975–, VII, 123; Fasmer 1967, II, 232; and Doerfer 1963, 471–72. On the office, see Poluboiarinova 1978, 18–22.

43. Khodarkovsky 2002, 44–45; and Serruys 1962, 21 and 23.

44. Sreznevskii 1989, III/2, 864.

45. *RMO*, 172 and 330; and *RCS*, I, 291.

CHAPTER 9

1. For a survey, see Wiedemann 1911, 345–58.

2. *LKA*, 241; *BGR*, §§ 5, 224, 237, 252, and 378. See also Niẓām 1931, 87, and Maqrīzī, II/1, 242.

3. Dunaysarī, 153–54.

4. Al-Bīrūnī/B, 144–49.

5. Al-Bīrūnī/K, pt. II, 24–27.

6. *'A-D*, 218 and 515.

7. Tao Zongyi, ch. 8, 104.

8. Pegolotti, 26, 28, 59, 62, 64, 66, 71, 79, 124, 126, 146, 182, 215, and 302–4.

9. *MTMW*, 283.

10. Vaṣṣāf, 336.

11. Al-Bīrūnī/S, I, 211.

12. Watt 1908, 557; and Kunz and Stevenson 1908, 103–9.

13. Brunhes 1920, 340–45.

14. See Landman et al. 2001, 189–201.

15. Niẓāmī, v.19.12; Ibn Khaldūn, II, 325; and *TTP*, 57 and 59.

16. Al-Bīrūnī/K, pt. II, 30.

17. On the modern cultured pearl industry, see Landman et al. 2001, 155–83.

18. Cf. Khoury 1990, 24–31; and Parry 2013, 52–59.

19. Grierson 1959, 123–40; and Cutler 2001, 245–78.

20. Xuanzang, II, 817; Xuanzang/B, II, 207; Marco Polo, 381; Nikitin, 79; and *CP*, 308–10.

21. Huan Kuan, I, 42.

22. Sima Guang, I, 94; Shiba 1970, 159–60; and Khiṭā'ī, 118.

23. Yazdī, II, 247; and *CP*, 93.

24. Al-Maqrīzī, II/I, 214; and Mufaḍḍal/K, 69 and 191.

25. Pearson 1996, 175–77.

26. *LMJT*, 31, 83–84, 136, and 151; Ibn Jubayr, II, 140 and 206–7; *'A-D*, 236 and 528; and Ma Huan, 176.

27. Pliny, IX.117–22.

28. *NITP*, 223.

29. *FCH*, 237; *BGR*, § 252; and Bar Hebraeus, 219.

30. *YS*, ch. 30, 676.

31. Tao Zongyi, ch. 7, 84–85; and *MREAS*, I, 173–76.

32. Mandeville, 150 and 160.

33. For examples, see Dasxuranc'i, 77 and 82.

34. Theophanes, 24.

35. Xuanzang, I, 117; Xuanzang/B, I, 44; al-Nadīm, II, 827, 828, and 830; *'A-D*, 75 and 368; al-Bīrūnī/K, pt. II, 30; al-Bīrūnī/ B, 71 and 157; al-Bīrūnī/S, I, 116, 119, and 121; Niẓām 1931, 86–122 and 124–25; Darmasvāmin, 70, 79, 90, 94, and 110; and Rashīd/J, 49 and 340r.

36. *BGR*, § 29; Niẓām 1931, 163, 211–13, and 221; and Bosworth 1963, 78–79, 135–37, and 140.

37. Cf. Donkin 1998, 171–73.

38. Darmasvāmin, 70.

39. Ye Longli, ch. 19, 182; and *YS*, ch. 47, 986.

40. *GC*, 71, 83, 84, 100, 115, 127, 134, 137, and 140; and *HG*, 617.

41. Al-Bīrūnī/B, 30-31. Cf. Nadvi 1979, 535.

42. Quintas Curtius, III.iii.24.

43. Theophylact, III.6.4 and 14.10; and Theophanes, 151, 171, and 180.

44. *YS*, ch. 128, 3137.

45. Yazdī, I, 188; and Maqrīzī, III/3, 1042–43.

46. Mīrzā Ḥaydar, 323–24 and 327–28.

47. Nasawī, 75, 94, 105, 107–8, 115, 203, 208, 223, 231, 277, and 300; Rashīd/K, I, 376; Juvaynī/Q, II, 199; Juvaynī/B, II, 466–67; and *HG*, 511 and 513.

48. Mīrzā Ḥaydar, 255–56.

49. Juvaynī/Q, I, 15–16; and Juvaynī/B, I, 22.

50. Quintas Curtius, IX.i.2.

51. Rashīd/K, II, 1081 and 1084–85; and Rashīd/M, pt. II, 169 and 181.

52. Nasawī, 130–31.

53. Kirakos/K, 175.

CHAPTER 10

1. *TMC*, 177 and 189; and *YS*, ch. 16, 352.

2. *BF*/D, 289—91; and *BF*/M, 202–3.

3. Neverov 1983, 123–35.

4. Ullmann 1972, 95.

5. Akimushkin 1967, 147–48.

6. Qāshānī/A, 84–107. Cf. Mikhailevich 1972, 107–9.

7. Rashīd/Q, CXIII–CXIV and CLVIII; and Lambton 1999, 131.

8. Wang Shidian, 207 (ch. 7, 14b); and Tasaka 1957, 100–101, and 114–15.

9. Anawati 1979, 437–53; and Ullmann 1972, 121–22.

10. For Chinese perceptions, see Schafer 1967, 207 ff., and Schafer 1970, 77 ff.

11. Pliny, IX.107–9. See further Donkin 1998, 1–8.

12. Isadore, 11.

13. Al-Shīrāfī, 128–29; Benjamin of Tudela, 119; *BF*/D, 290; *BF*/M, 203; Teixeira, 179; and Fryer, II, 362–63.

14. Al-Bīrūnī/B, 126–32; and Qadri 1979, 589–90 and 592.

15. Schafer 1967, 220.

16. *CMS*, 22, 140, 141, 247, and 249.

17. Song Yingxing, 437–38. Cf. Donkin 1998, 10–13 and 179–80.

18. Eberhard 1941, 241; Eberhard 1968, 239 and 246; Schafer 1963, 232–39; Schafer 1970, 50; Zhao Rugua, 137; and Zhao Rugua/H, 157.

19. Hara 1999, 155–74. Cf. al-Bīrūnī/K, pt. I, 406.

20. Tao Zongyi, ch. 21, 263.

21. Eberhard 1968, 205, 235, and 381.

22. Donkin 1998, 154–56.

23. *RTC*, 132–33.

24. Ammianus, XXIII.6.85–86.

25. Pelliot 1984, 25–26, 45 (XIV.114) and planche V in book pocket. Cf. Moule 1930, 40.

26. Lach 1970, 113–17. Cf. Olschki 1960, 48 and 162–65; Donkin 1998, 318–31; Landman et al. 2001, 13–21; and Phillips 1990, 83–85.

27. *SBM*, 515; and Qazvīnī, *ZSNQ*, 59.

28. *SBM*, 101–2, 109, 297–98, 301–3, and 502; *BF*/D, 290; *BF*/M, 203; Ibn Riḍwān/G, I, 38 and 83, and II, 167; Ibn Riḍwān/D, 31 and 141; Samarqandī, 139, 140, 142, and 150; and Donkin 1998, 181 and 260–61.

29. Schafer 1963, 245; and Needham 1976, 34–35 and 99.

30. Bailey 1962, 31–32; Bailey 1982, 14 and 33; and van der Kuip 1975, 24.

31. Ponder 1925, 686–87; and Thorndyke 1958, 80, 125, 177, 193, 241–44, and 246.

32. Al-Bīrūnī/K, pt. II, 22–23.

33. Teixeira, 180–81.

34. Al-Bīrūnī/K, pt. II, 28; and Goitein 1967–93, I, 155.

35. Pegolotti, 36 and 109; *CWT*, III, 168; and Fryer, II, 367–68.

36. *MTMW*, 111 and 113; and Pegolotti, 294 and 296.

37. Juvaynī/Q, I, 5; and Juvaynī/B, I, 8. Cf. al-Bīrūnī/K, pt. I, 411–12.

38. Pliny, IX.110; and Ammianus, XXIII.6.87.

39. Rockhill 1915, pt. III, 387; and Ibn Khaldūn, I, 138.

40. Narshakhī, 45; al-Sīrāfī, 130–31; and *GLR*, 286.

41. Arberry 1947–48, 36–38.

42. Pliny, IX.111. Cf. Arrian, *Ind.*, 8.11–13.

43. *ʿA-D*, 148 and 456.

44. Schafer 1952, 162.

45. Schafer 1952, 156–57 and 160.

46. *SCBM*, 20–21 (ch. 3, 10b–11a); Stein 1940, 95–102; Franke 1975, 151–53; Schlesinger 2017, 47; and Wang 2011, 110–18.

47. Sherratt 1995, 10–17 and 24–25.

48. Benn 2002, 55; Schafer 1951, 403–22; Schafer 1963, 242–43; and Rong 2005, 215–16.

49. Al-Bīrūnī/B, 204, 408, and 474. Cf. Grenet 1996, 75 and Livshits 1962, 60–62.

50. *'A-D*, 59 and 350.

51. Schafer 1967, 98–99 and 220.

52. Laufer 1915a, 5–21 and Laufer 1915b, 202–5, for the Chinese texts.

53. *MREAS*, I, 151–52; and Marco Polo, 395–96.

54. Quintas Curtius, VIII.ix.19.

55. Pollard 2013, 19–20.

56. Arrian, *Ind.*, 8.8–11.

57. See Mair 1990, 27–47.

58. Pliny, XXXVII.54, 118, 124, 135, 142, 144–45, 155–56, 165, and 169.

59. *FCH*, 103.

60. So Theophanes, 139, characterizes the Byzantine emperor Constantine VI (r. 780–97).

61. The views expressed in the following paragraphs owe much to the seminal works of Mary Helms, 1988 and 1993.

62. Pollard 2013, 20–23.

63. Freedman 2008, 223–26.

64. For ambergris, see Wheatley 1961, 125–30, and for asbestos, Laufer 1915c, 302–59.

65. Good 2006, 204–6.

66. Laufer 1913, 315–64; Laufer 1916, 348–89; Pelliot 1913, 365–70; Wittfogel and Feng 1949, 235; and Schafer 1963, 242.

67. Helms 1988, 68 ff. Cf. al-Bīrūnī/B, 48, and Lieu 1985, 71.

CHAPTER 11

1. See, for example, Makarov 2006, 130–31.

2. Lowenthal 1992, 189–90.

3. Donkin 1998, 42–44.

4. Needham 1971, 674–77.

5. Sivin 1968, 212–13; and Needham 1971, 677–78.

6. Benn 2002, 104–5.

7. Ḥāfiẓ-i Abrū/M, 35 and 56.

8. Al-Bīrūnī/K, pt.II, 23.

9. Nikitin, 82.

10. *ZS*, 15 and 80 (17a).

11. Al-Bīrūnī/K, pt. II, 22–23; and al-Bīrūnī/B, 99, 113, and 129. Cf. Donkin 1998, 261–63.

12. Jāḥiz, 155.

13. Bálint 1989, 152–53 (pls. 63.7 and 10), 200 (pl. 89.1–3), and 246 (pl. 116.7–10).

14. Levashova 1965, 298–300.

15. Al-Bīrūnī /B, 41, 71, 80–81 and 91.

16. Lucas 1934, 347–48; and Thompson 1936, 133–34 and 195.

17. Fryer, II, 363; and *AM*, 248 and 255.

18. Lach 1965, 374 and 403.

19. Needham 1962, 112–13; *'A-D*, 174 and 483; and Ibn Khaldūn, III, 230.

20. Pliny, XXXVII.51, 79, 83–84, 98, 112, and 197–200.

21. Al-Bīrūnī/B, 83 and 260.
22. Al-Nadīm, II, 867.
23. Song Yingxing, 443–44 and 449; and Clunes 1992, 151–52.
24. Laufer 1915a, 41–42.
25. Mandeville, 119.
26. *MKK*, 196.
27. *MTMW*, 138; and Holmes 1934, 195–96.
28. Needham 1970, 154–55.
29. MacCoull 1988, 101–4; and al-Nadīm, II, 856, 857, and 867.
30. Renfrew 1988, 148–49.
31. *HHS*, ch. 88, 2920.
32. Nappi 2009, 41–44; and Karimov 1991, 141–42.
33. On gold foil, see Shiba 1983, 97.
34. Al-Shīrāfī, 44–45; and al-Bīrūnī /B, 211–12.
35. Stanley 2010, 107–15.
36. Lang 1966, 143–49.
37. Li Zhichang, 347; Li Zhichang/W, 107; and Rawson 1984, 82–85 and figs. 63–65.
38. Elikhina 2010, 45; and Erdenebat et al. 2010, 57 and 59.
39. Gerritsen 2012, 267–72.
40. Fyodotov-Davydov 1984, 126, 195, and 238.
41. *CP*, 224; Wulf 1966, 149–50; and Christensen 1993, 173.
42. Al-Bākuwī 28 and 12b.
43. Pierson 2012, 9–39.
44. Pelliot 1959–73, II, 805–12. See also Wheatley 1961, 83, and al-Bākuwī, 20 and 8a.
45. Finley 1998, 141–87.
46. Rashīd/S, 189.
47. Pelliot 1959–73, I, 145–50.
48. *TYH*, 17.
49. Thaʿālibī, 141.
50. *ʿA-D*, 106-07, 184, 193, 409, 492, and 499.
51. Zhao Rugua, 81 and Zhao Rugua/H, 103. Cf. Laufer 1967, 539.
52. Ibn Baṭuṭṭah, II, 446, and III, 548; ʿUmarī/L, 27, 97, 100, and 156; Clavijo, 287, 327, and 353; and Mukminova 1976, 70 ff.
53. Cf. Serjeant 1972, 69.
54. Allsen 1997, 38–41.
55. Tikhonov 1966, 82–84; and Litvinskii, ed., 35–74.
56. Rashīd/S, 208.
57. For linguistic analysis, see Theodoridis 2002, 249–57. Cf. Jacoby 2003, 140–41, and Lessing 1960, 993.
58. Pegolotti, 23, 36, 79, 109, and 216; *CWT*, III, 155; *MTMW*, 358; and Lopez 1952, 74–75.
59. Marco Polo, 556–57; and Monnas 2001, 7–8.
60. Jacoby 2004, 209–12 and 216–22.
61. Jacoby 2003, 140–42; Jacoby 2007, 30–31; and Jacoby 2010, 78–81.
62. Yule and Burnell 1903, 484–85; Pelliot 1959–73, I, 146–47, *Slovar* 1975–, VII, 48–49; Monnas 2001, 7–8; and Serjeant 1972, 150 and 248.
63. On the diagnostic value of weave structures, see Gasparini 2012, 1–19.
64. See *CWT*, III, 98–99; Clavijo, 328; and Fletcher 1968, 213.

65. *YS*, ch. 78, 1942.
66. ʿUmarī/L, 33, text, and 113, translation; Allsen 2009, 152–53; and Nappi 2009, 41.
67. Cutler 2001, 260–78.
68. Abū'l Faẓl, II, 247.

CHAPTER 12

1. Kauz 2010b, 159–71.
2. On Muslim agencies, see Goitein 1964, 118–23.
3. Cf. Hambly 1966, 1.
4. For examples, see Tampoe 1989, 129–50; Yokkaichi 2008, 73 ff.; and Barendse 2000, 183 and 194. Others are cited below.
5. Aubin 1969, 21–37 and map on 36; Williamson 1973, 61; and Ashtor 1983, 323 and 397–98.
6. Marco Polo, 123.
7. Zhao Rugua, 108–9; and Zhao Rugua/H, 134.
8. Ma Huan, 165.
9. *CP*, 300.
10. Ma Huan, 171.
11. Pigulevskaia 1951, 266, 274, 388, and 393–97.
12. Sen 2003, 219–20.
13. Schafer 1963, 157–60 and 174–75; and al-Ṣābi', 79.
14. Noonan 1983, 239–43.
15. Pliny, XXXII.21–22; and al-Bīrūnī/B, 178 and 180.
16. al-Bakuwī, 54.
17. Schafer 1967, 159; Clark 1986, 26–28; and Rockhill 1915, pt. III, 383–84, and pt. IV, 624.
18. Ray 1998, 77–78; *PME*, 67 (28), 75 (39), 81 (49), and 85 (56); *Ḥ-ʿA*, 86; and al-Shīrāfī, 132–33.
19. *LMJT*, 88, 107, 118, 215, 247–48, 281, 284, and 286.
20. Schafer 1963, 246–47. Cf. *MREAS*, I, 151, and Rockhill 1915, pt. V, 624–25. On the Mediterranean coral industry, see Arbel 2004, 58–60.
21. Rapin 1996, 40; and Tolstov and Vainshtein 1967, 151–52, and 331, pl. 18.9–12.
22. Bailey 1982, 14; Bailey 1985, 73; Marco Polo, 140 and 272; Terent'ev-Katanskii 1993, 79–80 and 176; and Pinks 1968, 25, 26, 28, and 97.
23. Li Zhichang, 344; and Li Zhichang/W, 103–4.
24. Levashova 1965, 306.
25. Yang Yu, 15a.
26. *MTMW*, 153.
27. On the absence of pearls among the Mongols, see *PRDK*, 45 and 56.
28. Timkowsky 1827, II, 294 and 309; Przhevalskii 1876, I, 49; Rockhill 1891, 59, 184, and 282; Rockhill 1894, 69, 103, 234, 253, 273 and 284; Khabtagaeva 2003–4, 141–43 and 145; and Boyer 1952, 22 ff.
29. Laufer 1967, 223–25; Wheatley 1961, 77–80; al-Bīrūnī/B, 177; and Samarqandī, 119, 140, 144, and 150.
30. *BS*, ch. 97, 3230; Rong 2004, 27 and 34; and Ennin, 233 and 255.
31. See Liu 1988, 54–58, 92–94, 160–62, and 166.

32. Theophylact, IV.16.22 and V.1.8; Matthew 13.45–46; Donkin 1998, 92–93; and Colless 1969–70, 27–29.

33. *TTT*, II, 423, lines 11–12.

34. Sherratt 2006, 38–40 and 44–45.

35. My characterization draws on Bunker 1998, 604–18.

36. Stronach 1978, 172, 177 and pls. 156c, 159c and 161.

37. Rose 2001, 38, 40, and 42; and Baer 1989, 83–97.

38. Al-Bīrūnī/B, 42, 143–44 and 146–48; *BGR*, §§ 37, 93, and 198; Goitein 1967–93, IV, 203–4, 216–17, and 220; and Ibn Baṭṭuṭah, II, 403.

39. Benn 2002, 104.

40. Allsen 1997, 60–70.

41. Koryakova and Epimakhov 2007, 249, 307, 310 and pl. 8.2.

42. Treister 2004, 297–321; and Leskov 2008, 47 (fig. 55), 88–89 (figs. 113–14), and 121–22 (figs. 154–55).

43. Koryakova and Epimakhov 2007, 4, 104, and 281.

44. Rudenko 1960, 211; Rudenko 1962, 42 and pls. II.6 and XX.17; and Aseev 1985, 35.

45. Honeychurch 2015, 65–71; Koryakova and Epimakhov 2007, 247–48; and Kessler 1993, 55 and fig. 35.

46. Rolle 1989, 88–89; and Rostovtzeff 1922, 135 and pl. XXVI.1.

47. Rudenko 1962, 48 and pl. XXI.28.

48. De La Vaissière 2002, 22–26; Rapin 2007, 55, 57–58, and 60; Sarianidi 1980, 31–41; and Sarianidi 1987, 268–70.

49. *HHS*, ch. 47, 1580.

50. *FCH*, 249, 285, and 319; and Thompson 1947, 62.

51. *BS*, ch. 96, 3186; *XTS*, ch. 221a, 6224; Yang Xuanzhi, 226; and *TYH*, 17 and 47.

52. *BS*, ch.97, 3212 and ch. 98, 3257.

53. Yang Xuanzhi, 157.

54. Kiss 1984, 33–40; Xiong and Laing 1991, 163–73; and Dien 2007, 268 and 282–83.

55. Dickens 2016, 20 and 24. Cf. Menander, 119.

56. *JTS*, ch. 194b, 5180; and *XTS*, ch. 215b, 6056.

57. Cf. Kliashtornyi 1964, 78–80 and 92–103 and de La Vaissière 2002, 222–44.

58. Henning 1943–46, 468; Frye 1951, 142–45; Yoshida 2004, 129–30; and *Hex.*, 164 (195A10).

59. Yang 2005, 31, 45, and 43; Belenitskii 1959, 15, pl. IV, 21–22, pls. XXI–XXII, and 67, pl. XXXIX; and Haussig 1992, fig. 367.

60. Zhang 2005, 94–95; and Grenet 2005, 127, fig.3, and 138.

61. Kubarev 1984, 29–31 and fig. 5.1–8.

62. Ṭabarī, XXVII, 202. Cf. De La Vaissière 2002, 278.

63. Grenet 1996, 65–84.

64. Narshakhī, 18 and 49. My italics. Cf. al-Bīrūnī/B, 148.

65. *BS*, ch. 97, 3228.

66. *GOT*, 231 and 258 (KTS3) and 260 and 294 (KČE4); *XTS*, ch. 43b, 1149; and Kliashtornyi 1961, 24–26.

67. Bálint 1989, 23–24 (pl. 1.1–3), 25–26 (pl. 3.1–4), 29–31 (pl. 9.6 and 10.30) and 41 (pl. 16.1), and many others. Cf. Rudenko 1960, 211, and Kessler 1993, 55, fig. 43.

68. Haussig 1992, 98 (fig. 156), 118 (fig. 191), and 258–59 (fig. 445); Kliashtornyi et al. 1989, 8–15; and Hayachi 1975, 38 (fig. 25), 100, 142–43 (figs. 165, 166, and 169).

69. Ibn Faḍlān, 217–18.

70. Rong 2004, 19 and 34; Moriyasu 2012, 32 and 57; and Yūsuf, 184.

71. Pinks 1968, 96 and 98; and *TMC,* 43.

72. Ye Longli, ch. 21, 205, and ch. 26, 246.

73. *YS*, ch. 124, 3050.

74. Eberhard 1941, 220; Marco Polo, 139–40; *TMC*, 106; Dunnell 1996, 102 and 128; Darmasvāmin, 55; and *TLT*, II, 381 (A1); *GLR,* 286.

75. On the China connection, see Shiba 1983, 94–95.

76. Bóna 1990, 113–17; Fülöp 1990, 140 and 142; *XTS*, ch. 217b, 6147; and Sunchugashev 1979, 137–38 and fig. 43.

77. *MREAS*, I, 30.

78. Rashīd/K, II, 685.

79. *YS,* ch. 3, 46 and 47; Rashīd/K, I, 600 and 616; Rashīd/B, 223 and 246–47; Pelliot, 1959–73, II, 746–48; and Herman 2002, 297 and 301 ff.

80. Rashīd/ K, I, 638; and Rashīd/B, 272.

81. For details, see Buell 2009, 21–29.

82. *YS,* ch. 209, 4633–34; and Vu 2017, 13–19.

83. Vu 2017, 21–23 and 37. The appointment of Na-[su]-la-ding is noted in the *YS*, ch. 209, 4635.

84. *YS*, ch. 4, 87, and ch. 209, 4635.

85. Wheatley, 1961, 65–67, 68–72, 77, 81–83, and 111–12.

86. Farquhar 1990, 85, 101, and 102.

87. *YS*, ch. 209, 4635.

88. *YS*, ch. 209, 4636.

89. *YS*, ch. 131, 3198.

90. *YS*, ch. 8, 148; and Pelliot 1959–73, I, 5.

91. *CWT*, III, 234–35; and Rashīd/J, 41 and 336v.

92. *YS*, ch. 10, 204.

93. Cf. Ciocîltan 2012, 32.

94. Rashīd/K, I, 645; and Rashīd/B, 282–83. For an example of data they provided, see *YS*, ch. 210, 4669, and Pelliot 195-73, I, 5.

95. On Burma as a transition point, see Stargardt 1971, 38–62, esp. 40 and 45.

96. Yang 2004, 281–322.

97. Pelliot 1959–73, I, 543–47.

98. Yang 2011, 1–25.

99. See Vogel 1993, pt. I, 211–52, and pt. II, 309–53; and Franke 1949, 117–19.

CHAPTER 13

1. Artzy 1994, 131–40.

2. Beaujard 2010, 32–34.

3. Chaudhuri 1985, 161–81. Cf. Beaujard 2005, 447.

4. *DRI*, 63.

5. The classic formulation of this argument is Khazanov 1994, 202–12.

6. Golden 1987–91, 49, 57–58, 65–66, and 68–73; Golden 1991, 97–100; and Noonan 2000–2001, 216.

7. Allsen 2013, 177–83.

8. Barthold 1968, 397–400.

9. For an example of the latter, see Juvaynī/Q, III, 83–85; Juvaynī/B, II, 602–4; Rashīd/K, I, 609–10; and Rashīd/B, 237.

10. Het'um/B, 177–88.

11. *MREAS*, I, 122–55.

12. Olschki 1972, 77–94.

13. *MKK*, 134–40.

14. Rashīd/K, II, 755.

15. Olschki 1960, 12–28.

16. Bar Hebraeus, 456.

17. Cheng Jufu, ch. 5, 3b–4a.

18. Cleaves 1976, 181–203.

19. Vaṣṣāf, 505–6; and *HI*, 45–47.

20. Qāshānī/H, 31–32 and 41.

21. *LAÖPB*, 55–56.

22. Qāshānī/H, 49.

23. *YS*, ch.30, 667, 671, 672, and 675.

24. YS, ch. 30, 673; al-Ahrī, 153, Persian text, and 54–55, translation; and Ḥāfiẓ-i Abrū/B, 167.

25. My estimate of the distance is calculated in straight lines between the four capitals.

26. *YS*, ch. 34, 754.

27. *YS*, ch. 117, 2906; and *MREAS*, II, 13–14.

28. *YS*, ch. 43, 911; and Pelliot 1959–73, II, 640.

29. Al-'Umarī/L, 75, 77, and 142–43.

30. Li Zhichang, 288; and Li Zhichang/W, 76–77.

31. Marco Polo, 470–73. On earlier commercial routes in this region, see Lubo-Lesnichenko 1989, 4-9 and map on 5.

32. Rashīd/K, 654; Rashīd/B, 293–94; and Pelliot 1959–73, I, 5 and 77–78.

33. Kyzlasov 1962, 203–10.

34. Kerner 1946, 165–72; and Bell, 33–105.

35. *MM*, 226; and Moule 1930, 175.

36. *MM*, 228; and Moule 1930, 178.

37. On caravan routing, see Lattimore 1962, 37–72, quote from 56.

38. Steensgaard 1991, 5–6.

39. Shim 2014, 419–27, 432–40, and 461.

40. *HYYY*, I, 12, 30, 65, 72, and 101, and II, 98 and 103.

41. Cf. Martinez 2008–9, 136–39.

42. On the buildup in the eastern zone, see Wade 2009, 221–65.

43. Vaṣṣāf, 303 and 505–6; and *HI*, 35 and 45–47.

44. Qāshānī/H, 109.

45. Qāshānī/H, 182.

46. Ibn Baṭṭuṭah, IV, 895–96.

47. See Ziiaev 1983, 42–43, 51, 53, 61, 63–64, 69, 82–83, and 93.

48. Cf. Linschoten, II, 102.

49. So 1991, 117–37.

50. Marco Polo, 328, 348 and 351; Rashīd/K, 645; Rashīd/B, 283; Schafer, 1957, 83–84; and Schafer 1967, 36, and 77.

CHAPTER 14

1. Deng 1997, 1–8.
2. Pritsak 1979, 3–21.
3. Fong 2014, 475–92.
4. Clark 2009, 20–33.
5. Yokkaichi 2008, 83–84.
6. So 2000, 108–17, 207, and 301–5.
7. Chaffee 2006, 397, 409, 412, and 414; Liu 2008, 135–38; and Yokkaichi 2008, 101.
8. Cf. Sen 2006, 426–35; and Yokkaichi 2008, 87–90.
9. Schurmann 1956, 223–28; Pelliot 1959–73, II, 587–93; and Farquhar 1990, 374–75 and 380.
10. Jūzjānī/L, 388; Jūzjānī/R, I, 179–80, and II, 1118–19. For pearls from the Gulf, see Juvaynī/Q, I, 164; and Juvaynī/B, I, 207.
11. Juvaynī/Q, I, 205 and 212, II, 243, and III, 74; Juvaynī/B, I, 250, 257, 507, and 597; Jūzjānī/L, 382–83 and 423; and Jūzjānī/R, II, 1109–10 and 1228.
12. Rashīd/K, I, 664–65; Rashīd/K, II, 734, 743–44, 785, 811, 815, 821, 921, and 1053–54; Rashīd/B, 307; and Rashīd/M, pt. II, 101–4.
13. Vaṣṣāf, 302–3; *HI*, III, 35; and Rashīd/K, II, 926. For details, see Aubin 1953, 80–102; Spuler 1985, 122–27; Williamson 1973, 56–61; Kervan 1983, 2–24; Benjamin of Tudela, 118–19; Marco Polo, 101, 117, 386, 441, and 446; Pelliot 1959–73, I, 244–45 and 576–82, and II, 820–22; and Whitehouse 1976, 46–47.
14. Al-ʿUmarī/L, 96 and 156.
15. Wozniak 1979, 115–26.
16. Dunlop 1954, 94 and 206–7.
17. Ciocîltan 2012, 145–47.
18. Jacoby 2003, 131–40.
19. Di Cosmo 2013, 174–99; and Ciocîltan 2012, 152 ff. Cf. Meyendorff 1981, 48–53; Nicol 1992, 40–42, 59–64, and 88–89; Di Cosmo 2005, 406–12; and Martinez 2008–9, 139–44, 168–74, and 188–93.
20. Clark 2009, 1–33, esp. 30–33.
21. Chase 2003, 21–22.
22. Hall 1985, 41–43, 93–94, and 211–12. Cf. Lach 1965, 352.
23. On these polities, see Mair 2005, 54–84.
24. Hall 1985, 100–102, 212–13, 229–31, and 255–56.
25. Yamamoto 1981, 1–28; Whitmore 2006, 107 and 110–12; and Wade 2009, 239, 241, 243, and 259.
26. Xiao 1990, 177–200; and Wright 2007, 207–16.
27. Vu 2016, 23 ff.
28. Tampoe 1989, 127.
29. Allsen 1989, 117–20.
30. For China, see Ch'en 1979, 69 and 80–88.

31. The place to start is Constable 2003.
32. Martinez 1995–97, 132 and 134; and Di Cosmo 2010, 90–91, 95, and 104–5.

CONCLUSION

1. Deng 1997, 54–58. Cf. Ptak 1995, 47–75.
2. See Clark 1995, 50–65; and Sen 2003, 165–68 and 236.

BIBLIOGRAPHY

Abalahin, Andrew J. 2011. "Sino-Pacifica: Conceptualizing Greater Southeast Asia as a Sub-Arena of World History." *Journal of World History* 22: 659–91.

Akimushkin, O. F. 1967. "Novye postupleniia persidskikh rukopisei v rukopisnyi otdel Instituta narodov Azii AN SSSR." In V. V. Struve, ed., *Ellinisticheskii Blizhnii Vostok, Vizantiia, Iran*. Moscow: Nauka, pp. 140–56.

Allsen, Thomas T. 1989. "Mongolian Princes and Their Merchant Partners, 1200–1260." *Asia Major*, 3rd ser., 2/2: 83–126.

———. 1997. *Commodity and Exchange in the Mongol Empire: A Cultural History of Islamic Textiles*. Cambridge: Cambridge University Press.

———. 2009. "Mongols as Vectors of Cultural Transmission." In Nicola Di Cosmo et al., eds., *The Cambridge History of Inner Asia: The Chinggisid Age*. Cambridge: Cambridge University Press, pp. 135–54.

———. 2013. "Remarks on Steppe Nomads and Merchants." In Robert Hillenbrand et al., eds., *Ferdowsi, the Mongols and the History of Iran: Studies in Honour of Charles Melville*. London: I. B. Tauris, pp. 177–83.

Amitai, Reuven, and Michal Biran, eds. 2015. *Nomads as Agents of Cultural Change: The Mongols and Their Eurasian Predecessors*. Honolulu: University of Hawai'i Press.

Anawati, G. C. 1979. "The Kitāb al-Jamāshir fī Maʿrifah al-Jawāhir of al-Bīrūnī." In Said 1979, pp. 437–53.

Andrews, Peter Alford. 1999. *Felt Tents and Pavilions: The Nomadic Tradition and Its Interaction with Princely Tentage*. London: Melisende. 2 vols.

Anonymous. 1914. "Notes and Queries." *T'oung-pao* 15: 184–86.

Arbel, Benjamin. 2004. "The Last Decades of Venice's Trade with the Mamluks: Importations into Egypt and Syria." *Mamluk Studies Review* 8/2: 37–82.

Arberry, A. J. 1947–48. "Miracle of the Pearls." *Bulletin of the School of Oriental and African Studies* 12: 36–38.

Artzy, Michal. 1994. "Incense, Camels, and Collared Rim Jars: Desert Trade Routes and Maritime Outlets in the Second Millennum." *Oxford Journal of Archaeology* 13/2: 121–47.

Ascher, Abraham et al., eds. 1979. *The Mutual Effects of the Islamic and Judeo-Christian Worlds: The East European Pattern*. New York: Brooklyn University Press, distributed by Columbia University Press.

Aseev, I. V. 1985. "K voprosu o datirovka mogil typa chetyrkhugol'nykh ogradok." In K. S. Vasil'evskii ed., *Drevnie kul'tury Mongolii*. Novosibirsk: Izdatel'stvo Nauka, sibirskoe otdelenie, pp. 34–40.

Ashtor, Eliyahu. 1983. *Levant Trade in the Later Middle Ages.* Princeton: Princeton University Press.

Aubin, Jean. 1953. "Les princes d'Ormuz du XIIIe au XIVe siècle." *Journal asiatique* 241: 77–138.

———. 1969. "La survie de Shilau et la route du Khundj-o-Fal." *Iran* 7: 21–37.

Austin, David, and Leslie Alcock, eds. 1990. *From the Baltic to the Black Sea: Studies in Medieval Archaeology.* London: Routledge.

Babaian, L. O. 1969. *Sotsial'no-ekonomicheskaia i politicheskaia istoriia Armeniia v XIII–XIV vekakh.* Moscow: Izdatel'stvo Nauka.

Baer, Eva. 1984. "Jeweled Ceramics from Medieval Islam: A Note on Ambiguity of Islamic Ornament." *Muqarnas* 6: 83–97.

Bailey, Harold W. 1962. "The Preface to the *Siddhas*āra-Sāstra." In H. B. Henning and E. Yarshater, eds., *A Locust's Leg: Studies in Honour of S. H. Taqizadeh.* London: Percy Lund, pp. 31–38.

———. 1982. *The Culture of the Sakas in Ancient Iranian Khotan.* Delmar, N.Y.: Caravan Books.

———. 1985 *Indo-Scythian Studies.* Vol. VII, *Khotanese Texts.* Cambridge: Cambridge University Press.

Balard, Michel. 1978. *La Romanie Génoise, XIIe–debut du XVe.* Rome: École française de Rome. 2 vols.

Bálint, Csanád. 1989. *Die Archäologie der Steppe: Steppenvölker zwischen Volga und Donau vom 6. bis 10. Jahrhundert.* Vienna: Böhlau.

Barendse, R. J. 2000. "Trade and State in the Arabian Seas: A Survey from the Fifteenth to the Eighteenth Century." *Journal of World History* 11: 173–225.

Barker, John W. 1969. *Manuel II Palaeologus (1391–1425): A Study in Late Byzantine Statesmanship.* New Brunswick, N.J.: Rutgers University Press.

Barthold, W. 1968. *Turkestan Down to the Mongol Invasion.* 3rd ed. London: Luzac.

Bautier, R. H. 1970. "Points de vue sur les relations économiques des occidentaux avec les pays d'Orient, au Moyen Âge." In Mollat 1970, pp. 263–331.

Beaujard, Philippe. 2005. "The Indian Ocean in Eurasian and African World Systems Before the Sixteenth Century." *Journal of World History* 16: 411–65.

———. 2010. "From Three Possible Iron-Age World Systems to a Single Afro-Eurasian World System." *Journal of World History* 21: 1–43.

Behrens-Abouseif, Doris. 2014. *Diplomacy in the Mamluk Sultanate: Gifts and Material Culture in the Medieval Islamic World.* London: I. B. Tauris.

Belenitskii, A. M. 1959. "Novye pamiatniki istkusstva drevnego Piandzhikenta: Opyt ikonograficheskogo istolkovaniia." In A. M. Belenitskii and B. B. Piotrovskii, eds., *Skulptura i zhivopis drevnego Piandzhikenta.* Moscow: Izdatel'stvo Akademii Nauk SSSR, pp. 11–86.

Belenitskii, A. M., et al., eds. 1973. *Srednevekovyi gorod Srednei Azii.* Leningrad: Izdatel'stvo Nauka leningradskoe otdelenie.

Bemmann, Jan, et al., eds. 2010. *Mongolian-German Karakorum Expedition.* Vol. I, *Excavations in the Craftsmen Quarter at the Main Road.* Wiesbaden: Reichert.

Benn, Charles. 2002. *China's Golden Age: Everyday Life in the Tang Dynasty.* Oxford: Oxford University Press.

Berendei, Mihnea, and Gilles Veinstein. 1976. "La Tana-Azaq de la présence italienne à l'empire Ottomans." *Turcica* 8/2: 110–201.

Bokshchanin, A. A. 1968. *Kitai i strany Iuzhnykh morei v XIV–XVI vv.* Moscow: Nauka.

Bóna, István. 1990. "Byzantium and the Avars: The Archaeology of the First 70 Years of the Avar Era." In Austin and Alcock 1990, pp. 113–17.

Bosson, James E. 1961. "A Rediscovered Xylograph Fragment from the Mongolian 'Phags-pa Version of the *Subhāṣitaratnanidhi*." *Central Asiatic Journal* 6: 85–102.

Bosworth, Clifford E. 1963. *The Ghaznavids, Their Empire in Afghanistan and Eastern Iran, 994–1040*. Edinburgh: Edinburgh University Press.

Bowen, Richard. 1951a. "Pearl Fisheries of the Persian Gulf." *Middle East Journal* 5: 161–80.

———. 1951b. "Maritime Industries of Arabia." *Geographical Review* 41/3: 384–400.

Boyer, Martha. 1952. *Mongol Jewellery*. Copenhagen: Gyldendalske Boghandel, Nordisk.

Bratianu, G. I. 1929. *Recherches sur le commerce génois dans la Mer noire au XIIIe siècle*. Paris: Librairie orientaliste Paul Guethner.

Briant, Pierre. 1982. "Forces productive, dépendence rurale et idéologies religieuses dans l'empire Achéménides." In his *Rois, tributes et paysans*. Paris: Belles Lettres.

Broase, T. S. R. 1978. "Gazetteer." In T. S. R. Broase, ed., *The Cilician Kingdom of Armenia*. Edinburgh: Scottish Academic Press, pp. 145–85.

Brunhes, Jean. 1920. *Human Geography*. Chicago: Rand McNally.

Buell, Paul D. 2009. "Indochina, Vietnamese Nationalism and the Mongols." In Volker Rybatzki et al., eds., *The Early Mongols, Language, Culture and History: Studies in Honor of Igor de Rachewiltz on the Occasion of His 80th Birthday*. Indiana University Uralic and Altaic Series, vol. 173. Bloomington, Ind: Denis Sinor Institute for Inner Asian Studies, 21–29.

Bunker, Emma C. 1998. "Cultural Diversity in the Tarim Basin Vicinity and Its Impact on Ancient Chinese Culture." In Victor Mair, ed., *The Bronze and Early Iron Age Peoples of Eastern Central Asia*. Washington, D.C.: Institute for the Study of Man, vol. II, pp. 604–18.

Bushkevich, Paul. 1980. *The Merchants of Moscovy, 1580–1650*. Cambridge: Cambridge University Press.

Cammann, Schuyler. 1950. *Trade Through the Himalayas*. Princeton: Princeton University Press.

Chaffee, John. 2006. "Diaspora Communities in the Historical Development of Maritime Muslim Communities of Song-Yuan China." *Journal of the Economic and Social History of the Orient* 49: 395–420.

Chase, Kenneth. 2003. *Firearms, a Global History to 1700*. Cambridge: Cambridge University Press.

Chauduri, K. N. 1985. *Trade and Civilization in the Indian Ocean: An Economic History from the Rise of Islam to 1750*. Cambridge: Cambridge University Press.

Chen Da-sheng. 1992. "Sources from Fujian on Trade Between China and Hurmuz in the Fifteenth Century." In Lisa Golombek and Maria Subtelny, eds., *Timurid Art and Culture: Iran and Cental Asia in the Fifteenth Century*. Leiden: E. J. Brill, pp. 191–94.

Ch'en, Paul Heng-chao. 1979. *The Chinese Legal System Under the Mongols: The Code of 1291 as Reconstructed*. Princeton: Princeton University Press.

Christensen, Peter. 1993. *The Decline of Iranshahr: Irrigation and Environments in the History of the Middle East, 500 B.C. to A.D. 1500*. Copenhagen: Museum Tusculanum Press.

Christian, David. 2000. "Silk Roads or Steppe Roads? The Silk Roads in World History." *Journal of World History* 11: 1–26.

Ciocîltan, Virgil. 2012. *The Mongols and the Black Sea Trade in the Thirteenth and Fourteenth Centuries*. Leiden: Brill.

Clark, Grahame. 1986. *Symbols of Excellence*. Cambridge: Cambridge University Press.

Clark, Hugh. 1991. *Community, Trade and Networks: Southern Fujian Province from the Third to the Thirteenth Century*. Cambridge: Cambridge University Press.

———. 1995 "Muslims and Hindus in the Cultural Morphology of Quanzhou from the Tenth to the Thirteenth Centuries." *Journal of World History* 6: 49–74.

———. 2009. "Frontier Discourse and China's Maritime Frontier: China's Frontiers and the Encounter with the Sea Through Early Imperial History." *Journal of World History* 20: 1–34.

Clauson, Sir Gerard. 1966. "Three Mongolian Notes." In Walther Heissig, ed., *Collectanea Mongolica: Festschrift für Professor Rintchin zum 60. Geburtstag.* Wiesbaden: Otto Harrassowitz, pp. 29–34.

———. 1971 "A Late Uyğur Family Archive." In Clifford E. Bosworth, ed., *Iran and Islam in Memory of the Late Vladimir Minorsky.* Edinburgh: At the University Press, pp. 167–96.

Cleaves, Francis W. 1949. "The Sino-Mongolian Inscription of 1362 in Memory of Prince Hindu." *Harvard Journal of Asiatic Studies* 12: 1–133.

———. 1951. "The Sino-Mongolian Inscription of 1338 in Memory of Prince Jigüntei." *Harvard Journal of Asiatic Studies* 14: 1–104.

———. 1953 "*Daruγa* and *Gerege.*" *Harvard Journal of Asiatic Studies* 16: 237–59.

———. 1959 "An Early Mongolian Version of the Alexander Romance." *Harvard Journal of Asiatic Studies* 22: 1–98.

———. 1976 "A Chinese Source on Marco Polo's Departure from China and a Persian Source on His Arrival in Persia." *Harvard Journal of Asiatic Studies* 36: 181–203.

Clunas, Craig. 1991. *Superfluous Things: Material Culture and Social Status in Early Modern China.* Urbana: University of Illinois Press.

———. 1992. "Connoisseurs and Aficionados: The Real and the Fake in Ming China (1368–1644)." In Jones 1992, pp. 151–56.

Colless, B. C. 1969–70. "Traders of the Pearl: The Mercantile and Missionary Activities of Persian and Armenian Christians in Southeast Asia." *Abr Nahrain* 9: 17–38.

Constable, Olivia Remie. 2003. *Housing the Stranger in the Mediterranean World: Lodging, Trade, and Travel in the Middle Ages.* Cambridge: Cambridge University Press.

Cutler, Anthony. 2001. "Gifts and Gift Exchange of the Byzantine, Arab and Related Economies." *Dumbarton Oaks Papers* 55: 245–78.

Dale, Stephen F. 2015. *The Orange Trees of Marrakesh: Ibn Khaldun and the Science of Man.* Cambridge, Mass.: Harvard University Press.

Dardess, John. 1978. "Ming T'ai-tsu on the Yüan: An Autocrat's Assessment of the Mongol Dynasty." *Bulletin of Sung and Yüan Studies* 14: 6–11.

Dars, Jacques. 1992. *La Marine chinoise du Xe siècle au XIVe.* Paris: Economica.

Deng, Gang. 1997. *Chinese Maritime Activities and Socio-Economic Development, c. 2100 B.C.–1900 A.D.* Westport, Conn.: Greenwood Press.

Dickens, Mark. 2016. "John of Ephesus on the Embassy of Zemarchus to the Türks." In Zimonyi and Karatay 2016, pp. 103–31.

Di Cosmo, Nicola. 2005. "Mongols and Merchants on the Black Sea Frontier in the Thirteenth and Fourteenth Centuries: Convergences and Conflicts." In Reuven Amitai and Michal Biran, eds., *Mongols, Turks and Others: Eurasian Nomads and the Sedentary World.* Leiden: Brill, pp. 391–419.

———. 2010. "Black Sea Emporia and the Mongol Empire: A Reassessment of Pax Mongolica." *Journal of the Economic and Social History of the Orient* 53: 83–108.

———. 2013 "Connecting Maritime and Continental History: The Black Sea Region at the Time of the Mongol Empire." In Peter N. Miller, ed., *The Sea: Thalassography and Historiography.* Ann Arbor: University of Michigan Press, pp. 174–97.

Dien, Albert E. 2007. *Six Dynasties Civilization.* New Haven: Yale University Press.

Doerfer, Gerhard. 1963. *Türkische und mongolische Elemente in Neupersischen.* Vol. I, *Mongolische Elemente.* Wiesbaden: Franz Steiner.

Donkin, R. A. 1998. *Beyond Price: Pearls and Pearl Fishing*. Philadelphia: American Philosophical Society.

Dunlop, D. M. 1954. *The History of the Jewish Khazars*. Princeton: Princeton University Press.

Dunnell, Ruth W. 1996. *Great State of White and High: Buddhism and State Formation in Eleventh Century Xia*. Honolulu: University of Hawai'i Press.

Eberhard, Wolfram. 1941. "Die Kultur der alten zentral- und westasiatischen Völker nach chinischen Quellen." *Zeitschrift für Ethnologie* 71: 215–75.

———. 1968. *The Local Cultures of South and East China*. Leiden: E. J. Brill.

Eitel, Ernest J. 1976. *Handbook of Chinese Buddhism, Being a Sanskrit-Chinese Dictionary*. Reprint San Francisco: Chinese Materials Center.

Elikhina, Iulia. 2010. "The Most Interesting Artifacts from Karakorum in the Collection of the State Hermitage Museum, St. Petersburg." In Bemmann et al., 2010: 34–47.

Elverskog, Johan. 2010. *Buddhism and Islam on the Silk Road*. Philadelphia: University of Pennsylvania Press.

Endicott-West, Elizabeth. 1989a. *Mongolian Rule in China: Local Administration Under the Yüan*. Cambridge, Mass.: Harvard University Press.

———. 1989b. "Merchant Associations in Yüan: The *Ortoγ*." *Asia Major*, 3rd ser. 11: 127–54.

Enoki, K. 1957. "Marco Polo and Japan." In *Oriente Poliano*, pp. 23–44.

Erdenebat, U., et al. 2010. "Two Ceramic Deposits from the Territory of Kara Korum." In Bemmann et al. 2010: 49–62.

Farquhar, David M. 1990. *The Government of China Under the Mongols: A Reference Guide*. Stuttgart: Franz Steiner.

Fasmer (Vasmer), Maks. 1967. *Etimologicheskii slovar russkogo iazyka*. Moscow: Izdatel'stvo "Progress." 4 vols.

Al-Feel, Muhammad Rashid. 1965. *The Historical Geography of Iraq Between the Mongolian and Ottoman Conquests, 1258–1534*. Nejef: al-Adab Press.

Finlay, Robert. 1998. "The Pilgrim Art: The Culture of Porcelain in World History." *Journal of World History* 9: 141–87.

Fishel, W. J., ed. 1951. *Semitic and Oriental Studies: A Volume of Studies Presented to William Popper*. University of California Studies in Semitic Philology, vol. XI. Berkeley: University of California Press.

Fletcher, Joseph. 1968. "China and Central Asia, 1368–1884." In John King Fairbank, ed., *The Chinese World Order: Traditional China's Foreign Relations*. Cambridge, Mass.: Harvard University Press, pp. 206–24.

Fong, Adam C. 2014. "'Together They Might Make Trouble': Cross-Cultural Interactions in Tang Dynasty Guang Zhou, 618–907 C. E." *Journal of World History* 25: 475–92.

Franke, Herbert. 1949. *Gelt und Wirtschaft in China unter der Mongolen-Herrschaft*. Leipzig: Otto Harrassowitz.

———. 1967. "Eine mittelalterliche chinesische Satire auf die Muhammedaner." In Wilhelm Hoernerbach, ed., *Der Orient in der Forschung: Festschrift für Otto Spies zum 5. April 1966*. Weisbaden: Otto Harrassowitz, pp. 202–8.

———. 1975. "Chinese Texts on the Jürchen: A Translation of the Jürchen Monograph in the *San-ch'ao pei-meng hui-pien*." *Zentralasiatische Studien* 9: 119–86.

Freedman, Paul. 2008. *Out of the East: Spices and the Medieval Imagination*. New Haven: Yale University Press.

Frye, Richard N. 1951. "*Jamūk*, Sogdian Pearl?" *Journal of the American Oriental Society* 71: 142–45.

Fülöp, Gyula. 1990. "New Research on Finds of Avar Chieftain-Burials at Agar, Hungary." In Austin and Alcock 1990, pp. 138–46.

Fyodotov-Davydov, G. A. 1984. *The Culture of the Golden Horde Cities.* BAR International Series, no. 198. Oxford: British Archaeological Reports.

Gasparini, Mariachiara. 2012. "A Mathematical Expression of Art: Sino-Iranian and Uighur Textile Interrelations and the Turfan Textile Collection in Berlin." *Transcultural Studies,* no 1. Downloaded on 26 August 2016.

Gernet, Jaques. 1962. *Daily Life in China on the Eve of the Mongol Invasion, 1250–1276.* Stanford: Stanford University Press.

Gerritsen, Anne. 2012. "Porcelain and the Material Culture of the Mongol-Yuan Court." *Journal of Early Modern History* 16/3: 241–73.

Gode, P. K. 1957. "Some References to Persian Pearls in Sanskrit Literature." *Rocznik orientalistyczny* 21: 129–34.

Goitein, S. D. 1964. "The Commercial Mail Service in Medieval Islam." *Journal of the American Oriental Society* 84: 118–23.

———. 1967–93. *A Mediterranean Society.* Berkeley: University of California Press. 6 vols.

Golden, Peter B. 1987–91. "Nomads and their Sedentary Neighbors in Pre-Činggisid Eurasia." *Archivum Eurasiae Medii Aevi* 7: 41–81.

———. 1991. "Aspects of the Nomadic Factor in the Economic Development of Kievan Rus'" In Koropeckyj 1991, pp. 58–101.

———. 1992. *An Introduction to the History of the Turkic Peoples: Ethnogenesis and State-Formation in Medieval and Early Modern Eurasia and the Middle East.* Wiesbaden: Otto Harrassowitz.

Gonda, J. 1991. *The Functions and Significance of Gold in the Veda.* Leiden: E. J. Brill.

Good, Irene. 2006. "Textiles as a Medium of Exchange in Third Millennium BCE Western Asia." In Mair 2006, pp. 191–214.

Gordon, Steward, ed. 2001a. *Robes and Honor: The Medieval World of Investiture.* New York: Palgrave.

———. 2001b "A World of Investiture." In Gordon 2001a, pp. 1–19.

Grenet, Frantz. 1996. "Les marchants sogdiens dans les mers du Sud à l'époque préislamique." *Cahiers d'Asie centrale* 1–2: 65–84.

———. 2005. "The Self-Image of the Sogdians." In La Vaissiere and Trombert 2005, pp. 123–40.

Grierson, Philip. 1959. "Commerce of the Dark Ages: A Critique of the Evidence." *Transactions of the Royal Historical Society,* ser. VI, 6: 123–40.

Hall, Kenneth R. 1985. *Maritime Trade and State Development in Early Southeast Asia.* Honolulu: University of Hawai'i Press.

Hambly, Gavin. 1966. "Introduction." In Gavin Hambly, ed., *Central Asia.* London: Weidenfeld and Nicolson, pp. 1–18.

Hara, Minoru. 1999. "The Pearl in Sanskrit Literature." *Memoires of the Research Department of the Toyo Bunko* 57: 155–74.

Harada, Yoshito. 1971. "East and West (II)." *Memoirs of the Research Department of the Toyo Bunko* 29: 57–80.

Hartwell, Robert. 1988. "The Imperial Treasuries: Finance and Power in Song China." *Bulletin of Sung and Yüan Studies* 20:18–89.

Haussig, Hans-Wilhelm. 1992. *Archäologie und Kunst der Seidenstrasse.* Darmstadt: Wissenschaftliche Buchgesellschaft.

Hayachi, Ryōchi. 1975. *The Silk Road and the Shoso-in*. New York: Weatherhill.

Helms, Mary W. 1988. *Ulysses Sail: An Ethnographic Odyssey of Power, Knowledge and Geographical Distance*. Princeton: Princeton University Press.

———. 1993. *Craft and the Kingly Ideal: Art, Trade and Power*. Austin: University of Texas Press.

Henning, W. B. 1943–46. "Sogdian Tales." *Bulletin of the School of Oriental and African Studies* 11: 465–87.

Herman, John E. 2002. "The Mongolian Conquest of Dali: The Failed Second Front." In Nicola Di Cosmo, ed., *Warfare in Inner Asian History (500–1800)*. Leiden: Brill, pp. 295–334.

Herskowitz, Melville J. 1951. *Man and His Works: The Science of Cultural Anthropology*. New York: Alfred A. Knopf.

Holmes, Urban T. 1934. "Medieval Gem Stones." *Speculum* 9/2: 195–204.

Honeychurch, William. 2015. "From Steppe Roads to Silk Roads: Inner Asian Nomads and Early Interregional Exchange." In Amitai and Biran 2015, pp. 50–87.

Horst, Heribert. 1964. *Die Staatverwaltung der Grosselǧūqen und Ḫōrazmšāhs (1038–1231)*. Wiesbaden: Franz Steiner.

Hosie, Alexander. 1904. *Manchuria: Its People, Resources and Recent History*. New York: Charles Scribner's Sons.

Hsiao Ch'i-ch'ing (Xiao Qiqing). 1978. *The Military Establishment of the Yuan Dynasty*. Cambridge, Mass.: Harvard University Press.

———. 1990. "Meng-Yuan shuijun zhi xingchi yu Meng-Song zhanzheng." *Hanxue yenjiu* 8: 177–200.

Ioannisyan, Oleg M. 1990. "Archaeological Evidence for the Development and Urbanization of Kiev from the 8th to the 14th Century." In Austin and Alcock 1990, pp. 285–312.

Jacoby, David. 2003. "The Silk Trade of Late Byzantine Constantinople." In Sümer Atasoy, ed., *550th Anniversary of the Istanbul University International Byzantine and Ottoman Symposium (XVth Century)*. Istanbul: Istanbul Üniversitesi, pp. 129–44.

———. 2004 "Silk Economics and Cross-Cultural Artistic Interaction: Byzantium, the Muslim World, and the Christian West." *Dumbarton Oaks Papers* 58: 197–240.

———. 2006. "Marco Polo, His Close Relatives, and His Travel Account: Some New Insights." *Mediterranean Historical Review* 21/2: 193–218.

———. 2007 "Late Byzantium Between the Mediterranean and Asia: Trade and Material Culture." In Sarah T. Brooks, ed., *Byzantium: Faith and Power*. New Haven: Yale University Press, pp. 20–41.

———. 2010. "Oriental Silks Go West: A Declining Trade in the Later Middle Ages." In Catarina Schmidt Arcangeli and Gerhard Wolf, eds., *Islamic Artifacts in the Mediterranean World: Trade, Gift Exchange and Artistic Transfer*. Venice: Marsilio, pp. 71–88.

James, H. E. M. 1888. *The Long White Mountain or Journey in Manchuria*. London: Longmans, Green.

Jenkins, Marilyn. 1988. "Mamlūk Jewelry: Influence and Echoes." *Muqarnas* 5: 29–42.

Jones, Mark, ed. 1992. *Why Fakes Matter: Essays on the Problems of Authenticity*. London: British Museum Press.

Kara, G. 1965. "Le dictionnaire étymologique et la langue mongole." *Acta Orientalia Academiae Scientiarum Hungaricae* 18: 1–32.

Karimov, U. I. 1991. "Slovar meditsinskikh terminov Abu Mansurs al-Kumri." In P. G. Bulgakov and U. I. Karimov, eds., *Materialy po istorii i istorii nauki i kul'tury narodov Srednei Azii*. Tashkent: Fan, pp. 112–55.

Kauz, Ralph, ed. 2010a. *Aspects of the Maritime Silk Road: From the Persian Gulf to the East China Sea.* Wiesbaden: Harrassowitz.

———. 2010b "Paliuwan: Trader or Traitor?" In Kauz 2010a, pp. 159–71.

Kerner, Robert J. 1946. *The Urge to the Sea: The Course of Russian History.* Berkeley: University of California Press.

Kervan, Monik. 1983. "Famous Merchants of the Arabian Gulf in the Middle Ages." *Dilmun* 11: 21–24.

Kessler, Adam T. 1993. *Empires Beyond the Great Wall: The Heritage of Genghis Khan.* Los Angeles: Natural History Museum of Los Angeles County.

Khabtagaeva, Baiarma. 2003–4. "The Etymology of Some Buriat Jewel Names." *Ural-Altaische Jahrbücher*, n.s., 18: 141–48.

Khazanov, Anatoly M. 1994. *Nomads and the Outside World.* 2nd ed. Madison: University of Wisconsin Press.

———. 2015. "The Scythians and Their Neighbors." In Amitai and Biran 2015, pp. 32–49.

———. 2016. "Notes on the Scythian Political Culture." In Zimonyi and Karatay 2016: 171–88.

Khodarkovsky, Michael. 2002. *Russia's Steppe Frontier: The Making of a Colonial Frontier, 1500–1800.* Bloomington: University of Indiana Press.

Khoury, Eileen. 1990. "Servants of the Pearl." *Saudi Aramco World* (Sept.–Oct.): 24–31.

Kiss, Attila. 1984. "A Byzantine Jewel from the 6th–7th Century in China." *Acta Orientalia Academiae Scientiarum Hungaricae* 38: 33–40.

Kliashtornyi, S. G. 1961. "Iaxartes—Sïr-Darya." *Central Asiatic Journal* 6: 24–26.

———. 1964. *Drevnetiurkskie runicheskie pamiatniki kak istorichnik po istorii Srednei Azii.* Moscow: Izdatel'stvo Nauka.

Kliashtornyi, S. G., et al. 1989. "The Golden Bracteatus from Mongolia: A Byzantine Motif in Central Asiatic Toreutics." *Information Bulletin, International Association for the Study of Cultures of Central Asia* 10: 5–19.

Koropeckyj, I. S., ed. 1991. *Ukrainian Economic History: Interpretive Essays.* Cambridge, Mass.: Harvard University Press for the Harvard Ukrainian Research Institute.

Koryakova, Ludmila, and Andrei V. Epimakhov. 2007. *The Urals and Western Siberia in the Bronze and Iron Ages.* Cambridge: Cambridge University Press.

Kovalevskaia, V. B. 1979. *Poiasnye nabory Evrazii, IV–IX vv.: Prazhki.* Arkheologiia SSSR, E1-2. Moscow: Izdatel'stvo Akademii Nauk SSSR.

Kramarovsky, Mark G. 1992. "The New Style Filigree Work in the Mongol Era: A Problem of Provenance." In Gary Seaman, ed., *Foundations of Empire: Archaeology and Art of the Eurasian Steppes.* Los Angeles: Ethnographics Press, pp. 191–200.

Krippes, Karl A. 1992. "Mongol and Jurchen Words in a Middle Korean Text." *Mongolian Studies*: 97–109.

Kubarev, V. D. 1984. *Drevnetiurkskie izvaianiia Altaia.* Novosibirsk: Izdatel'stvo Nauka sibirskoe otdelenie.

van der Kuijp, L. W. J. 1975. "An Index to a Tibeto-Mongolian Materia Medica." *Canada Mongolia Review/Revue Canada Mongolia* 1/2: 15–46.

Kunz, George F., and Charles Stevenson. 1908. *The Book of the Pearl.* New York: Century.

Kyzlasov, L. R. 1962. "Pamiatniki musul'manskogo srednevekova v Tuve." *Sovetskaia arkheologiia* 2: 203–10.

Labib, S. 1970. "Les marchants Karīmīs en Orient et sur l'océan Indien." In Mollat 1970, pp. 209–14.

Lach, Donald F. 1965. *Asia in the Making of Europe*. Vol. I, bk. 1, *The Century of Discovery*. Chicago: University of Chicago Press.

———. 1970 *Asia in the Making of Europe*. Vol. II, *A Century of Wonder*, bk. 1, *The Visual Arts*. Chicago: University of Chicago Press.

Lambourn, Elizabeth. 2003. "Of Jewels and Horses: The Career and Patronage of an Iranian Merchant under Shah Jahan." *Iranian Studies* 36: 213–40.

Lambton, A. K. S. 1999. "The *Athār wa aḥyā* of Rashīd al-Dīn Faḍl Allāh Hamadanī and His Contribution as an Agronomist, Arboriculturist and Horticulturalist." In Reuven Amitai-Preiss and David O. Morgan, eds., *The Mongol Empire and Its Legacy*. Leiden: Brill, pp. 126–54.

Landman, Neil H. et al. 2001. *Pearls: A Natural History*. New York: Harry N. Abrams.

Lang, David Marshall. 1966. *The Georgians*. New York: Frederick Praeger.

Lattimore, Owen. 1962. "Caravan Routes of Inner Asia." In his *Studies in Frontier History: Collected Papers*. London: Oxford University Press.

Laufer, Bertold. 1913. "Arabic and Chinese Trade in Walrus and Narwhal Ivory." *T'oung-pao* 14: 315–64.

———. 1915a *The Diamond: A Study in Chinese and Hellenistic Folk-lore*. Field Museum of Natural History, Anthropological series 15, 1. Chicago: Field Museum of Natural History.

———. 1915b. "Optical Lenses, I, Burning Lenses in China and India." *T'oung-pao* 16: 169–228.

———. 1915c. "Asbestos and Salamander: An Essay in Chinese and Hellenistic Folk-lore." *Toung-pao* 16: 299–373.

———. 1916. "Supplementary Notes on Walrus and Narwhal Ivory." *T'oung-pao* 17: 348–89.

———. 1967. *Sino-Iranica: Chinese Contributions to the History of Civilizations in Ancient Iran*. Reprint Taipei: Ch'eng-wen.

La Vaissière, Étienne, de. 2002. *Histoire des Marchants sogdiens*. Paris: Collège de France.

La Vaissière, Étienne, de, and Éric Trombert, eds. 2005. *Les Sogdiens en Chine*. Paris: École française d'Extrême-Orient.

Ledyard, Gari. 1963. "Two Mongolian Documents from the Koryŏ Sa." *Journal of the American Oriental Society* 83: 225–38.

Leskov, A. M. 2008. *The Maikop Treasure*. Philadelphia: University of Pennsylvania Museum of Archaeology and Anthropology.

Lessing, Ferdinand D. 1973. *Mongolian-English Dictionary*. Bloomington, Ind.: Mongolia Society.

Levashova, V. P. 1965. "Busy iz Kara-Korum." In S. V. Kiselev, ed., *Drevnemongolskie goroda*. Moscow: Nauka, pp. 297–307.

Lieu, Samuel N. C. 1985. *Manichaeism in the Later Roman Empire and Medieval China: A Historical Survey*. Manchester: Manchester University Press.

Litvinskii, B. A., ed. 1995. *Vostochnyi Turkestan v drevnosti i rannem srednekov'e: Khozaistvo, material'naia kultura*. Moscow: Izdatel'staia firma "Vostochnaia literatura."

Liu, Xinru. 1988. *Ancient India and Ancient China: Trade and Religious Relations*. Delhi: Oxford University Press.

Liu, Yingsheng. 2008. "Muslim Merchants in Mongol-Yuan China." In Schottenhammer 2008, pp. 133–44.

Livshits, V. A., ed. 1962. *Sogdiiskie dokumenty s gora Mug*. Vol. II, *Iuridicheskii dokumenty i pisma*. Moscow: Izdatel'stvo Vostochnoi literatury.

Lopez, Robert S. 1943. "European Merchants in the Medieval Indies: The Evidence of Commercial Documents." *Journal of Economic History* 3: 164–84.

———. 1952. "China Silk in Europe in the Yuan Period." *Journal of the American Oriental Society* 72: 72–76.

Lowenthal, David. 1992. "Authenticity? The Dogma of Self-Delusion." In Jones 1992, pp. 184–92.

Lubo-Lesnichenko, E. I. 1989. "Uigurskii i kirgizskii puti v Tsental'noi Azii." *Trudy Gosudarstvennogo Ermitazha* 27: 4–9.

Lubsangjab, Choi. 1980. "Milk in Mongol Customs: Some Remarks on Its Symbolic Significance." *Entogafia Polska* 24: 41–43.

Lucas, A. 1934. *Ancient Egyptian Materials and Industries.* London: Edward Arnold.

MacCoull, Leslie S. B. 1988. "Coptic Alchemy and Craft Technology in Islamic Egypt: The Papyrological Evidence." In Marilyn J. Chiat and Kathryn Reyerson, eds., *The Medieval Mediterranean: Cross Cultural Contacts.* St. Cloud, Minn.: North Star Press, pp. 101–4.

MacKenzie, D. N. 1971. *A Concise Pahlavi Dictionary.* London: Oxford University Press.

Maenchen-Helfen, Otto. 1950. "Two Notes on the Diamond in China." *Journal of the American Oriental Society* 70: 187–88.

Mair, Victor H. 1990. "Old Sinitic *Myag, Old Persian Maguš and English Magician." *Early China* 15: 27–47.

———. 2005. "The North(west)ern Peoples and the Recurrent Origins of the Chinese State." In Joshua Vogel, ed., *Teleology of the Modern Nation State: Japan and China.* Philadelphia: University of Pennsylvania Press, pp. 46–84.

Mair, Victor H., ed. 2006. *Contact and Exchange in the Ancient World.* Philadelphia: University of Pennsylvania Press.

Makarov, N. 2006. "Traders of the Forest: The Northern Periphery of Rus in the Medieval Trade Network." In Kathryn L. Reyerson et al., eds., *Pre-Modern Russia and Its World: Essays in Honor of Thomas S. Noonan.* Wiesbaden: Harrassowitz, pp. 115–33.

Maquet, Jacques. 1993. "Objects as Instruments, Objects as Signs." In Steven Lubar and W. David Kingery, eds., *History from Things: Essays on Material Culture.* Washington, D.C.: Smithsonian Institution Press, pp. 30–40.

Martinez, A. P. 1995–97. "The Wealth of Ormus and of Ind." *Archivum Eurasiae Medii Aevi* 9: 123–251.

———. 1998–99. "Ducuts and Dinars, pt. I." *Archivum Eurasiae Medii Aevi* 10: 118–206.

———. 2008–9. "The Eurasian Overland and Pontic Trades in the Thirteenth and Fourteenth Centuries." *Archivum Eurasiae Medii Aevi* 16: 127–221.

———. 2010. "The Il-Khanid Coinage: An Essay in Monetary and General History Based Largely on Comparative Numismatic Metrology." *Archivum Eurasiae Medii Aevi* 17: 59–164.

Meyendorff, John. 1981. *Byzantium and the Rise of Russia: A Study of Byzantino-Russian Relations in the Fourteenth Century.* Cambridge: Cambridge University Press.

Mikhailevich, G. P. 1972. "Soobshchenie Nasir al-Dina Tusi o reznom izumrude khorezmshah Tekesha." In A. A. Ivanov and S. S. Sorokin, eds., *Srednaia Aziia i Iran.* Leningrad: Izdatel'stvo "Avrora," pp. 107–13.

Mokri, M. 1960. "La Pêche des perles dans le Golfe persique." *Journal asiatique* 248: 381–97.

Mollat, Michel, ed. 1970. *Sociétés et compagnies de commerce en Orient et dans l'océan Indien.* Paris: SEVPEN.

Monnas, L. 2001. "Textiles at the Coronation of Edward III." *Textile History* 32: 2–35.

Moriyasu, Takao. 2012. "Epistolary Formulae of Old Uighur Letters from the Eastern Silk Road (pt. 2)." *Memoirs of the Graduate School of Letters, Osaka University* 52: 1–98.

Morony, Michael G. 1984. *Iraq After the Muslim Conquest.* Princeton: Princeton University Press.

Mostaert, Antoine. 1927. "À propos de quelques portaits d'empereurs mongols." *Asia Major* 4: 147–56.

Moule, A. C. 1930. *Christians in China Before the Year 1550*. London: Society for Promoting Christian Knowledge.

Mukminova, R. G. 1976. *Ocherki po istorii remesla v Samarkande i Bukhare v XVI veke*. Tashkent: Izdatel'stvo "Fan" uzbekskoi SSR.

Nadeliaev, V. M. et al. 1969. *Drevnetiurkskii slovar*. Leningrad: Izdatel'stvo Nauka leningradskoe otdelenie.

Nadvi, Syed H. H. 1979. "Al-Bīrūnī and his Kitāb al-Jamāhir fī Ma'rifah al-Jawāhir." In Said 1979, pp. 530–44.

Nappi, Carla. 2009. *The Monkey and the Inkpot: Natural History and Its Transformation in Early Modern China*. Cambridge, Mass.: Harvard University Press.

Needham, Joseph. 1959. *Science and Civilization in China*. Vol. III, *Mathematics and the Sciences of the Heavens and the Earth*. Cambridge: Cambridge University Press.

———. 1962. *Science and Civilization in China*. Vol. IV, *Physics and Physical Technology*, pt. 1, *Physics*. Cambridge: Cambridge University Press.

———. 1970. "Abstract of Material Presented to the International Maritime History Commission at Beirut." In Mollat 1970, pp. 139–63.

———. 1971. *Science and Civilization in China*. Vol. IV, *Physic and Physical Technology*, pt. 3, *Civil Engineering and Nautics*. Cambridge: Cambridge University Press.

———. 1976 *Science and Civilization in China*. Vol. V, *Chemistry and Chemical Technology*, pt. 3, *Spagyrical Discovery and Invention*. Cambridge: Cambridge University Press.

Neverov, O. Ia. 1983. *Gemmy antichnogo mira*. Moscow: Nauka.

Nicols, Donald M. 1992. *Byzantium and Venice: A Study in Diplomatic and Cultural Relations*. Cambridge: Cambridge University Press.

Niẓām, Muḥammad. 1931. *The Life and Times of Ṣulṭan Maḥmūd of Ghazna*. Cambridge: Cambridge University Press.

Noonan, Thomas S. 1983. "Russia's Eastern Trade, 1150–1350: The Archaeological Evidence." *Archivum Eurasiae Medii Aevi* 3: 201–64.

———. 1991. "The Flourishing of Kiev's International and Domestic Trade, ca. 1100–ca. 1240." In Koropeckyj 1991, pp. 102–46.

———. 2000–2001. "Volga Bulgharia's Tenth-Century Trade with Samanid Central Asia." *Archivum Eurasiae Medii Aevi* 11: 140–218.

Olschki, Leonardo. 1946. *Guillaume Boucher, a French Artist at the Court of the Khans*. Baltimore: Johns Hopkins University Press.

———. 1960 *Marco Polo's Asia*. Berkeley: University of California Press.

———. 1972 *Marco Polo's Precursors*. Reprint New York: Octagon Books.

Oriente Poliano. 1957. *Oriente Poliano: Studi e Conferenze Tenute all' Is.M.E.O. in Occasione del VII Centenario della Nascita di Marco Polo (1254–1954)*. Rome: Istituto Italiano per il Medio ed Estreme Oriente.

Pakhomov, E. A. 1970. *Monety Gruzii*. Tbilisi: Izdatel'stvo "Metsniereba."

Parry, James. 2013. "The Pearl Imporium of al-Zubārāh." *Saudi Aramco World* (Nov.–Dec.): 52–59.

Pearson, Michael N. 1996. *Pilgrimage to Mecca: The Indian Experience, 1500–1800*. Princeton: Marcus Wiener.

Pelenski, Jaroslaw. 1974. *Russia and Kazan: Conquest and Imperial Ideology*. The Hague: Mouton.

———. 1979. "State and Society in Moscovite Russia and the Mongol-Turkic System in the Sixteenth Century." In Ascher et al. 1979, pp. 93–109.

Pelliot, Paul. 1913. "Addenda [to Laufer 1913]." *T'oung-pao* 14: 365–70.

———. 1928. "Des artisans chinois à la capitale abbaside en 751–62." *T'oung-pao* 26: 110–12.

———. 1930. "Les mots mongols dans le *Korye Să*." *Journal asiatique* 217: 253–66.

———. 1959–73. *Notes on Marco Polo*. Paris: Adrian Maisonneuve. 3 vols.

———. 1973. *Recherches sur les chrétiens d'Asie centrale et d'Extrême-Orient*. Paris: Imprimerie nationale.

———. 1984. *Recherches sur les chrétiens d'Asie centrale et d'Extrême-Orient*. Vol. II, 1, *La Stèle de Si-ngan-fou*. Paris: Éditions de la foundation Singer-Polignac.

Pelliot, Paul and Louis Hambis. 1951. *Histoire des campagnes de Gengis Khan*. Leiden: E. J. Brill, vol. I.

Phillips, Carla Rahn. 1990. "The Growth and Composition of Trade in the Iberian Empires, 1450–1750." In James D. Tracy, ed., *The Rise of Merchant Empires: Long Distance Trade in the Early Modern World*. Cambridge: Cambridge University Press, pp. 34–101.

Pierson, Stacy. 2012. "The Movement of Chinese Ceramics: Appropriation in World History." *Journal of World History* 23: 9–39.

Pigulevskaia, N. 1951. *Vizantiia na putiakh v Indiiu: Iz istorii torgovli Vizantii s Vostokom v IV–VI vv*. Moscow: Izdatel'stvo Akademii Nauk SSSR.

Pinks, Elisabeth. 1968. *Die Uiguren von Kanchou in der frühen Sung-Zeit*. Wiesbaden: Otto Harrassowitz.

Pollard, Elizabeth Ann. 2013. "Indian Spices and Roman 'Magic' in Imperial and Late Antique Indomediterranea." *Journal of World History* 24: 1–23.

Poluboiarinova, M. D. 1978. *Russkie liudi v Zolotoi Orde*. Moscow: Izdatel'stvo Nauka.

Ponder, Eric. 1925. "The Reputed Medicinal Properties of Precious Stones." *Pharmaceutical Journal* 61: 686–87.

Porada, Edith. 1969. *The Art of Ancient Iran*. New York: Greystone.

Pritsak, Omeljan. 1979. "The Role of the Bosporus Kingdom and Late Hellenism as the Basis for the Medieval Cultures of the Territories North of the Black Sea." In Ascher et al. 1979, pp. 3–21.

Przhevalskii (Prejevalsky), N. 1876. *Mongolia and the Tangut Country, and the Solitudes of Northern Tibet*. London: Samson Low. 2 vols.

Ptak, Roderich. 1995. "Images of Maritime Asia in Two Yuan Texts: *Daoyi zhilue* and *Yiyu zhi*." *Journal of Sung-Yuan Studies* 25: 47–75.

Qadri, M. A. H. 1979. "Kitāb al-Jamāhir fī Mā'rifah al-Jawāhir: Al-Bīrūnī's Contribution to Biological Studies and Concepts." In Said 1979, pp. 587–93.

Raman, K. V. 1991. "Further Evidence of Roman Trade from Coastal Sites in Tamil Nadu." In Vimala Begley and Richard De Puma, eds., *Rome and India: The Ancient Sea Trade*. Madison: University of Wisconsin Press, pp. 125–33.

Rapin, Claude. 1996. "Relations entre l'Asie centrale et l'Indie à l'époque hellénistique." *Cahiers d'Asie centrale* 1–2: 35–47.

———. 2007 "Nomad Migrations in Central Asia." In Joe Cribb and Georgina Herrmann, eds., *After Alexander: Central Asia Before Islam*. Oxford: Published for the British Academy by Oxford University Press, pp. 29–72.

Rawson, Jessica. 1984. *Chinese Ornament: The Lotus and the Dragon*. London: British Museum Publications.

Ray, Himanshu P. 1998. *The Winds of Change: Buddhism and Maritime Links of Early South Asia*. New Delhi: Oxford University Press.
Renfrew, Colin. 1988. "Varna and the Emergence of Wealth in Prehistoric Europe." In Arjun Appadurai, ed., *The Social Life of Things: Commodities in Cultural Perspective*. Cambridge: Cambridge University Press, pp. 141–68.
Rentz, E. 1951. "Pearling in the Persian Gulf." In Fishel 1951, pp. 392–402.
Rockhill, William W. 1891. *The Land of the Lamas*. London: Longmans, Green.
———. 1894. *Diary of a Journey Through Mongolia and Tibet in 1891 and 1892*. Washington, D.C.: Smithsonian Institution.
———. 1916. "Notes on the Relations and Trade of China with the Eastern Archipelago and the Coast of the Indian Ocean During the Fourteenth Century, Part II." *T'oung-pao* 16/2: 236–71; Part III, 16/3: 374–92; Part IV, 16/4: 435–67; Part V, 16/5: 604–26.
Rockstein, Edward. 1972. "The Mongol Invasion of Korea: 1231." *Mongolia Society Bulletin* 12/2: 41–54.
Rolle, Renate. 1989. *The World of the Scythians*. Berkeley: University of California Press.
Róna-Tas, András. 1982. "The Periodization and Sources of Chuvash Linguistic History." In András Róna-Tas, ed., *Chuvash Studies*. Wiesbaden: Otto Harrassowitz, pp. 113–69.
Rong Xinjiang. 2004. "Khotanese Felt and Sogdian Silver: Foreign Gifts to Buddhist Monasteries in Ninth- and Tenth-Century Dunhuang." *Asia Major* 17: 15–34.
———. 2005. "*Sabao* or *Sabo*: Sogdian Caravan Leaders in the Wall Paintings in Buddhist Caves." In La Vaissière and Trombert 2005, pp. 207–30.
Rose, Jenny. 2001. "Sasanian Splendor: The Appurtenances of Royalty." In Gordon 2001a, pp. 35–56.
Rostovtzeff, M. 1922. *Iranians and Greeks in South Russia*. Oxford: Clarendon Press.
Roux, Jean-Paul, and Marie-Madeleine Massé. 1976. "Quelques objects numineux des Turcs et des Mongols: Les plumes." *Turcica* 8/1: 28–57.
Rozycki, William. 1994. *Mongol Elements in Manchu*. Indiana University Uralic and Altaic Series, no. 157. Bloomington: Research Institute for Inner Asian Studies.
Rudenko, S. I. 1960. *Kul'tura naseleniia Tsentral'nogo Altaia v Skifkoe vremia*. Moscow: Izdatel'stvo Akademii Nauk SSSR.
———. 1962. *Sibirskaia kollektsiia Petra I*. Arkheologiia SSSR, D3-9. Moscow: Izdatel'stvo Akademii Nauk SSSR.
Rybakov, B. A. 1948. *Remeslo drevnei Rusi*. Moscow: Izdatel'stvo Akademii Nauk SSSR.
Said, Hakim Muhammad, ed. 1979. *Al-Bīrūnī Commemorative Volume*. Karachi: Times Press.
Sakip Sabanci Müzesi. 2006. *Cengiz Han ve Mirasçilari: B*üyük Moğol Imparatorluğu. Istanbul: SSM.
Sarianidi, V. I. 1980. "The Treasure of the Golden Mound." *Archaeology* 33/3: 31–41.
———. 1987. "Tillia-tepe iuvelirnoe iskusstvo rannikh Kushan." In G. M. Bongard-Levin, ed., *Tsentral'naia Aziia: Novye pamiatniki pismennosti i iskusstvo*. Moscow: Nauka, pp. 268–81.
Schafer, Edward H. 1951. "Iranian Merchants in T'ang Dynasty Tales." In Fishel 1951, pp. 403–22.
———. 1952. "The Pearl Fisheries of Ho-p'u." *Journal of the American Oriental Society* 72: 155–65.
———. 1957. "A Fourteenth Century Gazeteer of Canton." In *Oriente Poliano*, pp. 67–93.
———. 1962. "Notes on T'ang Culture." *Monumenta Serica* 21: 194–221.
———. 1963. *The Golden Peaches of Samarkand*. Berkeley: University of California Press.
———. 1965. "Notes on T'ang Culture, II." *Monumenta Serica* 24: 130–54.

———. 1967. *The Vermillion Bird: T'ang Images of the South.* Berkeley: University of California Press.

———. 1970. *Shore of Pearls.* Berkeley: University of California Press.

Schlesinger, Jonathan. 2017. *A World Trimmed with Fur: Wild Things, Pristine Places, and the Natural Fringes of Qing Rule.* Stanford: Stanford University Press.

Schneider, Jane. 1977. "Was There a Pre-Capitalist World System?" *Peasant Studies* 6: 20–29.

Schottenhammer, Angela, ed. 2008. *The East Asian "Mediterranean": Maritime Crossroads of Culture, Commerce and Human Migration.* Wiesbaden: Harrassowitz.

Schurmann, Herbert Franz. 1956. *Economic Structure of the Yüan Dynasty.* Cambridge, Mass.: Harvard University Press.

Sen, Tansen. 2003. *Buddhism, Diplomacy and Trade: The Realignment of Sino-Indian Relations, 600–1400.* Honolulu: University of Hawai'i Press.

———. 2006. "The Formation of Chinese Maritime Networks to Southern Asia." *Journal of the Economic and Social History of the Orient* 49: 421–53.

Serjeant, R. B. 1970. "Maritime Customary Law off the Arabian Coasts." In Mollat 1970, pp. 195–207.

———. 1972. *Islamic Textiles: Materials for a History up to the Mongol Conquest.* Beirut: Librairie du Liban.

Serruys, Henry. 1962. "Three Mongol Documents from 1635 in the Russian Archives." *Central Asiatic Journal* 7: 1–41.

———. 1967. *Sino-Mongol Relations During the Ming: The Tribute System and Diplomatic Missions.* Brussels: Institut belge des haute études chinois.

———. 1974 *Kumiss Ceremonies and Horse Races: Three Mongolian Texts.* Wiesbaden: Otto Harrassowitz.

———. 1975. "The Seven Jewels in Mongol Literature." *Mongolian Studies* 2: 133–40.

Shaffer, Lynda. 1994. "Southernization." *Journal of World History* 5: 1–21.

Sherratt, Andrew. 1995. "Reviving the Grand Narrative: Archaeology and Long Term Change." *Journal of European Archaeology* 3: 1–31.

———. 2006. "The Trans-Eurasian Exchange: The Prehistory of Chinese Relations with the West." In Mair 2006, pp. 30–61.

Shiba, Yoshinobu. 1970. *Commerce and Society in Sung China.* Ann Arbor: University of Michigan Center for Chinese Studies.

———. 1983. "Sung Foreign Trade: Its Scope and Organization." In Morris Rossabi, ed., *China Among Equals: The Middle Kingdom and Its Neighbors, 10th–14th Centuries.* Berkeley: University of California Press, pp. 89–115.

Shim, Hosung. 2014. "The Postal Roads of the Great Khans in Central Asia Under the Mongol-Yuan Empire." *Journal of Song-Yuan Studies* 44: 405–69.

Sivin, Nathan. 1968. *Chinese Alchemy: Preliminary Studies.* Cambridge, Mass.: Harvard University Press.

Skrynnikova, T. 1992–93. "Sülde—the Basic Idea of the Chinggis Khan Cult." *Acta Orientalia Academiae Scientiarum Hungaricae* 46: 51–59.

Slovar. 1975–. *Slovar russkogo iazyka, XI—XVII vv.* Moscow: Nauka. 28 vols. to date.

So, Jenny F., and Emma C. Bunker. 1995. *Traders and Raiders on China's Northern Frontier.* Seattle: Sackler Gallery and University of Washington Press.

So, Keelong (Billy K. L.). 1991. "Financial Crises and Local Economy: Ch'uan-chou in the Thirteenth Century." *T'oung-pao* 77: 119–37.

———. 2000. *Prosperity, Region and Institutions in Maritime China: The South Fukien Pattern, 946–1368.* Cambridge, Mass.: Harvard University Press.

Spuler, Bertold. 1985. *Die Mongolen in Iran: Politik, Verwaltung und Kultur der Ilchanzeit, 1220–1350*, 4th. ed. Leiden: E. J. Brill.

Sreznevskii, I. I. 1989. *Slovar drevnerusskogo iazyka.* Moscow: Kniga. 3 vols. in 6 pts.

Stanley, Tim. 2010. "Patterns of Exchange in the Decorative Arts Between China and South-West Asia." In Kauz 2010a, pp. 107–15.

Stargardt, Janice. 1971. "Burma's Economic and Diplomatic Relations with India and China from Early Medieval Sources." *Journal of the Economic and Social History of the Orient* 14: 38–62.

Steensgaard, Niels. 1991. "Asian Trade Routes: Evidence and Patterns." In Karl Reinhold Haellquist, ed., *Asian Trade Routes: Continental and Maritime.* London: Curzon Press, pp. 1–6.

Stein, Rolf. 1940. "Leao-che." *T'oung-pao* 35: 1–154.

Steingass, F. 1970. *Persian-English Dictionary.* Reprint Beirut: Librairie du Liban.

Stronach, David. 1978. *Pasargadae.* Oxford: At the Clarendon Press.

Sunchugashev, Ia. I. 1979. *Drevnaia metallurgiia Khakasii: Epokha zheleza.* Novosibirsk: Izdatel'stvo Nauka sibirskoe otdelenie.

Sykes, Percy M. 1902. *Ten Thousand Miles in Persia or Eight Years in Iran.* London: John Murray.

Tampoe, Moira. 1989. *Maritime Trade Between China and the West: An Archaeological Study of Ceramics from Siraf (Persian Gulf), 8th to 15th Centuries A.D.* BAR International Series, no. 555. Oxford: British Archaeological Reports.

Tasaka, Kōdō. 1957. "An Aspect of Islam[ic] Culture Introduced into China." *Memoirs of the Research Department of the Toyo Bunko* 16: 75–160.

Terent'ev-Katanskii, A. P. 1993. *Material'naia kul'tura Si Sia.* Moscow: Izdatel'stvo firma "Vostochnaia literatura."

Theodoridis, Dmitri. 2002. "Kulicarta: ein mongolischer Stuffname chinesischen Ursprungs." *Jahrbuch der österreichischen Byzantinistik* 55: 249–57.

Thompson, E. A. 1947. "Notes on Priscus Panites." *Classical Quarterly* 41: 61–65.

Thompson, R. Campbell. 1936. *Assyrian Chemistry and Geology.* Oxford: Clarendon Press.

Thorndyke, Lynn. 1958. *A History of Magic and Experimental Science.* Vol. VII, *The Seventeenth Century.* New York: Columbia University Press.

Tikhomirov, M. 1959. *The Towns of Ancient Rus.* Moscow: Foreign Languages Publishing House.

Tikhonov, D. I. 1966. *Khozaistvo i obshchestvennyi stroi uigurskogo gosudarstva X–XIV vv.* Moscow: Izdatel'stvo Nauka.

Timkowski, George (Grigori Timkovskii). 1827. *Travels of the Russian Mission Through Mongolia to China . . . in the Years 1820–21.* London: Longman. 2 vols.

Tolstov, S. P., and B. I. Vainberg, eds. 1967. *Koi-Krylgan-Kala: Pamiatnik kul'tury drevnego Khorezme, IV v. do n.e.–IV v. n.e.* Trudy khorezmskoi arkheologo-ethnograficheskoi ekspeditsii, vol. V. Moscow: Nauka.

Toynbee, Arnold J. 1934–54. *A Study of History.* London: Oxford University Press. 10 vols.

Treister, Mikhail. 2004. "Eastern Jewelry in Sarmatian Burials and Eastern Elements in the Jewelry Production of the North Pontic Area in the First Century A.D." *Iranica Antiqua* 39: 297–321.

Tsintsius, N. I., ed. 1975–77. *Sravnitel'nyi slovar tunguso-man'chzhurskikh iazykov.* Leningrad: Nauka. 2 vols.

Ullmann, Manfred. 1972. *Die Nature- und Geheimwissenschaften im Islam.* Leiden: E. J. Brill.

Vogel, Hans Ulrich. 1993. "Cowry Trade and its Role in the Economy of Yunnan: From the Ninth to the Mid-Eighteenth Century." *Journal of the Economic and Social History of the Orient* 36: pt. I, 211–52, and pt. II, 309–53.

Vorob'ev, M. V. 1972. "Pechati gosudarstva Tszin (1115–1234)." In R. Sh. Dzharylgasinova and M. V. Kriukov, eds., *Epigrafika Vostochnoi i Iuzhnoi Azii.* Moscow: Nauka pp. 81–98.

———. 1975. *Chzhurcheni i gosudarstvo Tszin.* Moscow: Nauka.

———. 1983. *Kul'tura chzhurchenei i gosudarstva Tszin (X v.–1234 g.).* Moscow: Nauka.

Vu, Hong Lien. 2017. *The Mongol Navy: Kubilai Khan's Invasions in Đai Viêt and Champa.* Working Paper, no. 25. Singapore: Nalanda-Sriwijaya Centre.

Wade, Geoff. 2009. "An Early Age of Commerce in Southeast Asia: 900–1300." *Journal of Southeast Asian Studies* 40/2: 221–65.

Wang Ting. 2011. *Neilu Yazhou shidi qinsuo.* Lanzhou: Lanzhou daxue chubanshe.

Watt, Sir George. 1908. *Commercial Products of India.* London: John Murray.

Wheatley, Paul. 1961. "Geographical Notes on Some Commodities Involved in the Sung Maritime Trade." *Journal of the Malayan Branch of the Royal Asiatic Society* 32/2: 5–140.

Whitehouse, David. 1976. "Kīsh." *Iran* 14: 146–47.

Whitmore, John K. 2006. "The Rise of the Coast: Trade and Culture in Early Đai Viêt." *Journal of Southeast Asian Studies* 13/1: 103–22.

Wiedemann, Eilhard. 1911. "Über den Wert von Edelsteinen bei den Muslimen." *Der Islam* 2/1: 345–58.

Wilkinson, Endymion. 2013. *Chinese History: A New Manual.* Cambridge, Mass.: Harvard University Press.

Willan, T. S. 1968. *The Early History of the Russia Company, 1553–1603.* Manchester: Manchester University Press.

Williamson, Andrew. 1973. "Hurmuz and the Trade of the Gulf in the 14th and 15th Centuries." *Proceedings of the Seminar for Arabian Studies* 6: 52–68.

Wittfogel, Karl A., and Feng Chia-sheng. 1949. *History of Chinese Society, Liao (907–1125).* Philadelphia: American Philosophical Society.

Woods, John E. 1990. "Timur's Geneology." In Michael M. Mazzoui and Vera B. Moreen, eds., *Intellectual Studies on Islam: Essays Written in Honor of Martin B. Dickson.* Salt Lake City: University of Utah Press, pp. 85–125.

Wozniak, F. E. 1979. "The Crimean Question, the Black Bulgharians and the Russo-Byzantine Treaty of 944." *Journal of Medieval History* 5: 115–26.

Wright, David C. 1207. "Navies in the Mongol-Yuan Conquest of Southern Song China." *Mongolian Studies* 19: 207–16.

Wulf, Hans E. 1966. *The Traditional Crafts of Iran.* Cambridge, Mass.: MIT Press.

Xiong, Victor Cunrui, and Ellen Johnson Laing. 1991. "Foreign Jewelry in Ancient China." *Bulletin of the Asia Institute*, n.s., 5: 163–73.

Yamamoto, Tatsurō. 1981. "Vân-dôn, a Trade Port in Vietnam." *Memoirs of the Research Department of the Toyo Bunko* 39: 1–28.

Yang Bin. 2004. "Horses, Silver, and Cowries: Yunnan in Global Perspective." *Journal of World History* 15: 281–322.

———. 2011. "The Rise and Fall of Cowrie Shells: The Asian Story." *Journal of World History* 22: 1–25.

Yang Junkai. 2005. "Carvings on the Stone Outer Coffin of Lord Shi of the Northern Zhou." In La Vaissière and Trombert 2005, pp. 21–45.

Yarshater, Ehsan. 1983. "Iranian National History." In Ehsan Yarshater, ed., *The Cambridge History of Iran*. Vol. III, *The Seleucid, Parthian and Sasanian Periods*. Cambridge: Cambridge University Press, pt.1, pp. 359–477.

Yokkaichi, Yasuhiro. 2008. "Chinese and Muslim Diasporas and the Indian Ocean Trade Network Under Mongolian Hegemony." In Schottenhammer 2008, pp. 73–102.

Yoshida, Yutaka. 2004. "Some Reflections About the Origin of Čamūk." In Takao Moriyasu, ed., *Papers on the Pre-Islamic Documents and Other Materials Unearthed from Central Asia*. Kyoto: Hōyū Shoten, pp. 127–35.

Yü, Ying-shih. 1967. *Trade and Expansion in Han China*. Berkeley: University of California Press.

Yule, Sir Henry, and A. C. Burnell. 1903. *Hobson-Jobson: A Glossary of Anglo-Indian Words and Phrases*. London: John Murray.

Zhang Qingjie. 2005. "*Hutengwu* and *Huxuanwu* Sogdian Dances in the Northern, Sui and Tang Dynasties." In La Vaissière and Trombert 2005, pp. 93–106.

Zhukovskaia, N. L. 1988. *Kategorii i simvolika traditsionnoi kul'tury mongolov*. Moscow: Nauka.

Ziiaev, Kh. Z. 1983. *Ekonomicheskie sviazi srednei Azii s Sibir'iu v XVI–XIX vv*. Tashkent: Fan.

Zimonyi, István, and Osman Karatay, eds. 2016. *Central Eurasia in the Middle Ages: Studies in Honour of Peter B. Golden*. Wiesbaden: Harrassowitz.

INDEX

ACKNOWLEDGMENTS

This volume is a by-product of my interest in Mongolian political culture and its manifold influences on the circulation of natural and cultural goods throughout the Eurasian landmass and its neighboring seas. In pursuing these issues that have so often led me far from the areas of my training and experience, I have relied heavily on friends and colleagues for guidance, bibliography, and copies of their own and others' works. For these many kindnesses, freely given, I offer my deep-felt thanks to Anne Broadbridge, David Christian, Nicola Di Cosmo, Jos Gommans, Roman Kovalev, Xinru Liu, Ruth Meserve, and Osman Ozgudenli.

As always, free-ranging discussions with Stephen Dale, Peter Golden, and Anatoly Khazanov over many decades have informed and sharpened my understanding of the nomads' role in the Asian continent's interactive history.

Once again I am indebted to Victor Mair, for his sponsorship of this volume in the Encounters with Asia series and for suggestions that improved its organization and argumentation.

I must also record my special thanks to Candice Etheredge, who willingly shared with me her long experience in the jewelry trade that provided me with a much-needed orientation to the field at large and that saved me from many beginner's mistakes and misunderstandings.

For her support and editorial skills, I record my gratitude to my wife, Lucille, who somehow always seemed genuinely interested in this, the most recent of my enthusiasms.

Last, it was during the course of informal conversations with Roxann Prazniak on the life portraits of fourteenth-century Yuan empresses that initially prompted my interest in pearls as a window on Chinggisid statecraft. Thereafter, we regularly discussed these matters, and her comments, insights, and arguments did much to frame and shape the direction of my subsequent research. For this and for the supply of much-needed materials I am pleased to register my deep appreciation and indebtedness.